Savory praise for
Julie Powell's
CLEAVING
A Story of
Marriage, Meat, and Obsession

"Anyone who loved *Julie and Julia* will want to follow Julie Powell into the butcher shop as she struggles to wield a cleaver and save her marriage." —Michele Kayal, *Atlanta Journal-Constitution*

"Ms. Powell is a wonderful prose writer."
—Moira Hodgson, *Wall Street Journal*

"You'll eat up this second memoir by the author of *Julie and Julia*. In it, Powell tries to end an adulterous affair by immersing herself in an apprenticeship at a butcher shop—and embarks on a world tour of meat. How she finds her way home is the marrow of this tell-all travelogue/love story. Well done!" —Elisabeth Egan, *Self*

"I've already recommended *Cleaving* to several friends—the ones who have wandering eyes but whose qualms won't quite let them stray. Julie Powell's follow-up to *Julie and Julia* paints a visceral, compulsively readable picture of what it looks like when you fully indulge with a fantasy object who isn't your spouse.... Tense scenes of Powell sitting in front of the TV angstily tapping her foot on the leg of her in-the-know husband of ten years while she waits for her lover's text-beckonings are as disturbing as her descriptions of band-sawing through a pig's head or drinking fresh blood poured from a steer's neck in Tanzania.... Powell has honed her writing chops along with her culinary skills, and her extended metaphor is dead on: how we can systematically hack each other apart without ever getting to the heart of our desires."
—Miranda Purves, *Elle*

"Unabashedly confessional....A compulsive, voyeuristic read. If you're a foodie, the recipes scattered throughout are a bonus, but the real meat in this book is Powell's relationship with her husband." —Lylah M. Alphonse, *Boston Globe*

"As intoxicating as baked bone marrow....Powell is reckless, yes, but also incredibly brave as she cuts through the raw flesh of her marriage, exposing every quivering nerve. It is an evisceration not without its insight and hard-won rewards. It's also funny....The book's joys are many. The butchers who take Powell in at Fleisher's Grass-Fed and Organic Meats in Kingston, New York, are so interesting they make you want to give up your career and take up the cleaver. In this meaty environment, Powell's writing becomes erotic, almost prurient....As unsure as the novice butcher is with a knife is how sure Powell is with her pen. In her self-gutting story we see our own fleshy vulnerabilities when it comes to the intricacies of love." —Greg Morago, *Houston Chronicle*

"I loved the parts of the book where she's learning how to butcher like the boys at Fleisher's butcher shop in Kingston, New York. The cold of the meat, her weary muscles, the boisterous banter in the store—Powell is a solid writer." —Addie Broyles, *Austin American-Statesman*

"A gutsy, profane, energetic writer." —Lisa Schwarzbaum, *Entertainment Weekly*

"From the title to the last page, former blogger Julie Powell's startling second memoir is smart and compelling....Like the best elements of the blogosphere, *Cleaving* gives readers an almost tactile sense of its author's vulnerabilities: Powell acknowledges right away that she is 'familiar with the landscape of addiction.'...Powell's steadfast femininity and confident voice are refreshing." —Laura Impellizzeri, *San Francisco Chronicle*

"An engaging writer. Fast, funny, and observant.... She's your mean best friend sending instant messages that make you snort at your desk.... Powell's sincere interest in butchery and love for the Fleisher's crew bring the book's slasher scenes to life."

— Christine Muhlke, *New York Times Book Review*

"It's all gross and strangely fascinating. Powell, being the cheeky writer she is, hilariously alludes to Jack the Ripper and *The Silence of the Lambs* while popping out ham hocks and bone marrow.... She's raw and complicated in trying to piece herself back together after achieving success. One of the things Powell learned at Fleisher's was how to tie perfect roasts. It sums up her second memoir quite well: 'It is both delicate and, sometimes, painful. The twine can bite into fingers, cut off circulation, but the swirling motions as I quickly make the knot and pull it tight are graceful and feminine.'"

— Nicole Chvatal, *Portland Oregonian*

"Powell's elegant yet matter-of-fact descriptions of butchery's physical work and her affectionate portrayals of the butchers comprise some of *Cleaving*'s best writing."

— Ellen Kanner, *Miami Herald*

"Powell is a strong and lively writer and manages to make a fine story out of her exploits with rolling roulades of turkey, de-cheeking pig heads, or negotiating racks of ribs with a band saw.... The likable train-wreck persona from the *Julie and Julia* days lives on in Powell's passionate curiosity about food. Whatever her sins may be, they don't include culinary snobbery. Powell slugs cheap pink champagne in her off-hours and narrates her butchery education and subsequent meat-based international travels in tones of wondrous excitement."

— Allecia Vermillion, *Chicago Sun-Times*

"How on earth could New York recipe nut Julie Powell top the triumph of her first book, *Julie and Julia,* an enchantingly honest account of the year the author, back then a depressed secretary lacking any ambition, spent cooking all 524 of American food writer Julia Child's French recipes?...She has had a jolly good stab at it—literally....Powell has returned for seconds with a new foodie experiment: training as a butcher....*Cleaving* is highly readable....Ultimately, Powell is saved by her beautiful writing, effortlessly filling pages with virtuoso descriptions of animal slaughter and human travail."

—Camilla Long, *Sunday Times* (London)

"If Julie Powell's debut was reminiscent of egg whites whipped into glossiness with sugar, this new book has the heft and complexity of, well, meat....No tidy aha moment arrives, but butchery brings order to chaos; Powell can 'take a knife and do something new, break something apart to make something else beautiful, understand something, a body, its parts, the logic of it.'...By the end, I felt a growing admiration for the risks this author takes. Looking unflinchingly at her messy life, she can name her obsessions, excesses, and destructive tendencies without trying to cut them away....Here we have something richer and more satisfying: canvas enough for complexity, for Julie Powell to write about the world she's 'managed to crack open for [herself], like a bone saw exposing the marrow.'"

—Paula McLain, *Cleveland Plain Dealer*

CLEAVING

ALSO BY JULIE POWELL

Julie and Julia

CLEAVING

A Story of
Marriage, Meat, and Obsession

Julie Powell

BACK BAY BOOKS
Little, Brown and Company
NEW YORK   BOSTON   LONDON

Back Bay Books / Little, Brown and Company
Hachette Book Group
1290 Avenue of the Americas New York, NY, 10104
www.hachettebookgroup.com

Originally published in hardcover by
Little, Brown and Company, December 2009
First Back Bay paperback edition, November 2010

Back Bay Books is an imprint of Little, Brown and Company.
The Back Bay Books name and logo are trademarks of
Hachette Book Group, Inc.

The names and identifying characteristics of some characters (persons)
in this book have been changed.

"Designs on You" by Old 97's. Copyright © 2001: Songs Music Pub-
lishing, LLC o/b/o Ram Island Songs (ASCAP), Burgermeister Music
(ASCAP), Pennycost Music (ASCAP), This Is My Piece of Sheet Music
(ASCAP), Wait Till Next Year Music (ASCAP). Reprinted by permis-
sion of Songs Music Publishing, LLC. "Red Right Ankle." Written
by Colin Meloy. Copyright © Music of Stage Three o/b/o itself and
Osterozhna! Music (BMI). All rights reserved. Used by permission.
"Willin'." Copyright © 1994. Written by Lowell George of Little Feat.
Lyrics reprinted with permission.

Illustrations by Diana Cone

Library of Congress Cataloging-in-Publication Data
Powell, Julie.
    Cleaving : a story of marriage, meat, and obsession /
Julie Powell. — 1st ed.
        p. cm.
ISBN 978-0-316-00336-0 (hc) / 978-0-316-00337-7 (pb)
1. Powell, Julie. 2. Powell, Julie — Marriage. 3. Women
cooks — New York (State) — New York — Biography. 4. Cooks —
New York (State) — New York — Biography. 5. Butchers —
New York (State) — Kingston — Biography. 6. Meat cutting —
Psychological aspects. 7. Fleisher's (Kingston, N.Y.). 8. New York
(N.Y.) — Biography. 9. Kingston (N.Y.) — Biography. I. Title.
    TX649.P66A3 2009
    641.5092—dc22
    [B]   2008054939

10 9 8 7 6 5 4 3 2 1

For Josh and Jessica,
who have the hearts of true butchers—
tough, generous, and enormous

CONTENTS

AUTHOR'S NOTE

It's the memoirist's privilege to tell her version of a many-faceted story; and any one facet may necessarily be incomplete, fractured, or polished to a sheen that the original stuff of experience didn't possess. Cleaving is a book that is faithful to my heart, but occasionally fuzzy on the odd physical detail. Other participants in the events recounted in these pages undoubtedly remember things differently; from them, and from the reader, I ask for a bit of patience and understanding.

Prologue

February 13, 2008

THIS IS REALLY not what it looks like.

The work is most often a delicate thing, and bloodless. In the year and more that I've been doing this, I've gone whole days with no more evidence of my labors by evening than a small bit of gore on my shoes or a sheen of translucent fat on my hands and face (it's excellent for the skin, I'm told). So this is unusual, this syrupy drip, my arms drenched up to the elbows, my apron smeared with crimson going quickly to brown.

I reach down into the plastic-lined cardboard box one more time, coming up with an organ weighing probably fifteen pounds, a dense and slippery deadweight, a blood-soaked sponge. I slap it onto the cutting table, and it makes a sound like a fish flopping on the deck of a boat; the risk of dropping it on the floor is not inconsiderable. The box is deep, and when I reached to the bottom of it my face brushed up against the bloody lining. Now I can feel a streak of the stuff drying stickily across my cheekbone. I don't bother to wipe it off. On what clean surface would I wipe it, after all? Besides, it makes me feel rather rakish.

I take my scimitar from the metal scabbard hanging from a chain around my waist. For most work I use my boning knife, an altogether smaller, finer thing, six inches long, slightly curved, with a dark rosewood hilt worn to satin smoothness by all the fat and lanolin that has been massaged into it. That little knife cracks open a haunch joint or breaks down muscle groups into their component parts like nothing else. But with this heavy, foot-long blade I can, while pressing firmly down on the flesh with my right palm, slice straight through the liver in one dragging stroke. Thin, even slices. With the boning knife I'd have to saw away to get through that bulk of organ meat, making for torn, jagged edges. And you wouldn't want that. You want the blade to slip through easily. Smooth. Final.

More than a year ago, when I first told my husband, Eric, that I wanted to do this, he didn't understand. "Butchery?" he asked, an expression of mystification, perhaps even discomfort, screwing up his face.

His suspicion hurt me. There was a time, just a few years before, when there was no trace of it in his heart. I knew I deserved it. But it was just so strange to have to try to explain; strange to have to explain anything to Eric at all. I'd known him by then for sixteen years, almost literally half my life. I knew him when he was a beautiful, shy, blue-eyed teenager in baggy shorts, a stretched-out sweater, and worn Birkenstocks, with a dog-eared paperback jutting out of one rear pocket. And almost at the beginning I picked him out, decided he was the one I needed. It took most of a school year to snatch him from the swarm of pretty girls that seemed always to be circling—he so oblivious, he so sweet and gentle—but I managed it. God, I was invincible when I was eighteen. When it came down to it, I got pretty much whatever I went after. *Want. Take. Have.* That was my simple motto. And I was right—to take him, I mean. From the beginning we were interlocking puzzle pieces. From the beginning we nestled into the notion that our two lives were to be irrevocably woven into one.

I now slice off eight pretty burgundy flaps of liver. The cut organ releases a metallic tang into the air, and yet more blood onto the table. Changing knives now, I delicately excise the tight pale ducts that weave through the slices. Perfectly cooked liver should be crisp on the outside with a custardy-smooth center. Nothing tough or chewy should get in the way of that sensual quintessence. Six of these slices are for the gleaming glass and steel case at the front of the shop; the last two I set aside, to wrap up and take home after work for a Valentine's Day dinner tomorrow. Once, I thought the holiday merited boxes of chocolate and glittery cards, but in these last couple of eye-opening years, amid the butchery and wrenches of the heart, I've realized life has gotten too complicated for such sweet and meaningless nothings; I've even learned I'm okay with that.

Valentine's Day Liver for Two

½ cup flour

2 ½-inch-thick slices high-quality beef liver, trimmed of any tough veins or filament

Salt and pepper to taste

2 tablespoons butter

1 tablespoon extra-virgin olive oil

Spread flour on a large plate. Season the liver slices with salt and pepper, then dredge in the flour, shaking off excess.

Set a skillet over high heat, and add butter and oil. When the butter foam has just subsided, add the liver slices. Sauté just until a crispy golden brown crust develops, about two minutes. Flip the slices and do the same on the other side. (Don't worry about undercooking. Overcooking is by far the worse fate for liver.)

Beef liver cooked like this—I keep telling people in the face of near-universal scoffs of disbelief—is one of the most, well, passionate things you'll ever eat. I don't know exactly why this is. It's as sexy as hell, but difficult too. Somehow faintly forlorn, like there is no denying that something was torn from something for your pleasure.

Eric and I married young, but that doesn't mean our union was precipitous. We'd already known each other for seven years by the time I donned that white organza princess gown and walked along that stone path on my father's arm to the bubbly notes of "My Baby Just Cares for Me." We could look right down to the bottom of each other and see what was swimming there, like fish flashing in clear mountain lakes. At our center wasn't sexuality or ambition, though we shared both. No, deep understanding, that's what we had. The nagging voice I've all my life heard in my head, the one people might call addiction or restlessness or wayward-ness, but which is to me almost an embodiment, some thing out-side of myself, impish, far from benign, but also inspiring and not entirely unconcerned with my self-interest—Eric believed in it. He feared it sometimes, but he believed in it. In 2002, when I turned twenty-nine, and we were living in Brooklyn, and I was stuck in yet another in a long line of ill-paid, dead-end jobs, loving my hus-band—clinging to him, in fact, as the sole solace in a world that I figured by and large didn't have much use for me—but unhappy and beginning to feel I just didn't in fact have much of a talent for happiness, Eric understood that when the voice spoke to me I had to listen.

"What if I cooked my way through *Mastering the Art of French Cooking*? Like, in a year?"

"What if you did?"

"That's—what?—five hundred recipes? More than that. That's crazy, right? Right?"

"Sure it is. You could blog about it. I think you should." He didn't even look confused. Eric could always divine for me just who I was and just what I could do.

So: I did this crazy cooking thing, and did it saucily, with style and courage. And I was rewarded. Suddenly I was successful. A book deal, a career! Using the very stuff of my despair and frustration, I'd turned my life around, transformed myself from a depressed secretary into an Author. I was, I thought, just what I wanted to be—confident, brave, and well paid. I was congratulated on my transformation, and because I was now a confident woman, I accepted the congratulations. But privately, I knew that I owed it entirely to Eric. He'd seen me as better than I was and had shown me the way to get there. If you'd told me then that he wouldn't understand when the voice spoke again, that I was capable of doing anything that could erode the faith of this most loyal of men, I'd never have believed you.

But by the time I followed the whisper here, to this butcher shop two hours from my home in the city, I'd learned through bitter experience that I was wrong. It turns out that things, even perfect things, pieces that seem to fit, to work together, can warp and crack and change.

After slicing the liver, I give my hands a quick rinse in the utility sink at the back of the shop. On my left hand, my cutting hand, I'm wearing a curious uncured leather bracelet that wraps around my wrist, then meets in a single thin band at the back of my palm, a slit in the end of which encircles the base of my index finger. A few coarse, snow-white hairs cling to it, though most of the hide has been worn bare. People mistake this for some sort of brace or therapeutic wrap, a treatment for carpal tunnel or a sprained wrist, but really it is a reminder of what I've experienced during these last years of marriage, butchery, obsession. I try to wipe some of the blood from it, but as much soaks into the leather as washes away. Then I retrieve a china plate, white with small cornflower blooms, like something you'd find in a quaint old kitchen, and I line it with an absorbent pad and a square of green butcher paper. I arrange the slices in an attractive floral pattern.

It was confusing and distressing to find myself, so soon after that whirlwind year came to a close, more or less where I'd been before. That wasn't really true, of course. I could not, without seeming churlish and ungrateful, deny my good fortune, the money and job offers and a book contract, the fans and friends and of course the devoted husband. Eric and I seemed calmer together after weathering what I'd spent the last year putting us through. I had every reason for contentment, pride, fulfillment. So why did it all feel like...I don't know, like cheating, somehow? If I pinched myself, I feared I'd wake up, disappear from this dream world in a puff of smoke.

I was starry-eyed and vaguely discontented and had too much time on my hands. It was exactly the wrong time for the phone call I got that summer of 2004, a year after my cooking project ended, as I was putting the final touches on my very first book. A call from someone I'd not heard from in years, a half-remembered murmur coming across the line, sparking uncomfortable memories of a handful of long-ago late nights I'd nearly succeeded in forgetting. "Hey, it's me," he said. "I hear you've been doing well for yourself. I've moved to New York. Let's get lunch sometime."

I realize that this could all look a little incriminating, a woman in a butcher shop in upstate New York, covered in blood and completely unruffled by that fact, wielding knives casually, lovingly manipulating offal with gore-begrimed fingers. No, I'm not a lover caught red-handed in the middle of a crime of passion, or a psychopath in the midst of a ritual dismemberment. No humans were harmed in bringing you this scene, but still, I get why it would all make some folks, well, speculate. Speculate, maybe especially, about the expression on my face, which betrays more than just the professional indifference I'm trying hard to project. If you look closely enough, if you get past the (formerly) white apron and the blood and the big knives bristling at my hip and up to my eyes, I'll confess you might see something a bit unnerving there. A secret glow. A little thrill. As my friend Gwen would say, "Makes a girl wonder where she's hiding the bodies."

It's a difficult thing to explain, made more difficult still by a phenomenon I've noticed many times since starting work here: it turns out that it's very hard for people to listen clearly to a woman holding a butcher knife. But, truly, the glint in my eyes is not about violence or vengeance or cruelty. The joy I take is not—well, not *only*—in the power I now have to hack and cut and destroy. It's about something else, something calm and ordered.

Just as Tinker Bell led Wendy astray from time to time, my inner whisper has sent me right into all manner of scrapes and heartbreaks. But I trust it, because I've also followed it to my apprenticeship. My haven. My butcher shop. I spend my days now breaking down meat, with control, gentleness, serenity. I've craved certainty in these last troubled years, and here I get my fix.

I wipe my hands on a towel I grab from the bin and bring the china plate with its glistening offal rosette up to the front of the shop. As I do I feel an insistent beelike hum at my left butt cheek—the BlackBerry tucked into my jeans pocket. I get phone service only at the front of the shop; the walk-in coolers at the rear block the signal. Though I do, if I'm honest with myself, still feel a small adrenaline-stoked surge in my chest whenever I feel this buzz, I ignore it, and instead hold out the plate to Hailey, who's ringing up a couple at the cash register. "For the case," I mouth at her.

She nods. A line is forming, the beginning of the afternoon rush. "Can you put it in for me? There should be room on the top shelf."

"Um, where?"

"By the oxtails?"

I slide open the glass door of the case, bending to rearrange the crowded array of meat to accommodate this new addition. It's full to bursting already, with dry-aged steaks and unctuous Berkshire pork chops, heaped bowls of ground lamb and rows of spice-spiked house-made sausage. I thought it beautiful the first day I entered this shop, nearly a year and a half ago. Now, as a contributor to it, I find it more beautiful still.

As I close the door and straighten up, I find myself eye to eye with one of *those* women. They come into the shop every now and again, these women, with their raised eyebrows and sourly flared nostrils, as if they're walking into a refugee-camp latrine. Vegetarian or merely squeamish, forced by whatever circumstance into a clean-smelling but unapologetic temple of meat, they exude supercilious disapproval, as if this place I have come to love is a barely endurable abomination. It's all I can do to be civil, honestly.

"Hi. Whaddaya need?"

"Two skinless boneless chicken breasts, please."

These women *always* want skinless boneless chicken breasts. "We've only got bone-in. Sorry."

The woman sighs noisily at this affront. I try, not entirely successfully, to repress a roll of the eyes. Of course, I could offer to bone them out for her. I now know perfectly well how to remove the breastbone and cartilage from that insipid slip of white meat. But I am offended by the very notion of skinless boneless chicken breasts, and the boring sticklike women who eat them. This is why I don't work the counter; my people skills leave something to be desired. "Well, that will do, I suppose," she mutters. I turn to one side to reach for a pair of latex gloves.

"Ex—, excuse me?"

I look up from the tray of breasts to see the customer's suddenly stricken face. She brushes a finger fitfully against her own cheek. "You have a—"

I remember the red streak on my face and realize with a certain savage glee how I must look to her, bloody and wild-haired under my wide-rimmed leather hat. I want to bare my teeth and hiss vampirically at her. Instead I pull off the gloves I've just put on. "Actually, I'm going to let Jesse help you," I say cheerfully, nodding to a tall, bespectacled boy behind me who's just pulled on his newsboy cap and is washing his hands in preparation to return to the counter after his lunch break. Then I hold up my hands to her, turning them back to front so she gets a good look at the brown gunk under my nails, the stains and unidentifiable bits of goo stuck to my skin, the blood-stained leather band around my wrist. "I'm a little messy right now." I grin toothily, just to provoke a shudder, then turn on my heel.

As I throw the gloves into a garbage bin with a snap, the Black-Berry in my back pocket buzzes again. I pull it out, not worrying about the grime I just tried to scare a customer off with. (My

PDA, like my hat, my sneakers, and my iPod—currently resting in a dock balanced atop the Cryovac bags, blaring Modest Mouse—gets coated with meat schmutz as a matter of course. Even the setting of my engagement ring is clotted with bits of flesh and fat.)

An e-mail. Eric, of course. *How's it going?* he writes. The meat I bring back home when I return from Fleisher's, the butcher shop where I've trained and worked, helps, but after more than a year, my husband still doesn't understand what it is I'm trying to do here, what I'm finding that's so important. He gets lonely. So do I. Still, I elect not to answer; not now.

Instead, I take a break. It's four o'clock, and there's a fresh pot of coffee, our third of the day. Since I started cutting at Fleisher's I've become a coffee fiend. It's not just that the caffeine keeps me spry during the long hours on my feet. It's also that the heat warms fingers icy from slipping into the freezing crevices between muscles, and the moments spent loosely cupping the mug seem to soothe my hands and wrists, so often swollen from gripping the knife, working it into joints, then twisting to open them up.

I pour myself a mug and clasp it between my palms, leaning up against the table opposite the stove in the kitchen. Something on the cooktop smells wonderful, heady with garlic. The soup of the day. I peer into the pot, then grab a ladle for a taste. Spice and rich pork. Posole. Warms me to the core, reaches where even the coffee doesn't, in this place that must of necessity remain nippy all the time. Resting against the counter, thawing my hands, I stare, dreamy with weariness, at the lion's share of liver still sitting on the table a few feet away, as smooth as a river stone, though of a more vivid color.

Those familiar with grisly nineteenth-century British history might know that one popular theory among Jack the Ripper armchair criminologists posits that the killer was a practicing butcher. I have developed a small addendum to this hypothesis. I am by now fairly confident that should I want to surgically excise a streetwalker's liver, I could manage it. I will even confess that I can sort of imagine the appeal. Don't get me wrong: I'm not an advocate for slashing prostitutes' throats and rummaging through their innards as a valid lifestyle choice. But in a weird way, I see the butchering part of what Jack did as separate from the killing, the frenzy, the rage. And I see it as maybe containing the tiny kernel of sanity still left to him. Maybe it was his forlorn way of trying to fit the pieces back together, or at least understand how they once fit. I look at that crosscut organ sitting on the table, its workings so mysterious but its dimensions so satisfying, dense and symmetrical and glassy-smooth, and I feel a sort of peace, a small piece of understanding.

My hands are blue with chill, my lower back throbs, my left wrist aches, and in the cooler in back is a towering stack of pork sides waiting to be broken down before closing in three hours. I smile into my cup. I am far from home. Right where I want to be.

PART I

Apprentice

...And how it whispered,
"Oh, adhere to me, for we are bound by symmetry
And whatever differences our lives have been
We together make a limb."
    —THE DECEMBERISTS, "Red Right Ankle"

When are you going to get this, B? The life of a
slayer is very simple. Want. Take. Have.
    —FAITH, *Buffy the Vampire Slayer*

1

Love and a Butcher Shop

A year and a half earlier, July 2006.

I GUESS I really have been in the city too long; I've acquired, among other traits of the native New Yorker, a blanket disdain for the entire state of New Jersey. I was irrationally hesitant to come here. But on this day NJ Route 202 is leading me through an unexpectedly lovely landscape of gentle hills and dilapidated barns. I'm getting no service on my BlackBerry, which sends a slight frisson of panic through my body, making my teeth buzz in my gums; this must be another one of those New Yorker things I've picked up. I keep lighting up the screen and scrutinizing it for bars, but it's no-go.

The air breezes in through my rolled-down windows, warm and smelling heavily of honeysuckle and freshly cut grass, rather than the diesel fumes and sour chemical smoke that clung to my nostrils during the run down the turnpike. It calms me. I breathe deeply.

It's been a frustrating few months.

• • •

I GUESS the truth is that butchers intimidate the hell out of me. I've long had a bit of a thing for them, akin to the way many women feel about firefighters. Burly Irishmen covered in soot are okay, I guess, if you're into that. But I prefer this world's lock-pickers to its battering rams. Anybody with enough resolve and muscle can bust down a door; that kind of force I comprehend completely. I myself possess it, psychologically if not physically— just call me Julie "Steamroller" Powell. But a man who can both heave a whole pig over his shoulder *and* deftly break down the creature into all its luscious parts, in a matter of moments? That's a man whose talents I can really use.

I'm attracted to a butcher's intimate knowledge. Romantically, I imagine it's innate, that his nicked hands were born knowing how to slice those whisper-thin cutlets. I'm attracted to his courtly, old-world brand of machismo. Butchers are known for their corny jokes and their sexism, but when the man behind the counter calls me "sweetheart" or "little lady," I find myself flattered rather than offended. Most of all, I'm attracted to his authority. There's an absolute sureness to a butcher, whether he is chining lamb chops with a band saw or telling his customer just how to prepare a crown roast. He is more certain of meat than I've ever been about anything. Rippling deltoids and brawny good looks are nice, of course, but to me a butcher's sureness is the definition of mascu-linity. It strikes me as intoxicatingly exotic, like nothing I've ever experienced. (Well, not for years, anyway, not since I was a kid. I think of the teenager I was when I found Eric and took him to me, and it's like remembering an entirely different person.)

Maybe that's why I seem unable to open my mouth around butchers.

IF I'M dreading a conversation, I tend to practice it over and over in my head beforehand, perhaps not the most effective of preparation techniques. "I want to learn how to—"... "I was hoping you could teach me to—"... "I'm really *so* interested in what you do..." Ugh.

This is far from the first butcher I've tried to ask for this favor. Weeks ago, I asked the guys at Ottomanelli's—my first butcher shop when I moved to New York City, and still my favorite. It's a tidy storefront on Bleecker Street with hams and ducks hanging in the meticulously polished windows and a tight awning overhead, red and white stripes as neat as the trimmed and tied meat and bones within. I used to be a regular there, and the guys behind the counter—brothers, I think, all of them in their sixties or seventies, white coats spanking clean despite days of blood and ooze—still always make a point of greeting me when I come in. It's not quite a "Norm!" sort of welcome, but there's warmth there.

But when I managed to ask, stammering, if they had a place for an apprentice with zero experience, they demurred. Not particularly shocking, I suppose. Instead they suggested one of the culinary schools downtown. I briefly entertained this notion, but it turns out culinary programs don't offer one-off classes on butchering, and I wasn't about to shell out twenty thousand bucks for a yearlong program teaching restaurant management and pastry making, my personal vision of hell. I proceeded to ask around at the handful of other butcher shops in the city, or try to, anyway. Half the time I couldn't even get the words out. When I did, the men behind the counter looked at me as if I might be a tad touched and shook their heads.

I press my lips together as the beseeching words run through my mind. And then, inevitably perhaps, *he* pops into my head, the one whom the word *beseech* sometimes seems to me to have been invented for, the man who called, two years ago, to ask me to lunch, the man I've wound up spending much of the last two years pleading with—for attention, assurance, sex, and love. The exception proving the rule of my marriage, the one man who, when he was not much more than a boy, small and dark, not so very attractive, found he could make me open my dorm room door in bewilderment, late at night, with a single knock. The one who, nine years later, discovered he could still do essentially the same thing. In my phone's contact list he is represented by a single towering initial, D.

But no. I'll not let him in, not now. I shake my head sharply, as if I could physically dislodge the errant thoughts. *Find a butcher. Get him to teach you how he does what he does. Do it now.* I don't know why I want this so much, what I have to gain from learning to cut up animals. Yes, I have a thing for butchers, but it hasn't ever before occurred to me to try to *be* one. What's going on here?

Maybe I just need distraction. D and I have been sleeping together for nearly two years now. I'm familiar with the landscape of addiction, and I recognize that I've built up a habit for him, no less real and physical than my habit for booze, which has itself grown stronger in the wake of all the various stresses of being an adulterer. And something is wrong lately, slightly off. Just thinking about that makes me crave a drink.

Eric, of course, knows I'm fucking someone else, has known for almost the entire period of my affair with D. He even knows that, in distressing point of fact, I'm in love with this other man. I don't have to tell him this. We basically share the same mind, after all. Once, I was proud of and comforted by this nearly paranormal connection. That my husband knew me so well, and I him, seemed proof of a love superior in all ways to all others. Then D happened. We fought about it when Eric first found out, of course, or rather I cried and Eric yelled and marched out of the house into the night for a few hours. But after that, there was only exhaustion, and quiet, and in all the months since we've barely spoken about it at all. Sometimes, even most of the time, everything seems fine this way. But then, this talent we share emerges and proves itself the stealthiest, most vicious weapon in our arsenals. We can delve into each other's heart and deftly pull out the scraps of filthy hidden longing and unhappiness and shame. With a look or a word, we can deftly rub these into the other's face as we'd push a dog's nose into its mess on the living room rug.

We'll be sitting in front of the TV, say, into our second bottle of wine, watching some Netflix DVD. I always have my phone on silent when we're together, so Eric doesn't hear the trill or feel the buzz against the sofa cushions. But still I'm tense, glancing at the BlackBerry screen whenever Eric gets up to go to the bathroom or stir the soup. When he gets back to the couch and sits, I'll press the soles of my feet up against his thigh in a gesture of affection intended to make me seem comfortable and happy. But eventually, unconsciously, the nervous energy builds, and I'm tapping my bare feet against his pants leg. "What's the matter?" Eric will say, grabbing my feet to still them, not taking his eyes from the TV screen. "He not paying enough attention to you tonight?" I'll freeze, stop breathing, and say nothing, waiting to see if there will be more, but there won't be. There doesn't need to be. We'll stare at the television as if nothing at all has been said; when D does send me a message, if he does, I'll be afraid to answer it.

I can do the same to him. Some night my husband will go out. "Drinks with work buddies," he will say. "Back by nine." Nine o'clock and then ten will, inevitably, come and go. The first time this happened, a month or two after he discovered I was sleeping with D, I was surprised and worried. He came home that morning at two thirty and woke me up to confess, remorsefully, that he'd been on a date with another woman, that it wouldn't happen again, though I told him—ah, the pleasure of being the sainted one for once—that he deserved to be able to see anyone he wanted. By now I'm used to it; I don't expect him home, probably until dawn. I can instantly tell, from the tone of voice when he calls or the phrasing of his e-mail, that he's going to be with the woman he's been seeing off and on for nearly as long as I've been fucking D. I'm not even angry; I'm pleased. The text I send him at a little after eleven is always more than gracious: *Sweetie, can you let me know if you'll be home tonight? I totally understand if you won't be. I just don't want to worry.*

It might take him twenty minutes to write back, or an hour,

or three. But he'll always write the same thing. *I'll be home soon. I know I'm fucking up everything.*

No, I'll write, all sweetness and light, *you're not fucking anything up. Have fun. Come home whenever you like.* When I hear the lock in the door I'll initially feign sleep while he undresses and cuddles up guiltily beside me in bed, but I'll make sure I give his hand a reassuring squeeze so he knows. In the morning I'll pretend not to see his wish that I'd scream or cry, show my hurt and thus my love. I'll poach an egg for breakfast, smiling. Nothing will be said. This is how I punish him.

When he leaves for work I'll report everything that happens to Gwen, the friend I go to with all of this. "I really don't mind. He cares for her, you know? He deserves some relief."

"Julie, honestly? I love you, but I don't know why Eric stays. I really don't."

Gwen says all the things a good girlfriend should, and every once in a while she offers to beat up my husband or my lover for me, depending on who is driving me more crazy, which is nice. But at the end of the day, she can't quite fathom the situation I find myself in.

"I know. When did we start being so nasty to each other? I mean, it's not all the time, it's really not. But—"

"Do you really see this getting any better?"

I don't know the answer to her question. I do know that through all this, Eric still doesn't leave. And as for me, as bad as it is, I can't even comprehend the pain of leaving him. (As so often happens in my life, I find that a character from the much-mourned TV show *Buffy the Vampire Slayer* puts it best: "It's like I lost an arm. Or worse. A torso.") I just need a place to hole up from time to time, from this constant silent seep of toxic hurt and anger, and also, lately, from D's hot-and-cold ambivalence, which I feel like too-tight clothing. Bafflingly, when I think "sanctuary," what comes to mind is the gleam of steel and tile, the moist red of a lamb roast, the pungent smell of aging beef, and the grip of a knife in my hand.

But it turns out that this is a tricky thing I'm trying to do, and not just because I seem to be constitutionally terrified of men in white coats. There also just aren't a lot of butchers out there anymore, not real ones, not in this country. That seems impossible, doesn't it? I mean, there are a lot more of us Americans than there were, say, a hundred years ago, and a whole lot of us are eating meat. But butcher shops have been largely replaced by meat-processing plants, giant factories that swallow up animals and excrete vacuum-packed steaks. A crude analogy, I know. But the invisibility of the procedure is as complete as that of your own bodily processes. We know there are lots of heavy, sharp machines in there, since the workers inside are constantly getting hurt and killed. (Meatpacking is one of the most dangerous jobs in America, and that's probably why it employs more than its share of illegal immigrants.) We know that there are probably men in there with terrific knife skills, presumably fitted into the industrialized process, fleshly cogs in the vast machine, clad in chain-mail aprons and repeating the same cut on the same body part over and over until their hands cramp and backs throb.

But I'm guessing about all this, because Big Beef doesn't generally tend to roll out the red carpet and start throwing backstage passes around. In this age of nanotechnology and liability, you've got a better shot at taking a journey through the digestive tract of an industrially farmed steer than at witnessing exactly how that same animal moves from on the hoof to on your plate. And that's not what I want anyway. I want to be taught by an artisan, not an assembly-line worker.

So, after exhausting all the possibilities in the city, I've made a few calls and obtained another few names from farther afield, seasoned guys who still know how to go about the old-fashioned trade of ushering animal into meat. I'm following one of those leads now, straight into the far reaches of southern New Jersey.

I've been riding the curves of the road a bit too fast, declining to apply the brakes, so that on the sharper turns I can feel the weight of the car edging out along the grassy verge. But as I get closer to Bucktown, I slow up. At least, I think I'm close to Bucktown. I've been on the East Coast for fifteen years now, since graduating from high school back in Texas and moving up to Massachusetts for college, plenty of time to have accustomed myself to the fluid notions of townships up here. But I still find myself occasionally nostalgic for the decorous distances of my home state, not these villages and localities endlessly bunched and inextricable, but blank landscapes clarifying the separation between well-marked city limits, leaving me always assured that I can find out where I am, at least on a road map. I miss that sense of separation.

Generally I like driving, especially by myself. I never really lost that teenage thrill, the fantasies of flight that accompany going fifteen miles over the speed limit, curling smoothly around more earthbound drivers, knowing that whatever exit I need to take is still miles ahead. But this part of driving I don't like—the looking, the poking about, the squinting to catch sight of numbers on the sides of mailboxes. Trying to figure out the details of where the hell I'm headed. I guess maybe no one likes this part. I'm tempted to text Eric, always am when I'm lost. He is out there somewhere, eager to help, but I still have no phone service.

Finally I find the place. It's more retiring than I'd imagined, more countrified. I've been in the city long enough that I expected, even in this rural setting, a city sort of butcher shop. I'd been imagining a redbrick storefront in the small town center, shining glass panes, and the white tiles and stainless steel of a meat counter visible within. So I'd missed the rambling old clapboard building set some yards back from the road, with the weather-beaten sign propped up on the pitched roof of the front porch—an Italian family name in unprepossessing lettering. I pull into the little unpaved lot with a crunching roll of tires. For most of the drive from Queens I've been filled with that lovely sense of purpose that comes from having embarked upon a quest without yet having begun to grapple with any of the nitty-gritty; yet for the past half hour I've been overcome with the frustration and irritation of unfound addresses. And now, as I put the car into park and take the key out of the ignition, all of that goes away and I'm stuck with that old lurch of the heart. Now I have to walk in there and ask these guys for a favor. A job. That this time I've driven for two hours at the behest of the raving voice inside my head doesn't make this any easier at all.

The air smells like flowers. With a little extra push of will I open the car door and get out. Inside the front screen door, the shop is dim and has a whiff of something not exactly clean, though not unpleasant either, the same class of aromas to which horse barns belong. There's something unsavory, yet covertly exciting, about the place; it's like sneaking into an abandoned hunting lodge. A glass-fronted freezer against one wall to the left holds an untidy pile of hand-labeled bins and packages. The wide planks of the wood floor are worn, dark, stained, and strewn with a light sprinkling of sawdust. The meat counter seems to be an improvised affair; the coolers look old, perhaps secondhand, and rather than the high piles of fresh beef and lamb on neat trays adorned with parsley sprigs I'm accustomed to seeing at Ottomanelli's, there's a haphazard scattering of meat, some of it looking a little gray and tired. The end of a busy week. There's a blond woman in her late thirties smiling at me directly behind the counter, and an old man, stooped, in the farther reaches of the space behind her, winding trussing string around thick, stiff fingers. One of the brothers from the sign, of course. You can always tell a butcher. He looks up at me and nods, not unfriendly but weary. "Can we help ya?"

So once more I give my spiel about wanting to learn butchery, of being willing to do anything to get behind that counter every day and watch him do his thing, that I've driven all the way from New York to ask him for this favor. The brother smiles sadly. But once again I get a shake of the head. "We don't have enough work to go around as it is. Nobody wants butchers anymore. When we retire, we'll have to shutter this place." He says it kindly enough, and it's not my place to argue with him. Maybe he thinks I'm a dilettante, and maybe I am. Maybe this irrational passion is going to pop like a soap bubble, evanesce. Maybe I'll change my mind tomorrow, decide I'm really into, I don't know, dog racing.

But if there's one thing I've learned about myself, it's that my passions don't tend to run out. Would that they did.

It occurs to me as I duck back into my car that all the butchers I've been speaking to remind me of my granny. She lived to be ninety, never really had anything wrong with her, physically anyway, and presented herself as a cheery, tough old broad. It took me the longest time to realize that the same woman who used to make me the world's best fried chicken, who I shared a bed with as a kid, who I'd wake up in the morning with my giggling, toothless "Yet's yaff!" (that's "Let's Laugh!" in toddler), lived every day of her life harboring a blackness in her, a profound dissatisfaction with the confines she'd placed herself in when she was still just a beautiful young woman of limited prospects in Brazoria, Texas, that had settled into a sort of dry rot of the imagination. So what must it be like to see your entire profession—not just your job, or your business, but the entire profession, what you have always done for a living—crumpling up and blowing away? I don't know, but I know that Granny fought a feeling of pointlessness her whole life, that it curdled her sense of humor (she was never not funny, but she got to be funny in a darker, sour way) and led to the inordinate consumption of Taylor sherry. I know it because I see her in my mother, and I feel her in me, more and more. It leads me to drink too—though not sherry, yet—and to other things, to things that are bad for me, harmful urges succumbed to. My fear of butchers is nothing in the face of my fear of this curse that seems to run through the veins of the women in my family. Maybe that's what the voice I hear is telling me; it's trying desperately to help me outrace an inevitable future. One thing I've learned about my voice is that it prefers indulging dangerous cravings to the prospect of tamping down those cravings into bitter resignation. I make a U-turn in the gravel lot and head for home.

A few miles before I hit the interstate, I come over a hill and my BlackBerry goes all atwitter in the cup holder. I pick it up eagerly, though with a pang as well. I'm surprised in the moment that I'm almost disappointed the thing is working again.

Two messages, two men.

The first: *How's the meat?*

The second: *Mhm.*

Does everyone talk like this, in these codes? I decipher both perfectly. One pulls at me with a thousand strands of anxiety and obligation and love and solicitude and guilt; the other with a single knowing yank, the secret guttural syllable that brings me to heel.

To both my answer is the same: *I'm on my way.*

2
Boned Out

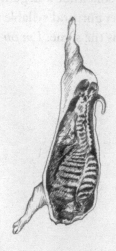

AND THEN, A month later, I find it.

Another clue has led to another long drive, all the way north to Kingston, New York, nestled in the Catskills. I head up early in the morning in my Outback. (Yes, I've become the sort of thirty-three-year-old woman who drives a silver Outback, bought new. Somehow, funky, colorfully dilapidated wrecks became one of those categories, along with funky, colorfully grotty shithole apartments, that I outgrew without noticing.) I am nervous and not too hopeful as I park, feed a meter, walk through the glass door of the shop on Wall Street. But I know the second I step in: this is it.

Fleisher's is more than a butcher shop, really. It's almost a market, with fragrant soaps made of beef tallow on the shelves, local vegetables in baskets in the middle of the floor, T-shirts for sale pinned to the walls: 100% GRASS-FED, LOCALLY GROWN. It's a place equally quixotic and inevitable. It might be a neighborhood butcher shop, or it might be a political movement masquerading as a neighborhood butcher shop; either way, it's not quite the shop of my fantasies. It's something else, a place I'd not quite imagined.

I introduce myself to the guy behind the counter, a big man with a seventies porn mustache, small, smirking blue eyes behind wire spectacles, and a long rusty braid running down his back from under a black Kangol cap. He's surprisingly young, not much older than I am. Maybe that's what finally gives me the push I need. "My name is Julie, and I—" At the last moment I abandon all my carefully rehearsed phrasings. "Honestly? I just want to learn how to turn a cow into a steak."

Raised eyebrows. And then: "Cool."

The butcher's name is Joshua. He invites me back to watch him cut up a pig. And then he feeds me the best pork chop I've ever tasted.

"ALL RIGHT, *chica,* you're going to bone these bad boys out." As he passes on his way to the front office, Josh tosses two bewilderingly large pieces of pig onto the cutting table, adding to the collection already there. Back legs, with the hooves still on—do pigs have hooves, is that what you call them?—and the skin, laced with dark veins and pocked with pores and the occasional wiry hair. They're shaped rather like giant pork drumsticks, which is exactly what they are. "Watch Tom," he calls over his shoulder as he strides away. "He'll show you what to do."

It's my first day as a butcher's apprentice. I woke up at six this morning. I'll grant you that's not hideously early by your average working stiff's standards, but sometimes it's a struggle just to get out of bed in the morning at all. I swear I sometimes think if I didn't have a dog to walk and cats to feed, I just never would. Eric has been having the same problem. He barely stirred when I slipped out from under the covers and into the shower. By seven I was on the road, and now, at five minutes after nine, I am tying on a white apron, which I grabbed from an old plastic laundry bin, and taking a knife from the magnetic strip on the wall.

Josh passes again. He keeps barreling up and down the length of the shop from counter to office to cooler to kitchen to back stair: arranging the case, grabbing invoices, pulling out primals to be cut down, checking on how the sausages are coming, going out back for a smoke break. A bear of a guy, with a big voice to match and a cheerfully profane word for everyone, he's like an animal in a well-designed, spacious zoo, relatively comfortable but still prone to restless pacing. I briefly try to picture this guy submitting to a suit and tie, a maze of cubicles; the image is laugh-out-loud funny.

"You got your lid?" he says without pausing in his circuit, tapping the brim of his own cap.

"Oh, right! I do actually!" I trot back to the table and chairs in the back of the shop, behind the front cooler, where I've dumped my stuff. I'm pretty proud that I remembered, on my first day, to bring a hat, and a good one, too—a brown leather New Zealand bush hat that fits me like I was born to it. I wear it at a slight tilt over one eye, jauntily. I have lost and found this precious object enough times to bring to mind the phrase "God looks after fools and drunks." I have had many dreams in which this hat has featured prominently. So the idea of wearing it all day, every day, to keep my hair in place while I'm learning to cut up large animals— the air of sexy, tomboyish bravado this hat will help me exude—is privately exciting. I yank it onto my head and almost dash back to the table, where Tom, a tall man with a slight stoop, a black mustache, and a goofy grin, is already pulling a second leg toward the edge of the table. Tom is a master butcher, has been doing this all his life, just as his father taught him. When Josh decided to open a shop a few years ago, he knew no more about butchering than what he had gleaned from some visits to his grandfather's kosher butcher shop in Brooklyn as a child, so he hired Tom not just to help cut meat, but to teach him and his employees. Of which I suppose I'm now one, sort of.

"Start by taking off the trotter, here." Holding the hoof in his left hand and the knife in his right, he runs his blade around and straight through the first joint, taking off the foot with one smooth spiraling motion. He tosses the foot to the table. "Go ahead, you do it. Piece of cake."

I pull a leg toward me, feel around to make sure I know where the joint is, and make a circular cut around, through the tough skin and flesh, but I've misjudged, for I hit only bone. "Shit," I mutter.

Tom grins over at me. "Wiggle it. Ya gotta *wiggle* it."

And when I move the foot back and forth I see what he means. When I work the foot I get a better sense of where the axis of the joint is, and after some digging around I hit cartilage and shove the tip of my blade through, between the bones. A bit more sawing and I have the foot off. It ain't pretty, but it's done. "Okay."

"Now off with the hock. You can do that with the band saw, if you're a hack."

"Oh, I'm a hack. I aspire to hackhood."

"Nah. This is how the *real* guys do it." He simply slides the blade through the skin, across what would be the base of the buttock, to mark his cut, then switches the grip on his boning knife so that he is fisting it with his pinky at the base of the hilt and with the sharp of the blade facing toward him. With his elbow bent at a right angle he pulls it through the meat, blade all the way to the table—a scarred wood surface, maple I think, four feet by six, on wheeled, metal legs—until, again unerringly, he hits the joint. Some blade tipwork gets him through that, and he finishes by smoothly raking through the flesh on the other side. Ham hock thrown to the side.

"They call this here a pistol grip." I nod, though I don't really understand how it pertains to firearms; it looks more like the clutch of a frenzied serial killer in a horror flick. Then he makes a quick gesture, pulling the knife blade first, fast, toward his groin. "They also call it the widowmaker," he says with a cackle. "Gotta be careful. You putting force behind that, it comes free and flies straight into you."

"Maybe you should show me the band saw."

"Eh, wimp. Go on, do it. You can learn the shortcut after you get the real way down. Band saw'll kill ya, anyway."

"Oh, all right..." So I apply myself to the job, getting used to the new grip. I actually prefer it; it feels so much stronger. Which, I realize, is exactly the danger. I'm able to put a lot more power behind the blade this way, pulling it toward me with my biceps. I can see what Tom means; if I pulled a bit too enthusiastically, things could get ugly. I scoot my body off to one side a little just to be safe, then slice through. Again I hit bone, again I have to dig messily around in the meat until I find the joint, wedge my knife tip down into the small, curved space between the bones, a cup and ball, as tightly knitted together with white bands of sinew as a devoted husband and wife. (I wince away that maudlin metaphor as quickly as I can.) My knife makes uncomfortable squeaky noises as it works in, hitting cartilage and bone. I get through it, though. The edge is ragged, the skin abraded, but the hock is off. "Okay," I breathe. "Now what?"

Tom is already on his third round, lapping me with practically every step I complete. I suspect he's showing off a little. "Peel away the skin. You want to leave the fat on, though." He demonstrates, loosening up the tough, slightly translucent skin at one edge and then, holding the flap between thumb and forefinger to keep it taut, pushing the blade away from him in a long sweeping motion just under it so that it lifts off easily, revealing a thick layer of fat, as white and sticky as a spread of Marshmallow Fluff. He pulls the skin off that entire ham—it is now recognizable as such—in one great piece, almost completely clean of any white fat residue. The woman-suit-making freak from *The Silence of the Lambs* would have been impressed. I certainly am.

Needless to say, I don't manage with nearly such finesse. I quickly find that there is something particularly satisfying about this job, though, something about how, when you get the pressure right, along with the angle of the blade, the knife skims across the underside of the skin with an easy scraping noise like ice skates. There is a trick to it, and when you're doing it right, you know it. I whisper under my breath, in nearly unseemly pleasure, "Thaaaaat's what I'm talkin' about."

But I don't always do it right. I sink into the bed of fat or pierce the skin, and wind up getting it all off only in several ragged pieces. No woman-suit for me.

Next I take off the top round, a cap of flesh on what I guess was once the pig's tush. Tom shows me how to find the seam. "Seams are the key. You can follow a seam, you can break down anything."

So. Between any two neighboring muscles, be they housed in a pig, a steer, or, one presumes, me, it turns out that there is a thin layer of connective tissue: clear, threadlike, easily cut. It looks rather like what would happen if you rubber-cemented two pieces of pink construction paper together, then pulled them apart again before the rubber cement dried. I don't know what this stuff would be called by a biologist or a doctor, but in the meat fabrication biz it is called a "seam." Seams seem (seams seem, heh) magical to me; they are what give butchery its best chance at grace. If you know what you're doing, you can peel two muscles clean apart, smooth and untorn, with the tip of a five-inch knife, or even just with your fingers. I go along painstakingly, but as I pull up on the cap of meat with my right hand, all those clear connecting threads show the seam's path. As timidly as I jab at them, still they fall away before me.

"Don't gotta be so delicate with. It's pork! You can't screw it up!" Tom cackles again. He's got a nasal voice, always amused, his words accented into a slight New Yawkese. He looks and sounds like a Muppets character. "Chop, chop!"

But I'm rather mesmerized by the slow, easy peel. Like the muscles knew from the beginning that it would end with this, this inevitable falling apart. It's actually rather moving, though I know better than to try to explain why aloud. It's sad, but a relief as well, to know that two things so closely bound together can separate with so little violence, leaving smooth surfaces instead of bloody shreds.

And off comes the top round. This will later be sliced into cutlets for the case, to be fried into schnitzel or rolled up into stuffed involtini. But for now it'll be bagged and put into the front cooler until the case needs to be refilled.

"And that's it. The rest goes into the grind. Just sausage."

A white plastic bin on the cutting table is piled high with pig meat, roughly sliced into big strips. Juan has come over to stuff the meat into big clear plastic Cryovac bags. He's a short, barrel-chested guy I guess to be a little younger than I am. I'm instantly attracted to his smile, though I've not yet gotten to talk much with him, just a hello after Josh introduced him this morning as "the only guy with any brains in the whole place. That's including me."

"I like your hat," he says to me now.

"Thanks!" I find myself blushing with pleasure. It *is* a good hat.

Tom has by now broken down almost all of the pile; he's leaving one more round for me to practice on, while he moves on to shoulders. He speaks quickly. "Pull out the aitchbone, that round one there."

"H bone? H as in hip?" For the bowl of bone protruding from the fat end of the round, with its hole in the middle, clearly has to be some part of the pelvis bone. It looks like something that—if picked clean of flesh and left out on the desert floor for a month or two—Georgia O'Keeffe would paint, as the bright New Mexico sky gleamed through its smooth white curve.

"Nah. Aitch. A-I-T-C-H."

"What does that mean?"

Tom shrugs his loose cartoonish shoulders. "Dunno. Homework for you, eh?"

So I pull it out as Tom shows me, with the help of a meat hook. With the big knob end of the drumstick facing me, I scoop out the divot of flesh from the middle of the hole, then come behind the bone to scrape meat free from the top edge. Then I can work the tip of the meat hook over that edge, then back and through the central hole. The hook is a C-shaped curve of steel about the size of my curled thumb and forefinger, with a viciously sharp point on one end and an orange plastic grip on the other. I hold it as if it were a bicycle handle, the base of the hook emerging from between my index and middle fingers. With it I can get a sure grasp on the bone, and a means to turn gravity to my advantage.

(Funny, about meat hooks. I've had the phrase *meat hooks* in my vocabulary for as long as I can remember, accompanied by the vision of a broad-chested, letter-jacketed thug pawing at a comely bobby-soxer. And I never gave the origin of the word any thought; I think I was picturing fleshy, too-big mitt-hands. Actually, using this meat hook, a sharp, small, thin tool that fits so coolly and easily in the palm, provokes a tiny, almost imperceptible shift of perspective. Meat hooks aren't like "meat hooks" at all. They're much more effective and terrifying. I find myself wondering idly if the first fifties coed to utter the phrase "Get your meat hooks *off* me!" was a butcher's daughter.)

As I pull down on the orange handle now, the bone gets looser. I help it along, scraping, sawing through the sinews marrying it to the rounded edge of the thigh bone. As more of the bone loosens, the rest of it comes away easily, until by the end I'm hardly using the knife, just yanking down and toward me with the hook.

"We keep the bones?"

"Keep the bones! *Always keep bones!*" Tom bellows. (In addition to working and instructing here at Fleisher's, Tom teaches butchery at the Culinary Institute of America in nearby Hyde Park and has therefore developed his comically stentorian delivery.)

"*Shut the fuck up!*" Josh bellows right back. (Not sure where Josh developed his stentorian delivery, but he sure as hell has.)

"*Josh, would you stop yelling?*" This from Jessica, Josh's tiny wife, ensconced in her office, working over invoices. "*The store is fucking open!*"

I like this place.

After the aitchbone is out (that's going to keep bothering me, what the hell kind of word is *aitch* anyway?), it really is pretty simple. There are two connected bones remaining in the hunk of meat, each of them shaped like a Flintstones sort of thing, what Pebbles would have stuck through her hair (bigger, of course). I stab down through the meat at the top edge, where the evident shiny white end of one of these bones sticks out, and I slice down along its top, to the next joint, until I've exposed its entire length. Then I get in there, the fingers of my right hand sunk deep in the meat crevice I've just made, peering inside, while with my left hand, my cutting hand, I scrape down along both sides of the bone and down under. The meat is cold from its time in the cooler; every once in a while I take my hands out and shake them around, blow into my cupped palms.

"Careful there," says Tom. "Get numb, you could lose a finger without feeling it. And we have a hell of a time moving finger sausage." (Tom thinks he's pretty funny.)

I gradually reveal the bones, peel them out, and all that's left is a messy mound of pig flesh, probably fifteen pounds of it. This I just carelessly cut into large chunks with my scimitar—rolling my eyes a little, inwardly, when Tom hands me the hugely impressive knife, one of his own personal collection, and tells me what it's called. Between the scimitars and the scabbards and the chain-mail gloves, it sometimes seems like the butchery industry was created by a bunch of testosterone-poisoned D&D nerds. More meat for sausage.

"All done."

"Good. There's the next one for you."

So I attack the second one. It's gratifying how much more quickly it goes than the first did; I do love me a steep learning curve. Tom is finished up and heading out, off to teach his evening class, and so now I'm alone at the table, mostly, except when Aaron passes on his way from the front counter, which he's working today, to the kitchen, where he's monitoring roast beef in the oven, slowly bubbling beef stock on the stove. "How's it coming, Jules?" he calls out with extravagant good cheer. "Can I call you Jules?"

"I answer to pretty much anything."

He throws some arched eyebrows my way. "Anything, huh? I'll have to think on that."

Aaron is a CIA grad—CIA culinary school, not exploding-cigars-and-covert-arms-deals CIA—and about my age, with close-cropped dark hair, startling blue eyes, and almost palpable enthusiasms. I barely know him, but I have known a few CIA grads in my time, and he has the vibe. Boyishly eager, impressed with himself. Sort of like a Harvard grad without all the money. I like him, but he's a little intimidating. I try not to let him see it. I throw some eyebrow action right back at him. "Do that." I don't even know what we're talking about, it's just random innuendo, locker talk without a subject matter.

I'm almost through with my round when Josh strides up from the back with a whole side of pork—eighty pounds of pig—slung casually over his shoulder. Without a word he rolls the thing onto the table. He takes his knife from the metal scabbard chained around his waist with a pink bicycle lock. "Yo, Uncle Sweet Tits!" he calls to Aaron, who's in the kitchen stirring around some chicken bones roasting in the oven. "I'm gonna kick your ass now." Jesse, the tall, thin, beaky kid who works the front of the shop—he's quiet, a reader of *Harper's* and *Wired,* who is teased mercilessly for drinking green tea—leans up against the case to watch. He evidently knows what's coming. Josh points with his knife to the clock on the wall, like Babe Ruth pointing his bat at the center-field bleachers at Wrigley Field. And sets to work.

Pulls off the kidney and kidney fat with a single yank. Gets in and quickly carves out the tenderloin nestled in under the spine, tosses it to the table. With thick but quick fingers, he counts five ribs down from the shoulder. Works his knife tip intricately between those two vertebrae, then, once they're separated, slices the shoulder away from the loin with one sweeping pistol-grip cut, straight down to the table. Picks up the butcher saw, like a hacksaw writ large, and with three swipes cuts across the ribs a couple of inches out from the triangular column of meat that runs along the rib cage's outer curve, against the backbone. Once he's through the bone, he puts down the saw, picks up his knife, and runs it along the saw cut he's just made, down to the table, curving up closer to the spine as he gets past the ribs, toward the hip joint, separating the belly from the loin. Then pulls the carcass to the edge of the table so that the rear leg is hanging off, leans hard with one thick forearm on the loin that rests on the table, while pushing suddenly, heavily, on the hoof with his other arm, really putting some serious pressure into it. A mighty *crack!* And the hip joint is opened up. One more raking slice through to wood and the round is off the loin, swinging floorward, held tight in Josh's big muff of a hand.

He slams the ham to the table with a meaty smack, staring at the clock. "Hey, pussy!" he yells. "One twenty-five!"

("We have *customers,* goddammit!" Jessica calls, not really expecting to be heeded.)

Aaron sticks his head out from the kitchen. "Fuck you. Really?"

"Booop!" Making an eloquent upward gesture, low down, middle finger extended. "Right up your rectum."

Aaron shakes his head, as a timer alarm goes off from somewhere over the stove. "Okay, man. I'm coming for you." He jabs the greasy end of a meat thermometer in Josh's direction. "I'm comin'. Don't mess with Chocolate Thunder." (Aaron and Josh, cochairs of the Nickname Committee, seem to disagree on Aaron's moniker.)

Jessica walks by on her way to the back of the shop in her padded orange vest and jeans, her frizzy hair twisted up on top of her head. She rolls her eyes in my direction as she passes, muttering "Jesus *Christ,*" with equal parts exasperation and affection.

I *really* like this place.

I go back into the remains of my pork round...and immediately send the tip of my knife skittering across the meaty flesh of my thumb. It doesn't so much hurt as startle me; I yank my hand out of the meat with a little whispered "shit!"

Josh turns to me with mild eyes. "You lose a finger, genius?"

It's a tiny thing. Blood, though, welling up through the smooth translucent smile of the sideways slice. "It's nothing."

Jessica calling from the back, "Oh, yes, please let's have the unpaid, uninsured apprentice cut off a digit on her first day."

"It's nothing."

"Lemme see." He roughly grabs my hand, peers at it. "Dude, that's *nothing!*"

"That's what I said."

"C'mon." He leads me to the back of the kitchen, where there's a shoebox full of first-aid supplies on a shelf over the big metal restaurant sink. "Rinse that out real good," he says as he rummages through the box. When I've finished washing and drying my hand—blood is still running in more-than-expected amounts—he dabs me with a drop from a dark green vial. OREGANO OIL, it says.

"What kind of hippie crap is that?" It is a testament to Josh's ability to put people at ease that a good girl like me is flipping shit to the boss before the first day is out.

"Beats Neosporin all to shit." He wraps a Band-Aid around the cut. "You put a glove on that. Don't want you bleeding all over my meat."

I SPEND the rest of the day helping out as I can, learning the ins and outs of boning pork shoulders, even breaking down my first side. (It, of course, takes me considerably more than one minute, twenty-five seconds.) I make sure to complain aloud about the glove I now have to wear: "Now I know why men hate condoms." I say it not just because it's true—I'm surprised at how that thin layer of latex between my skin and the meat makes me feel clumsier, less sure—but also, of course, because I want the guys to know I'm one of them, as obscene as they are. My cut keeps bleeding for a surprisingly long time, soaking through two Band-Aids and filling the fingers of two gloves before it finally stops. I'm obscurely proud of this.

Later, as we're cleaning up at the end of the day, I learn how to operate the great creaking Cryovac machine that vacuum-packs boned-out meat for the cooler until it's ready to be trimmed for the case or taken back to Juan. As the shop's sausage maker, he has his own little kingdom in the back dedicated to the work. I clean the cutting table with a metal scraper and wipe it with a towel soaked in a bleach solution before spreading on a thick layer of coarse sea salt, rubbing it into the cracks in the table. By seven thirty, my apron is in the dirty clothes bin, my leather hat is hanging from a hook in the bathroom, and I'm on my way out the door, a bag in hand full of meat Josh wouldn't let me pay for.

("Oh, come on. You can't give me this." "Fuck you. You worked for ten and a half hours for no pay." "But you're doing me the favor here. You're teaching me. I *suck* at this." "If you don't put that credit card away, I'm going to stick it up your butt.")

As I'm headed for the door, Aaron calls out to ask if I want to kick back with a beer before I leave.

"Nah, I got to get back."

Aaron is cracking open a bottle of his own, some dark local brew. "To the city? Man."

I shrug. "It'll be fine. Not so far."

"So, we gonna see you again, Jules?"

"Oh, yeah. Count on it."

I'm physically exhausted when I climb into the car, my hands aching, my back throbbing, my skin sheened in pig fat, and my hair limp and hat-headed. When I fill up for gas, I buy a couple of Diet Pepsis, as I'm a bit worried about this solo drive. But my mind is almost too busy, and it turns out that the two-hour evening drive back to Queens, the traffic quick and smooth at this hour, is just the gateway I need to calm myself a little. I glide down the thruway, keeping the speedometer at just under eighty. My iPod is plugged in and playing Old 97's, as I busily thumb-type away on the BlackBerry. (It is going to be really embarrassing if I wind up dying by careening off the road whilst texting, though I suppose I wouldn't be the first.) I give Eric my ETA—he's been checking in with me throughout the day, a few e-mails, a couple of texts, but I've been too busy to answer, plus I've found that reception is completely lousy in the shop—and babble to him about my fantastic first day. He writes back immediately; I picture him on the couch, watching the *NewsHour with Jim Lehrer,* his phone close at hand, waiting for me. "That's great, babe. Drive safe."

I babble, too, to D, the other one, this twitter being of a slightly different cant, self-consciously witty, flirtatious, downright dirty by turns. Once, not that long ago, he'd have answered all these in kind, hitting all the notes of our familiar cyber-foreplay routine. But he's grown chary with his responses lately; on this evening, he's totally silent.

By the time I get back to the apartment at nine thirty, I'm still giddy—the Diet Pepsi, as it turns out, was unnecessary and possibly a bad idea; I now am both overcaffeinated and in desperate need to pee. I take the two flights up two steps at a time, jiggle the key in the lock, swing it open with a flourish.

"Mommy's home!" Eric calls. Robert the Dog, our 110-pound German shepherd–Rottweiler mix, meets me at the door in his usual quiet style, tail wagging at a metronomic pace that possibly only Eric and I can recognize as an expression of enthusiasm. He is nosing at my bag as Eric comes to greet me, folding me into his arms. "My *God,* you smell like meat."

"Is it really that strong?"

He holds me at arm's length, his nose wrinkled not in disgust so much as a slight sense of bafflement. "Um. *Yeah.*" Robert is licking my shoes.

"Well, sorry. But I come bearing pork chops!"

Eric cooks us up some chops while I visit the bathroom, then sit at one of the stools at the kitchen island and pop open a bottle of Portuguese red. Eric's always in charge of pork chops. His favorite thing to do with them, usually, is a paprika cream sauce (Eric is an annoyingly thin man with a cream obsession that he foists off most inconsiderately on his gradually spreading wife). The recipe calls for loads of paprika, loads of fat (he never pours off the excess as some might do and, to be fair to him, it's not like the deracinated pork we usually get produces much), vermouth, and half a cup or more of cream. For most pork chops it's an excellent way to go, but here it would just be gilding the lily. "I'm telling you, you're not going to believe this meat. Don't do a thing to it."

So tonight Eric makes his pork chops a simple new way.

ERIC'S FLEISHER'S PORK CHOPS

½ tablespoon vegetable oil
2 1-inch-thick Berkshire pork chops
Salt and pepper to taste

Preheat the oven to 375°F. Set a heavy ovenproof skillet on the stovetop, over high heat. Heat the oil until almost smoking. (Don't you love it when recipes say things like "almost smoking"? Reminds me of that Beckett story about a stage direction reading that a door should be "imperceptibly ajar." Fuck you, Beckett. The oil can be smoking a little. Or not. Just make sure it's good and hot.)

Place the chops in the skillet and cook until deeply golden brown, just a couple of minutes per side.

"Finish off" the chops in the hot oven, a matter of about 5 to 10 minutes, depending. You can tell they're done by measuring the internal temperature with a meat thermometer—it should be, contrary to what the FDA would have you believe, about 120 to 125°F; the temperature will continue to rise as it rests—or, if you know your pork, pressing down with one finger to detect that moment when the flesh beneath the sear has begun to firm up but still has some give. Or you can do what Eric does, cheat—cut into it and peer at the juices, which should run almost clear, with just a hint of pink, and at the flesh, which also should retain a slight blush.

Let rest for 5 minutes. Salt and pepper to taste. Serves two.

While Eric cooks, I prattle on about Josh and Tom and Jessica and Aaron and Juan and Jesse and pigskin and look at my first cut! (I shove my bandaged thumb into his face.) And this is Berkshire pork, it's a heritage breed, andandand... "I'm a little manic, aren't I?"

"A little." He grins over at me, his eyes widening in that look of mock dismay he makes whenever his dismay is not entirely mock at all. I've not yet really been able to explain to Eric why I want to be doing this. Hell, I can't really explain it to myself.

Though we have a late start on the wine, we get through two bottles as usual. The pork chops are, as I promised Eric they would be, a revelation, moist and full of flavor, like a whole different animal from what you get in the grocery store, which of course it is. "Jesus *Christ*," he whispers. "Isn't this the best thing in the fucking world?"

I smile to hide a sudden pang of memory. "Pretty much."

I eat with other people in the world, of course. I cook for other people and take them to restaurants I hold dear. It's one of the ways I share myself and communicate with the people I love, probably the primary way, other than books maybe. (My dad and I, for instance, adore each other uncomplicatedly, but we almost never address that fact directly. Instead what we do is read together. One of my favorite earlyish memories is of reading aloud to him in the morning from Doonesbury comic strips, which I didn't entirely understand, to get him to laugh. And the last time I spoke to him on the phone, the first thing he said was "Have you read the latest Richard Price? I really think it's just great." This is how we tell each other we love each other.) And there is no one I share so satisfyingly with as Eric. We eat revelatory pork chops, we read revelatory novels, and when our eyes meet, our mutual understanding of these pleasures is utterly complete; we are one person who just happens to inhabit two bodies. I have this tenor of connection with no one else.

So why do I find myself anxiously fingering my infuriatingly quiet BlackBerry, retiring to the bathroom to text D behind Eric's back, to tell him I'm pining for him, that I love him? Why do I spend so much time feeling this alone?

To Eric, I am beloved. The Julie I am with him is mercurial, both too much and too weak, someone to be coddled and feared, kept in line and depended upon. The Julie who D knows is someone just a little different. A coconspirator. A playmate. Mischievous, sexy, thrillingly amoral. Someone to whom you'd murmur, as you slid inside her, and felt that answering clench, "Isn't this the best thing in the fucking world?" The me I feel I am with D is unfamiliar, exhilarating, someone I am constantly sidling up to, excited and frightened. But which one of me is real, the cherished, starstruck girl or the sultry, winking woman? I don't know these days, have not since the first day D tossed me back onto his bed.

Luckily, the wine does the job I've employed it for; that and a hot shower fold my overexcitement and confused contradictions back into my exhaustion and I am able to sleep. I think the night ends well; we go to sleep together, spooning, not one of those nights when I pass out early while Eric is left to his own devices.

But something happens while I'm sleeping, with uncharacteristic soundness. Something that I should by now expect, but that I snore right through—one of my husband's typical bouts of four a.m. wakefulness, his dream-inspired suspicion, his tiptoeing search for my red BlackBerry Pearl...

This affair of mine and D's would not have been possible for me, say, three years earlier. Not because I was a better, more stable person then. And not because I was working seventy hours a week in a cubicle, though that certainly put a damper on things. No, one simple technological innovation is really completely to blame for the whole thing: the SMS text message.

You'll have of course already noticed by now that I am the sort of person who uses *text* as a verb, the sort who conducts a disproportionate percentage of her interpersonal communication with her thumbs. This is a relatively new development. Historically, phones have been a phobia of mine, exacerbated greatly by my various stints in secretarial jobs over the years, during the last of which I came to regard the things as unpredictable and potentially vicious wild creatures. I didn't even own a cell until 2003. One of my most distinct memories of September 11 is walking the streets of midtown shaking my head in wonder at all the people wandering around staring perplexedly at the screens of their non-functioning phones. As soon as I did get one, though, I became enamored of this lovely new thing called "texting."

Many people will argue that e-mail and SMS and instant messaging and all the rest of it have destroyed our capacity as a race for gracious communication. I disagree. In fact, I would go so far as to say that we've entered a new golden epistolary age. Which is another of the reasons I hardly ever use my phone as a phone. Why stammer into a headset when I can carefully compose a witty, thoughtful missive? With written words I can persuade, tease, seduce. My words are what make me desirable. So it's really no wonder that I barely ever use my phone for actually speaking to people.

From almost the beginning, D and I did most of our flirting and plotting in cyberspace, either through e-mails or, later, the text messages that eventually flew fast and furious between us whenever we were apart. The same technologies that Eric and I used to discuss grocery lists and share random moments of charm we witnessed when we were away from each other—*Just saw Parker Posey watching kids on a playground!... Oh, can you pick up paper towels?*—transmitted between D and me dirty murmurs and teary yearnings and postcoital sighs, all read and tapped out on my BlackBerry's tiny screen, during any shred of a moment I could get to myself. (Eric must have thought my bladder had shrunk to half its former size, I started visiting the bathroom so often.) We signed off our missives with goofy pseudonyms (Ingritte Frottage, Laine Cable); we invented elaborate scenes of comic distress and romantic inevitability; we negotiated risky assignations. We turned each other on with words. We competed with them. Played with them. Message after message blinking into my in-box like spaceships popping into existence from some warp-speed jump. The trill from my phone provoking a response Pavlov would have made much of—racing heart, flushed skin. All for words, D's words and mine. They made what might have been simply tawdry, exotically illicit. They gave poetic weight to what by all rights ought to have been the stuff of soap opera. Words, to be pored over, analyzed late at night when I couldn't sleep for wishing I could just leap out of my own bed and run to his.

But of course that's exactly the problem with words, isn't it? There they are, kept, findable. Evidence. Who knows if my affair with D would have survived as long as it did, or even begun, without all those secret communiqués, but assuming that it had, it certainly would not have been discovered so quickly. Eric would have continued on, suspicious but unable to confront me, for who knows how long, allowing me to explain away the marks on my body and the glazed giddiness in my eyes, if it were not for that underwater river of words. As it was, it took almost nothing for him to divine the truth. The water table was so high, he barely had to dig to find it. He knew my e-mail password because it was the same as his own (the name of our eldest cat). He had access to my BlackBerry, from which I rarely wiped old messages, because I enjoyed rereading them. I was so blatantly careless that it began to verge on cruelty, and when his suspicion became unbearable to him, my behavior simply beyond innocent accountability, my cyber-breadcrumb trail of guilt was all too easy for him to follow. My scarlet phone spilled its secrets; my e-mail account opened easily beneath his typing fingers.

By now I've become accustomed to, and accepting of, my husband's snooping. I've learned to cover my tracks. But this time, I fall asleep before intercepting the missive that finally arrived, late in the night. *I love you too, sweetheart. Good night. xoh~D.*

Coded, the *h* our little shorthand to make something naughtier out of the traditional *x*s and *o*s, but not nearly coded enough. In truth, no code could suffice. D could be writing to me in binary, but the Portland area code he still uses nearly two years after he's moved to New York (it shows up on every communiqué issuing from his phone) would be enough.

The next morning, I don't know anything is wrong (I mean anything immediate; everything is wrong, of course, everything has been wrong, quietly or explosively, for two years now) until after I've fed the three cats their morning portions of wet food. Eric has climbed into the shower; we've not yet said good morning to each other. I reach over for my phone sitting on the counter, compulsively checking it like I always do, though there is no unread-message light. I open up the screen and see that in fact there is one message unread—unread, at least, by me. It is familiar now, that taste of my heart in my mouth.

The water stops running in the shower. I step into the bathroom, the door of which stands perceptibly ajar, and take a towel from one of the hooks behind the door to hand him as he slides the glass door open and steps out onto the wet floor.

(The tub has an incorrigible leak, in addition to being constantly, chronically clogged. Our new apartment is beautiful, with high ceilings, exposed brick walls, a skylight in the kitchen. But something seems to be going on, water-related, something that my inwardly superstitious mind finds worrying. Moisture seeping through where it shouldn't, lingering where it should drain away. I have to keep repeating to myself: it's faulty plumbing, it's a leaky roof. Yes, I've spent far too many days and nights sobbing in confusion and guilt and frustration, but tears, no matter how fiercely repressed, can't fuck up the paint job.)

The second I see him not meeting my eyes I know how it's going to go down. And I know I should just walk back out the door, let him come to me with his complaint. I know I should be angry, that I should not make this easy for him. I know I should be angry, but I can't make myself feel it. Instead, as usual, I offer myself up to *his* anger: "You okay?"

He sighs, for a second stands, his dirty blond hair dripping, and stares at his feet. I've always loved Eric's feet, first noticed them back when we were in high school, improbably shapely in their hippie sandals. Then he groans, grabs me roughly by the arms, gives me one tight shake. "Our marriage is falling apart and we're not talking about it!"

There is nothing I can say to that, not one thing. He's right, of course.

3
Fajita Heartbreak

"YOU KNOW IT's over when he'd rather show you *Team America* than his penis."

D is imagining the story I will one day tell about the day we broke up. He's holding me in his arms at the time. Smiling. I laugh when he says it. "That's a good line. I'm totally stealing it."

It doesn't feel like a breakup at all, not at first.

SO I'VE TOLD you a little bit about seams, those networks of filaments that both connect muscles and define the boundary between them. Now, the difficulty is that seams can be thick, or they can be thin. The seam of a tenderloin, for instance, is very thin indeed, and therefore hard to follow. It's easy to lose your way, which is apt to make you nervous, seeing as how the tenderloin is the single most expensive cut of meat on the steer, thirty-nine bucks a pound at Fleisher's. If you lose the seam in one direction you waste tenderloin, and there's only something like eight pounds of it per animal. If you lose it in the other direction, especially right at the head of the muscle, what's called the "chateaubriand," you cut into the eye of the sirloin, another expensive cut and one that short-tempered chefs won't buy mangled. Beginning butchers, needless to say, don't get assigned to pull out many tenderloins.

I have been allowed to do one so far, under Tom's close supervision. It's a long column of muscle, nestled up against the spine on the loin primal, tapering to a point up near the forward end of the cut, burying itself graspingly into the sirloin at the other end, at the hip. Using the very tip of my knife and my fingernails, bending close to peer at my progress, I flicked away, endeavoring to keep from tearing the meat, leaving precious shreds behind. It eventually rolled off the spine, but reluctantly. It clung to its cradle of bone. At its thick head, especially, right under the tailbone, it hung on tight. I had to be braver than I really was, get down under, skim along the silver surface of the sirloin, force it loose. I left a little behind. You always do, I guess, when you're dealing with two things so resolutely fused. By the time I was done, I was stinking with nervous sweat and my knife hand was aching, like your hands ache after surviving a car accident—a near collision or breathtaking slide on black ice—and you realize you've been gripping the wheel like a lifeline.

D is a great mythologizer. I learned this about him years ago, during those few nights in my college dorm room, and I rediscovered it when he moved back to New York nine years later and easily coaxed me back to his bed. He loves (well, once loved, as it looks now like I'm going to have to get used to this goddamned past tense) to pull up the sheets and lie in bed, entangled and sweaty, spinning tales and theories about the romantic logic of our journey to this one particular inevitable afternoon. It was destiny, he said. I remember photographically the conversation of more than a year ago, when he laid out his theory.

"Obviously fated from the start."

I was gazing fondly at the bruise his teeth had left on my upper arm. "How so?"

"Well, among many other factors, how about the first time I ever saw you? When you came to the door of my parents' house with Eric, while he was up visiting colleges." Eric was a year behind me in school and did his grand senior-year college tour the fall of my freshman year of college, using the excuse to make his first visit to me. D lived in my college town, but went to another college very nearby. (This whole thing is so intricate and incestuous and endless, I get breathless and discouraged just trying to get all the details down. It's like trying to explain the plotlines of a *Buffy* episode six seasons in.)

"So my do-gooder parents regularly give over their spare bedroom to visiting prospective students, and generously volunteer their son to do any dirty work involved. So I'm the one assigned to sit around waiting for this Eric guy. All day, I'm waiting. Then he finally comes around, with this sexy girl." Here he bit my shoulder until I squealed, and pressed his naked front up against my naked back.

"Ooh, what's that you've got there?"

"Don't interrupt, I'm talking." Digging his fingers deeply into my hair, pulling me onto my back. "And this guy is saying, 'Oh no, thanks, but I'll actually be sleeping with my *girlfriend*.' Uh-huh, so *that's* how it's going to be..."

"I don't remember this at all."

"You *forgot* this?" Atop me now, one arm hooking under my knee, drawing it up over his shoulder.

"Mhm..."

What I remembered was that I didn't notice that lean, dark young man who'd one day be D until nearly four years later, when he was introduced to me at a party. Eric, to whom I'd been unfailingly faithful all this time, was away on his junior year abroad; I wrote him long rambling letters and mailed care packages. I didn't think about the boy from the college down the road.

Until one night, not too long before graduation, I was invited to another dorm party at this other school. There was quite a bit of drinking, expectedly, and then, unexpectedly, disastrously, deliciously, there was kissing, a closed door, Al Green on his hip retro turntable, and, inevitably, sex. We've always differed, D and I, on who seduced whom; he says me, I say him. But I guess the real question is not Who? but Why? If you asked me then, I would say it was just hormones, that I wasn't even attracted to the guy, skinny, with hooded eyes, Mick Jagger lips, and a weak chin. I wouldn't talk about the judder in my veins when I heard his knock, knowing it was him, couldn't be anyone else at that hour. I wouldn't tell you about the sounds he made me make, despite my shame and thin dormitory walls.

I didn't talk to him in the daytime, though we chattered on enough at night. My guilt was too great. I didn't even say a proper good-bye when I graduated. But I have a snapshot from the day I moved out of my dorm. My father took it, and I to this day have no idea why. It's an odd photo, blurry and focused on nothing in particular, just a forgettable image of me hauling out a load of stuff, seemingly oblivious to the boy mooning, some feet away, at the edge of the photograph. In fact my heart pounded at his presence. My horror made me awful.

You'd have thought that was the end of it.

TENDERLOINS ARE hard. Skirt steak, on the other hand, is cake. A flap of meat totally encased in its seam, which is thick and white, less like the usual half-dried rubber cement than like an envelope of flaky, ancient paper. The whole package is laid out flat along a solid wedge of white fat and rib bone. Pulling out skirt steaks is the job you assign to the cutters who don't know what the hell they're doing. It's an obvious muscle, neither expensive nor delicate, and you don't need any mad knife skills to remove it. You practically don't need a knife at all. All you have to do is get a grip on one edge of the flap, push down on the fat with the heel of your other hand, and tear the thing right out—riiiip!—using your knife only at the very end, maybe, to cut loose a stubborn filament or two. Yes, skirt steak is a snap. I should know. This past week, I've torn dozens of them off dozens of beef flanks. There's a rhythm to it. Like pulling lots of Band-Aids off lots of knees.

THIS IS not the first time D and I have broken up.

The first time we broke up—that is, if you don't count me piling into my parents' Suburban without so much as a fare-thee-well on the day I graduated college—was right after Eric snuck into my e-mail and found his first hard evidence about D, just a couple of months into our affair.

This breakup happened at a bar—Eric's and my local bar, actually, in Long Island City, Queens. D got on a train to come to me as soon as I texted him. ("He knows," I wrote, having a great gift for melodrama.) I remember that I took Robert the Dog with me, more as an alibi, should Eric come home to find me gone, than as a nod to my pet's well-being. I remember that I cried a lot, and that we kissed a lot, and that the bartender, who of course knows me, and Eric, and knows that D is not Eric, disapproved.

I was the one who called it off. "I have to try to fix my marriage," I said. D didn't disagree. He wiped my tears from my face, which I thought was sweet. "I can't hurt Eric like this," I continued.

D nodded and pulled me in for a tender hug. He wasn't crying, but he looked like he might.

"We have to stop seeing each other."

We lingered at the subway entrance for a long time. (Robert the Dog thought all this standing around was *bullshit*, but he put up with it resignedly.) D and I hugged, and kissed, and made out, and generally made fools of ourselves. And I was thinking about how all this had started. An afternoon fuck, and then another, just a friendly exchange of fluids. I was thinking that he should be easier to give up, and wondering why it was so hard. And so

I said I loved him, for the first time, which made his face do this odd wavering thing for a moment, like I was seeing him through a haze of diesel exhaust.

"Well, maybe we can get together tomorrow," I said. "Since we had it planned."

D didn't disagree.

"But that's the last time."

Who did I think I was kidding?

THERE ARE actually four skirt steaks in every cow, two on each flank, just below the brisket, which is cut from the sternum, and even as I'm writing this sentence I can sense thousands of eyes glazing over in a more-than-I-needed-to-know fog. The two pieces on each side are called the inner skirt and the outer skirt. One of them is thicker and wider and longer than the other, and one is supposed to taste better, but I can never remember which is which. (I fall into fogs, too.) Josh has explained it to me a few times, and I don't want to ask again, even though I'm still not sure. But I do know that skirt steaks, along with hanger steaks, are diaphragm muscles, separating the chest cavity from the abdomen and making the whole in-and-out thing happen with the animal's lungs.

Anyway, the point is, there are lots of opportunities, even just on one animal (and there is *never* just one animal; Josh always brings back at least three whole steer from the slaughterhouse), to practice the grab-and-pull motion of skirt-steak removal. Get some good music cranking on the iPod. Eminem works well, something with a good high macho reading. Make a show of chatting nonchalantly as you go about your business, not even looking at what you're doing, exchanging filthy Michael Jackson jokes. ("What does Michael Jackson like about twenty-eight-year-olds? That there's twenty of 'em!") Build up a whole pile of skirts. You'll have to trim them later, make them palatable, and that is *not* the fun part. Avoid that part as long as possible.

D AND I broke up the second time about a year after the first split had failed to take. By this time, the entire tenor of the whole messy situation had changed. After Eric found out about D, we wrangled, tearily and angrily, for months and months, about what our next move would be. Many couples would just have called it quits, but instead we occasionally cried, drank, watched a lot of TV, and went to bed together nights, except when he stayed out, because this was when Eric began seeing the other woman, sometimes staying out all night without explanation, trailing home the next morning full of a remorse that was actually something else, a recrimination. Also around then, a bronchial infection landed some codeine cough syrup in my hands, which I found I liked very much indeed. It was the only thing other than the brief release of an afternoon with D that made me feel like maybe one day everything would work out—until Eric made me pour it down the sink.

At last we'd decided on a trial separation. I rented a small studio at 86th and York Avenue, and for four months I led a small, quietly satisfying, if slightly lonesome existence up in that unfashionable corner of Manhattan. I enjoyed having a space of my own, however tiny. I enjoyed the times, rarer than I'd have liked, when D came up and spent the entire night with me, just as though we were a regular couple, and I enjoyed the dinner dates with Eric, the sensation of simply liking his company, of having missed him. But then, four months into my six-month lease, my landlady had me kicked out early, not because the neighbors complained about some untoward three a.m. noises—though they did—but because she'd had a change of plans and needed her place back. I had nowhere to go. I would never in a million years have suggested living with D, he'd have laughed me out of the state, and besides, the bottle of beer he'd offered me the second time I came over to his apartment was still sitting on his windowsill a year later. I could have found another apartment, I suppose. But that had seemed like a stark choice, a separation more complete than moving out in the first place had been. In the end, I wasn't able to pull the trigger. I was moving back in with Eric, it seemed, because of the vagaries of New York real estate.

The second breakup went much the same as the first, except with less expectation of success. I performed it at Eric's explicit behest. He had broken up with his lover by this point, and, quite naturally, thought I should do the same. I knew it was the only fair thing to do, but the thought of giving up D made me feel as rebellious and petulant as an unjustly punished child. That morning, D and I sat together on the floor, leaning against my futon mattress, which was already tied with twine and ready to be loaded into the U-Haul van. I was still flushed from the Last Sex We Would Ever Have. Again I cried. "It's not fair!"

He stroked my hair.

"It makes no sense, breaking up with someone I don't want to break up with!"

He rested his chin on my head, which I'd tucked against his breastbone, like I was six years old and had dropped my ice cream cone. He hushed me gently. He didn't even come close to crying that time. I think he knew that his sex life was in no immediate danger of drying up.

I held out about a week.

So, as I've mentioned, the hard part, or rather the frustrating part, with skirt steak is the trimming. The thick filament that makes the muscle easy to remove is also so thick as to be inedible, or at least not very fun to eat. It must be removed, but it doesn't want to go, and clings determinedly. Some of it you can peel off with your fingers in strips, which is satisfying, rather like peeling nail polish, if your fingernail was four inches wide and two feet long. But like nail polish, bits of it stick stubbornly. Peeling also gets dangerous because sometimes you pull up a lot of meat with it, and if this happens at a thin space in the muscle, the steak can tear right in two. This is where your knife comes in.

Skirt steaks have a deeply striated grain, running up and down all along the narrow span of the muscle. It's best to marinate skirts before cooking, and always to slice them against the grain, because that striation leads to toughness. Any risk of chewiness is completely worth it, though, because, for some reason, the difference in flavor between Big Beef meat and that of a grass-fed "happy steer" shows most extraordinarily in this cut. It's a dark, concentrated, almost liverish taste that is not for everyone, but which I find wickedly enjoyable. This is how Jessica told me to cook the first skirt steak I brought home from Fleischer's. It's completely delicious, and so easy it's almost embarrassing.

JESSICA'S SUPER-EASY SKIRT STEAK SALAD

¾ cup balsamic vinegar
¼ cup extra-virgin olive oil
Several sprigs rosemary
3–4 cloves garlic, crushed
1 skirt steak
Arugula, spinach, or other salad green of your choice
Pecorino, Asiago, Parmesan, or other hard, salty cheese
    of your choice
Sea salt and freshly grated pepper to taste

In a nonreactive baking pan, combine the vinegar, olive oil, rosemary—slightly crushing the leaves between your fingers—and garlic to make a marinade for the steak. Let the steak stand in the marinade at room temperature for 45 minutes or so, turning once or twice.

(You may want to cut the skirt steak into a couple of pieces, if you don't have a huge skillet or a pan big enough to accommodate the marinating steak. Skirt steaks are rather long and can be unmanageable.)

When ready to cook, just heat a large skillet over very high heat until a drop of water flicked into it skitters madly across the surface. Lift the steak out of the marinade, shake off a bit but not all of the excess marinade clinging to it, and put it in the skillet. It will hiss and pop rather alarmingly. Cook only until brown on each side, flipping it over once—about 90 seconds per side. Remove and let rest for 5 to 10 minutes.

To serve, pile a handful of arugula or other green onto each of two plates. Slice the steak thinly, at a diagonal across the grain, and lay several strips over each bed of greens. Shave cheese over the top. I like to use a wide cheese slicer for this, to make substantial curls, but that's up to you. Season with salt and especially pepper, to taste. Serves two, with leftovers.

Easiest thing in the world. Assuming you've gotten your butcher to do the cleaning part, which is not so embarrassingly easy.

To clean a skirt steak, you must slice along the grain carefully, so as not to take off too much meat with it. It's a time-consuming process, slicing gingerly at all the stringy bits, judging just how clean is clean enough.

Sometimes, I'll confess, if I've been cleaning up skirts for too long, I'll take the easy way out. I'll tell myself, perhaps a self-serving justification, that there's no such thing as perfectly clean. And when Slave-Driver Aaron isn't looking, I'll roll up the steak with whichever is the prettier side facing out, hiding the last bits of chewy white shreds, and just tuck it into the case at the front of the shop, where it won't be closely examined. I do this furtively, guiltily. Sometimes I just can't take any more of the endless fretful picking.

THIS LAST breakup isn't like the others. It takes hours—in point of fact, from D's perspective, it probably has taken months—yet in the end it's quick and cruelly final.

During the two-hour drive back to the city from Kingston one Saturday afternoon in early October, I decide that something has to be done. D and I haven't been sleeping together for several months, not really. He keeps citing a busy schedule, and, to be fair, my being married and also driving upstate all the time for the butchering isn't making things easy either. Since he's returned from his most recent business trip more than a month ago, we've met in parks and bars, we've kissed and giggled, cooed sweet words and cuddled like bear cubs, but have managed sex exactly once, and that was because I lured him with a wildly expensive hotel room directly across the street from where he works. What's next? Is he going to start asking for a monetary exchange? Enough is enough. So I text him, just tell him straight up, *I'm coming over tomorrow. What's your apartment number?*

(He's just been forced out of his old apartment and has made the peculiar choice to move to a new one right down the street, staying in the Murray Hill neighborhood I find so dreadfully dull. I guess it's funny what you can get attached to. Anyway, I haven't seen it yet, which is my trumped-up excuse for inviting myself over.)

I'm in a good mood as I ride the elevator up to his apartment. Here I am, making a stand, going for what I want. No meek, whimpering adulteress, I! When he opens the door, I'm grinning, and I neatly ignore the distinct ambivalence of the smile he gives in return. I grab hold of his hand as he gives me the tour of his tiny, rather sad, new apartment. Once he's closed the door to his sunny, small room, still scattered with packing boxes, we collapse onto his bed—it's the same bed, but stuffed into this much smaller room, pushed up against a wall, it seems depleted, a double instead of a vast expanse of California king—and commence some serious making out. After two years, kissing him still leaves me breathless; it seems worth both the harrowing guilt over Eric and the nasty little holes of self-contempt that my neediness for D opens up in me over and over again.

But something's not right, even willfully clueless I must eventually admit. I keep going for the buttons of his shirt, his belt buckle, but he handily evades my gropings. He cops the occasional halfhearted feel but doesn't even attempt to get a hand under my shirt. (*Highly* unusual, that. D is what I believe is referred to as a "breast man.") After a while, the kissing trails off, and though I keep trying to make inroads, conversation takes hold. Increasingly frustrating conversation, about not all the deliciously dirty things we'd like to do to each other, but movies. Animated movies. D is simply shocked that I've never seen *Team America*. The laptop comes out.

I go along for a bit, fuming. He laughs loudly. It's the same laugh he bestows upon himself when he's feeling clever, which, I think meanly, is more often than is warranted. I don't think it's all that funny. I last perhaps twenty minutes before slumping onto my side with an irritable sigh. He presses the space bar to pause.

"What's the matter?"

"Nothing."

"Well, that's clearly not true." He's smiling at me. D never gets mad, not really. Occasionally condescendingly exasperated. He's always smiling, no matter how angry I get, and, in truth, I have often gotten too angry, demanded too much. I've wanted certainty, resolution—have needed it. He has been, all along, the wrong person to ask it from. We were both happier, I think, before I told him I loved him, when that was a hidden thing.

I flop onto my back, unable to stop a small answering smile to his despite my annoyance. "What the hell is going on here? What's the point of this anyway?"

"What's the point of what?"

"*This!* What's the point of a torrid love affair without any sex, goddammit?!"

And so, still in each other's arms, we talk.

"Look, I'm a total fucking mess, I'm miserable at the thought of losing you—"

"*Losing* me? You're not going to lose me."

"But I'm terrified that if we sleep together at this point, you'll be mad at me for not living up to what you're expecting—that I won't be funny or brilliant or even good in bed."

I laugh, cuddle into his side. "Don't be silly."

"Or else it'll be great and then you and Eric will get divorced and you'll blame me for wrecking your marriage when you realize that I'm not as good a catch as he is and then we'll both just get bitter and I'll lose my teeth and end up being an embarrassment to you for the rest of our lives."

I punch his arm. "Now you're just making up crap for the sake of it. And what is it with you and your obsession with your teeth?"

This is where we should be having the Fight Sex. Where I say something sufficiently angry, petulant, ultimatum-y, that leaves nothing for him to do but flip me over and fuck the living daylights out of me. In the past year this has happened countless times; I almost look forward to our fights now. But not this time. This time he just talks and talks. And it takes me so long, so agonizingly long to realize what's happening. He even speaks his immortal *Team America* line, and still, still, I don't get it. But finally I realize: He's not saying he can't have sex with me now. Or next week. Or until I'm happier, less needy. He's saying he can't ever. Not ever again.

I clamber from the bed in a panic, as if my abrupt epiphany is some kind of nasty crawling bug I can brush off. With my back pressed up against the window, as far from him as I can get, I stare at D. He's flat on his back, still smiling. He makes a gesture that in the last two years has become all too familiar. Without lifting his head from the pillow, he reaches his arms out to me like a hungry baby, his hands flapping toward his chest, his eyebrows raised in mock distress, dark eyes wide, soft lips parted to emit an urgent whine. It's an exasperating, endearing, indolent gesture of desire, and in the past has had the unfailing effect of drawing me back into his arms, comforted, laughing indulgently. But now at last I see what it really means. *I want to hold onto you a while longer. But it will never mean what you want it to mean.*

Oh, *Jesus.*

When I begin to sob, he doesn't come to me, not at first. He knows I've finally figured it out, something I've been ignoring for a long time, something that he's known. I cry and cry, and this isn't like the crying all the times before, not lusty and somehow at root pleasurable. This is the coldest, loneliest feeling in the world.

Now I will become part of another of D's favorite postcoital mythologies. Not the romantic epic of how the stars aligned to bring us together, but the litany of D's Lunatic Exes. The leggy blond model who didn't know the difference between Herbert and J. Edgar Hoover. The withholding Spanish exchange student who wound up being very impressed with his private parts. The dull grad student he narrowly avoided marrying. And now the crazy, clinging, married chick.

"I can't do this. Can't. Have to go." I pick up my purse, and then he does try to hug me. But I can't have it. I cringe in his arms. I'm not angry—oh, how wonderful anger would feel! I'm just...done. I'd so wanted certainty, and now that I have it, I can't breathe for the weight of it.

He takes me down to the street, helps me catch a cab. He wipes away my tears, even cries himself. It's the first time I've ever seen him cry, but it doesn't make any difference. He kisses me once more as the cabbie waits, which makes my heart blossom and die.

My brother, when he was eleven or so, had a baby iguana for a pet, whom he'd named Geraldo. One night we had been out, for dinner or something, and when we got back to the house he went to his room. The rest of us were still in the kitchen when he came running out, sobbing. "Geraldo is dead!"

In fact the poor thing was gray and cold but still, barely, alive. My mother took it into her cupped hands, blew onto it, trying to keep it warm, help it breathe. The creature would turn briefly green again, would seem to get better, but it couldn't last more than a few seconds without Mom's warm breath on it. I remember that moment more vividly than almost any other moment in my childhood. Our entire family gathered, crying, trying to summon enough breath to keep this animal alive. That's what my heart feels like. Like a goddamned lizard, upon whom entirely ineffective CPR is being performed.

At first I think I've been the one to do the ripping. I've made a decision. Painful, but clean. And there is a little consolation in the action of it. It takes me a while of picking off the bloody bits that remain to realize that I'm not the tearer, but the thing that's been torn away. And I pick and I pick and I pick at these connecting shreds that cling to me. They catch in my craw unexpectedly. A trip to the dentist can do it. (Always obsessed with his teeth, D, a winking Woody Allenish mannerism that irritated and amused me in equal measure.) A store window. (Zales. A kiss we once shared on the sidewalk in front of the store, impassioned enough to inspire the salesman inside to come out and encourage us to do a bit of impulse shopping.) A once-admired sweater or lingerie set. (Snapping on my bra in the morning, I flash on his eyes as he stands behind me in a hotel bathroom, his hands on my hips, eyeing me in the mirror: "That just hits you in all the right places, doesn't it?") *Team America,* of course. So what I thought at first would be clean and final is endlessly prolonged. The city is his body now, all those corners and bars and restaurants and uninspired blocks that inspire such specific wants in me. He's been part of my muscle and bone, one of the joints that I cling to, for two years—give or take a decade—and now he's gone. And I text and write and make phone calls that go unanswered. I pick and I pick and I pick.

There's no such thing as perfectly clean. Not really.

4

Stuffing Sausage

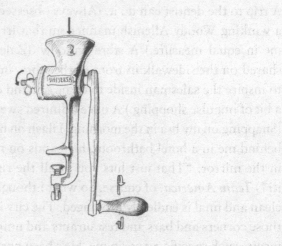

WHEN MY BROTHER and I were both in high school—this would be my senior year, his freshman—someone in the family obtained one of those Magnetic Poetry boxes. You know, those Lucite boxes with all the tiny refrigerator magnets with words printed on them, which you can put together in different ways. My brother, who never showed much inclination toward writing in any other context, turned out to be the Refrigerator Magnet Poetry King. Over the next several years, every time I came home from college, I would immediately read the refrigerator for new masterpieces. (To this day they remain, in the garage, where our old refrigerator was banished to when Mom bought her sexier stainless-steel model.) His lines could be witty and pithy and absurd (*Who put the knife in bed, man?* is one of my favorites), but perhaps his best one was this:

> *I wanted a life of*
> *Blue skies shining*

Diamonds and lusty
Spring shadows.
I have an apparatus
To produce sausage

JUAN IS teaching me how to make the Italian sweets. We're together in the small room at the back of the shop, hardly more than a pantry-cum-broom-closet, that is Juan's domain. The meat grinder, a stainless-steel contraption about five feet tall, dominates the room. The meat goes into the big bin on top, the bottom of which slants toward one end. Inside that is a hole not unlike a sink disposal, which houses the grinding apparatus. Below, on one side of the machine, is an opening over which Juan has fitted a metal plate dotted with holes, like a large shower drain. He and I are both standing on coolers on either side of the receptacle, up to our elbows in meat. Meat and ice. The meat is in chunks, perhaps five inches long by three inches wide, emptied from huge Cryovac bags marked "Pork Trim" that we toted in from the cooler. The ice is from a machine pushed into a corner of the kitchen. I'm not sure what the reason is for the ice, but it must be mixed in thoroughly.

I HAVE terrible circulation. It's one of those little niggling health things that has bugged me my whole life. When I was in high school, a bunch of us used to go to a place out near Wimberley, Texas, called the Blue Hole. As I remember, it was on private land, but whoever owned it had set up a slightly shabby park, with outhouses and rope swings over the river. The water wasn't exactly *blue*—Texas water, in general, tends more to the green—but it was as cold as all get-out, something to do with springs in the riverbed. I remember one specific time when my friend Paul suggested a trip, a little earlier in the year than was customary. It was March, I believe, which in Texas is an extremely tempting month—sunny days, cool evenings, bluebonnets. It's one of the best months Texas has to offer, actually, and how many places on the planet can say that March is a highlight? But in truth, even in Texas March is really too early for swimming in frigid spring water. We went anyway; we swung into the breathtaking water with manly fortitude, we splashed around and cursed and showed off like the kids we were, and then I got out...and I was blue. I mean *blue*. Not pale, not waxen. *Blue*. Like, as Paul said at the time, "comic-book-villain blue."

THE MEAT and ice mixture is ten times colder than the Blue Hole. I'm sure this could be proven scientifically, but lacking the necessary instruments and travel stipend I will rely instead upon the aqua shade my hands are turning.

"How on earth do you do this?" I ask Juan.

He just shrugs. "Yeah, it's cold, right? Put your hands under warm water."

Well, that's a good idea.

Except, *Jesus*, that hurts. Christ. Feels like my hands are going to fall off. Once the initial burning wears off, though, my hands are at least working again. I don a pair of gloves and go back to work. Juan is now grinding the meat. This is the easy part. He pushes a big button, and the meat starts going down the grinder, spilling out through the plate below into a white plastic lugger set on top of a third cooler. It snakes out in pink coils that make me think of some macabre child's toy—Sweeney Todd's Play-Doh Barbershop®. I return to my place atop the cooler and nudge the meat down toward the grinding apparatus—rather gingerly, because it turns out I have a bit of a phobia about all things that grind, fantasize about fingers caught up and drawn bloodily in.

So I'm a little wimpy in my efforts toward getting all the meat down there, but down it all goes, eventually, into the grinder's gullet.

Once the meat has finished slithering out, Juan pushes the button again to stop the machine, then shoulders the lugger of meat—seventy-five pounds of it—and dumps it right back into the grinder's metal bin. I add another couple of scoops of ice and stir it around while he switches out the plate at the grinder's mouth with another just like it, but with holes about half as wide in diameter, then pushes the big button again. And again we push the meat through, grinding it finer, and then one more time, using a plate with smaller holes still. Then once more the meat goes into the grinder's bin. This time I add to it the spice mix Juan measured out before we got started: a two-gallon container full of fennel, sage, garlic, salt, onion powder, basil, parsley, and white pepper. Burying my arms deep again, I churn the pork, now a sticky puree, until the spices are evenly blended in. Meanwhile, Juan is replacing the latest metal plate with a spigot, perhaps seven inches long, wider at the base than at the end. When he sits on the cooler in front of it, with the lugger in front of him between his spread legs, the spigot points squarely at his collarbone.

From a plastic Tupperware container, he lifts from milky water a length of pork middles, a category of sausage casings, which of course are just meticulously cleaned intestines. "Middles" are, obviously, the middle section of the intestines. Casings are also made, for larger sausages like those big dried salamis, out of lower intestines of pig or lamb or steer. These are called "bungs," which is a little lacking in euphemism for my taste.

Juan finds the end of the casing and blows lightly across it, as you'd blow on a bag off the roll in the supermarket produce section to get it open. The casing is several feet long, thin and pale, translucent. Once he can hold it open with two fingers, Juan bunches it onto the spigot, up to the base, with a quick back-and-forth motion that is embarrassingly recognizable.

(Jessica recently said, "Men always make the best sausage makers. They've all been practicing the necessary motions since they were twelve years old." And I, still so vulnerable, my skin as thin as some amphibian hatchling, had another of those flashes that come so often now, to a lazy afternoon interregnum: *"So if you define adolescent hell as the period between the moment you realize exactly what it is you want to be doing"*—*his mouth moving unhurriedly down my flank toward what he wants to be doing*—*"and the moment you first have the opportunity to do it, I was in hell for five long years. Being ten* sucked. *I managed to keep myself entertained, of course…"*)

I shake the memory loose as Juan finishes getting the next casing on and pushes the grinder's button. Meat starts shooting down through the spigot's end, filling the casing, the whole length of sausage spilling in a thick coil down into the lugger, helped along by another back-and-forth motion of Juan's, opposite the first, that encourages the casing off the spigot and, stuffed with meat, into the bin. Juan is an expert sausage stuffer, and so he knows, just by eyeing the rate at which the folds of the casing he's crumpled onto the base of the spigot unfurl, when to stop the grinder. Still, inevitably, after the last of the casing comes off and falls, a final burst of pink pork ooze spurts out of the spigot, which Juan catches in cupped hands and dumps back into the top of the grinder before he slides another casing on to start the process again.

Okay, it's true that since we broke it off I've had D, and sex, on the brain a lot, so maybe I'm more inclined to read into stuff. But surely it's not just me, right? "Wow. That's—"

Juan just grins and nods. "Yeah, I know."

Well, glad I'm not the only one.

"You should make blood sausage some time."

"Blood sausage? You do that?"

"Only once or twice. My mother told me how to do it, last time I was home. I'll show you sometime. With the blood filling especially, the casings look, I don't know, veiny and…" He makes a gesture, holding his thumbs and forefingers into an O of expansive girth while blowing out his cheeks.

"Okay, okay. Enough!"

I have no problem with sausage making, don't care about snouts and lips and assholes. (Though I know Fleisher's puts nothing in its sausage but good clean meat and fat.) But at this moment, I think I'll never be able to eat sausage ever again, no matter how delicious, without feeling in some little part of me that I'd rather be engaging in one way or another with D's penis. I know, that is so terribly crude that I, not exactly a prim person, cringe to write it. But then, that's making sausage.

Once Juan has turned the seventy-five pounds of pork into a great looping bin full of sweet Italian sausage, he puts it in the back cooler to rest. Later we will twist the filled casings into four-inch links. But first we take a break to warm our hands on some coffee mugs.

We lean up against the shelves in the kitchen, shaking out our numb fingers and listening to Juan's mix CD, a combination of Latino pop and Nashville country. Dolly Parton's "Little Sparrow" is playing. We're not saying anything. Juan and I tend to talk in bursts, just small stuff mostly. We'll talk music. As a Texan living in New York, I have relatively few opportunities to discuss country music with anyone outside of my immediate family. Or I'll ask him to sniff a burst Cryovac bag for his opinion on whether the meat in it has gone bad.

(Juan has the most trusted nose in the shop, which is a dubious honor, since it means he's the one people come to holding out a thawed turkey by splayed legs, saying, "Smell this." Perhaps associated with that, he's also the best taster around. Every day Fleisher's serves a soup of the day, and Jessica and Juan share responsibility for making it. Once Jessica was pulling together a beef stew, sort of making it up as she went along, and something was definitely missing. She and I both tasted and discussed, suggesting this or that ingredient to add that extra needed punch. Then we called in Juan. He took one spoonful, literally said "Aha!" with a finger in the air, and proceeded to boil a small pot of water, drop four dried guajillos into it, then immediately drain them, pound the softened peppers to paste in a mortar, and stir it into the vat of soup. The result was smoky, spicy perfection.)

But he's also a guy in whose company it is very comfortable just to be quiet. Which is what we're doing now, until suddenly Juan chuckles.

"What is it?" I ask, smiling in expectation of a funny anecdote.

And he starts telling me a story. It takes me a few seconds to catch up with what he's saying. Juan speaks completely fluent English, but it's accented enough, and he is soft-spoken enough, that occasionally I miss a word or two. Anyway, he's talking about walking a long way in the cold, and at first I think he's talking about walking to work.

(What I was thinking of was: I once overheard Josh asking Juan if he had a winter coat. "I'm *getting* you a coat. It fucking *kills* me thinking of you walking to work in this weather without a real coat." This from a man who had, not ten minutes earlier, cacklingly locked one of his employees into the cooler for fun.)

So then Juan says something about stopping in the middle of the night for a couple of hours' sleep, and I'm slowly beginning to understand what it is he's telling me and I am obscurely embarrassed, as if he's sharing something with me more intimate than our relationship bears up to.

"I woke up, and I was so, so cold, I thought I was going to die. I couldn't feel my hands. Lying there, freezing, and I look up at the sky, and there are so many stars. It was beautiful. Now whenever I'm really cold, I think about that." He laughs again.

"Where was this?" I ask, not exactly sure how to respond to this disclosure, however casually bestowed.

"Arizona, I think."

"The desert," I say moronically, "gets cold at night."

"Yeah."

I have been secretly feeling kind of sorry for myself ever since the spurting sausage. Pitying myself for my flailing marriage, for my lost lover, for getting older and maybe never having sex again. And then Juan tells me his story about crossing the border in the middle of the night, an experience so arduous and uncertain and frightening that rich tourists pay money, this is true, to get a Disneyfied version of the experience. And he tells it with a giggle. It's just what he has to do whenever he wants to visit his mother.

And I think, I really ought to get over myself.

JUAN'S MOTHER'S BLOOD SAUSAGE

    4 quarts unsalted pig's blood, as fresh as possible
    4 cups finely diced pork fat
    About 4 tablespoons kosher salt
    About 3 tablespoons coarsely ground black pepper
    1 quart chopped onion
    1½ cups finely chopped jalapeño, seeds removed
    2 cups shredded mint
    A quart container of pork "middles" (from your
        butcher—ordered along with the blood and fat)

    Kitchen twine, trimmed up into three-inch lengths
    Special equipment: a manual sausage-stuffing funnel,
        basically a metal cup with a nozzle at the bottom,
        either handheld or on a stand of some kind

If the blood is not basically straight out of the animal, it will
have congealed; reliquefy it with a blender, food processor,
or immersion mixer. Then simply stir in the fat and all the
remaining ingredients. It will be very, very liquid, and you'll
wonder how you'll ever make anything solid from it. There is
reason to wonder.

Untangle a length of casing, maybe three feet or so of it,
and bunch it up on the nozzle with the aforementioned up-
and-down motion. Tie the end into a knot and reinforce by
knotting a length of twine just above it.

Over a bin or large baking pan, begin spooning the blood
mixture into the cup of the stuffer, while with the other hand
urging the casing off the nozzle as it fills. When the chunks of
fat get stuck in the mouth of the funnel, push them through
with the handle of a wooden spoon or something similar. This
is all easier to accomplish if you have more than one pair of
hands. Sausage making, like the activity it often resembles, is
more fun with two people.

Stop filling when you still have about four inches of casing left. While one person holds the empty bit up and pinches it closed, the other person will twist the length of sausage into links. About four or five inches from the bottom end, make a double twist, then reinforce it with a tie. Continue like this until you've divided up the whole length. At the top of the last link, make a knot with the end of the casing. The sausages will feel to the touch like, well, pig intestines filled with blood.

Drop the length of sausages into simmering water and poach it for about ten minutes. This is tricky; keep the water at a very gentle simmer. After about five minutes, begin testing for doneness. Gently lift a link out of the water with tongs. First touch the surface; the sausage should have solidified. Then poke the sausage with a toothpick or skewer; the sausage is done when a puncture in the center of the link oozes clear juice rather than blood. Lift the sausage from the water and let cool to room temperature.

In an ideal world, this recipe would yield about two dozen four-inch links of sausage. However, all boiled sausages are delicate, especially blood sausage, due to the liquid filling. You will lose many lengths to burst casings—which make a disturbing mess in the simmering water—and more to undercooking (you can fry up the undercooked links and use them as you might chorizo). But the ones that do turn out are lovely—spicy and rich, with the mint providing an unexpectedly refreshing note. You'll find that you can live with the few links you have and not mourn too much over your mistakes.

5
Break Down

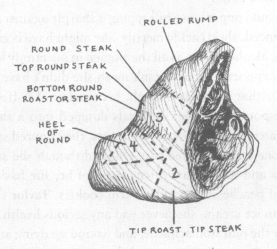

ROLLED RUMP

ROUND STEAK

TOP ROUND STEAK

BOTTOM ROUND
ROAST OR STEAK

HEEL
OF
ROUND

TIP ROAST, TIP STEAK

"IF YOU CAN dodge a wrench, you can dodge a ball." I don't quote Vince Vaughn movies, as a general rule, but this line pops into my head as I start in on my fourth beef round of the day. I've been working at the shop for a couple of months now, and I'm stronger than I was, but beef rounds still get me winded. After practicing on these buggers, going back to petite pig hindquarters will be a snap.

Beef rounds are enormous things, and more obvious than some of the other primal cuts. There is no question that this is a hundred-pound ass-end of cow. They are obvious in other ways as well. They have lots of interlocking parts, but the pieces all have a pleasing distinctness about them. The muscles have simple shapes, like those games for very small children, with the plastic blocks in different shapes that are meant to be fitted into different indentations: top round, a circle; bottom round, a trapezoid; eye round, a cylinder; knuckle, a cone. Breaking down a beef round is splendidly clear-cut work, but, given the sheer weight of the thing, it's also *hard* work.

The wrist of my left hand, my cutting hand, is now visibly thicker than my right, with muscle and also with chronic swelling. My left thumb has started to occasionally catch, just as my granny's used to do.

(She would pop it loose by rapping it sharply against a tabletop; when I winced, she'd cackle merrily. She might have been a manic-depressive alcoholic, but as all the women in my family know from personal experience, that doesn't mean she didn't have a sense of humor. Or that she wasn't tough: her version of coffee was several tablespoons of Folger's crystals dumped into a saucepan of boiling water, cooked down five minutes, then poured straight out into her one stained coffee cup. Oh, and though she smoked for fifty years and for the last fifteen years of her life basically lived on canned peaches, Pepperidge Farm cookies, Taylor sherry, and Neapolitan ice cream, she never had any serious health problems, except for the odd stomachache, and wound up dying at the age of ninety, mostly out of sheer cussedness.)

Sometimes, after a day of hard cutting, the ache in my wrist keeps me from sleeping. My hands and arms are adorned with nicks and scrapes, mostly from the featherbones that bristle along the cut edges of the spines on sides of pork, thin shards that can scrape like hell. I find all these marks, like the ones D used to bestow, perversely satisfying, a coded diary of my experience. Josh and I have begun talking tattoos. His arms are heavily inked already, and he's looking to accompany me when I decide what to get to commemorate my Butchering Endeavor.

It's a Wednesday afternoon, slow, so Jesse has joined me for a bit of knife practice. He normally works the counter, and so doesn't get a lot of table time. He and I, junior butchers, toil away on the rounds while Aaron and Tom go after the chuck shoulders. Chuck shoulder is the most challenging primal to break down. Aaron and Josh and Tom will get into three-way tiffs over the best technique for doing it. For now I pretty much stay away; I certainly can't yet navigate a shoulder without assistance. So I stick with rounds. The Jackson 5 is playing on Josh's iPod. (Josh's musical collection is something of a hoot—opera, sugary pop, Eminem, world music. My favorite, I think, is the album of themes from classic seventies porn movies. Actually really great, hummable tunes, with much amusing wakka chikka. And the sight of a bunch of butchers cutting meat to the theme of *Debbie Does Dallas* is not to be missed.)

I start by breaking off the shank. With a mighty pull I grab hold of the narrow end of the round—what would be the handle of the drumstick if this were a chicken—and swing it around until it's jutting out over the table edge. Checking first to make sure that no one is near the knife's path, I cut through the thick rope of tendon where it emerges from the muscle and stretches, exposed, to meet the bony knob of the shank's lower end, with one sawing slice away from me. The blade always springs up a bit once it's through. Then I follow the seam of the shank muscle up to where I estimate the joint to be. To find it, I press down against the meat and fat with my thumb and grab the bone by the end to wiggle it back and forth. My fourth round of the day, and finally, this time, when I stab my blade tip in, I hit the crack of the joint on the first try. "Gotcha!" I mutter as I dig in, working through the sinews until I'm able to break open the joint. The shank comes away in my hand and a lazy drip of clear, silky synovial fluid falls from the end to the ground. I toss the shank to the far end of the table. The inside of the joint's cup is bright white, wet with the lubricating fluid, and impossibly smooth. I can never resist running my fingers, ever so briefly, inside that bowl of cartilage.

"So tell me again where this place is? I've ridden my bike around there."

Jesse is asking about the apartment I've just rented, about twenty minutes away from Kingston. Eric doesn't like that I've done this, of course, but the drive up from the city and back at the end of each day I spend at the shop is exhausting and burns unseemly amounts of gasoline, and besides—who am I kidding?—I look forward to the nights of solitude, to the escape from our fights that aren't fights, our silences full of reproaches. It's a plain, pretty, often chilly set of rooms on the second story of a slightly shabby Victorian. When Eric and I were separated, I never told him that I was, much of the time, happy, just having that tiny apartment to myself, to be able to sleep until ten or stay up until four, to cook my own dinners for myself, to read in a room no one else resided in. Though this place is twice as large as my Yorkville sublet, and in an upstate so-called town—really just a post office, a volunteer fire department, and a curve in the road—it reminds me of that first room of my own, of the small pleasures of living alone.

"It's in Rifton." Now, the name is a bit of a problem, just a tad too ironic, as if I need more reminders of all the gaping crevasses opening up in my life. "South of here, off 213. Close to New Paltz, past Rosendale."

"Okay.... Yeah, there's great biking out that way. You have a bike?"

"Nah."

It seems like everyone in the shop is a serious biker, even Josh, who I can't imagine on a bicycle. (He even sells a biking shirt in the shop on which the cuts of meat are marked out, so that you can see where my brisket is, where my flatiron steak. I wear it sometimes while butchering, and Aaron says I look like a superhero, by which he means, though he doesn't say, that the top is brightly colored, very tight, and has a zipper that, when pulled halfway down, as I wear it, exposes a certain amount of cleavage.) Tom and Jesse, particularly, are always relating their latest cycling adventures. I have been trying to avoid getting sucked into an outing. That sounds nasty but isn't meant that way. I just feel so daunted.

I've taken up a meat hook and I'm working at pulling out the aitchbone. "Aitchbone," I've now figured out, by the way, is derived from the Middle English "nache," meaning "buttock." But it's still a hip bone, so I stand by my initial theory. Anyway, same process as with the pork rounds, just bigger and thus harder. I get the hook up through the eye of the bone.

"You could borrow one of mine sometime."

A small grunt as I begin to pull down on it with my right hand, scraping up under it with the knife in my left. "Thanks, that's nice of you. But I don't really ride."

"Everybody can ride."

"Yeah, well, not me. I'm ridiculous. Must be some repressed childhood thing."

"You were molested by a Schwinn?" Tom calls out.

"Something like that." I spend a moment contemplating something sufficiently locker-talky to distract from the cycling invitation I feel coming on. "Never take candy from a strange banana seat, kids."

"I did *not* just hear that." Aaron groans as everyone erupts into preadolescent guffaws, except for Jesse, who doesn't much go in for locker talk and is satisfied just listening in, smiling from time to time.

I sometimes feel like I spend an inordinate amount of energy evading social engagements lately, and I don't even know why—well, other than the fact that I really am pretty ridiculous on a bike. I like these people, a lot. Jesse, for instance, sweet and quiet, with a good laugh, enjoys talking politics with me, and is fond of recommending various holistic remedies, which he most of the time manages to do without sounding like a twit or a fanatic. He is sometimes a little, I don't know, floaty—easily distracted, slow moving. Josh and Aaron, straight-ahead, maniacally ambitious guys both, can get impatient with him. Occasionally they're inspired to lock him in the cooler with the lights out or to see how long they can string him along on a prank call. On one of his days off, Aaron once kept Jesse on the phone for close to ten minutes with a put-on voice, a false name, and a claim that a turkey he'd bought in the shop had had three wings. Jesse's nickname is "1480," a reference to Josh's disbelief that anyone with such an SAT score could be so out-to-lunch. But he's great with the customers, knows their names and somehow has time for a bit of conversation with each of them, even when it's busy. And I like having him around the place. The cutting table is surrounded by a constant flow of testosterone. Normally I enjoy being one of the guys, all of us competing to out-trash-talk one another. But sometimes I'm really thankful for a calm, simply kind presence like Jesse's. So why not take him up on a bicycle outing, after all? Or a drink after work? Why do I more often than not decline Josh and Jessica's invitations to dinner, Aaron's elaborate weekend agendas? (He's in the process now of formulating a shop-wide mustache contest and has been cultivating a great handlebar monstrosity with the care of Mr. Miyagi trimming a bonsai tree. He tells of combing and waxing and shaping endlessly. "We have an extra bathroom at home just for the mustache," he says, and I believe him.) It's not just exhaustion, which I often plead, or my anxiety to get back to the city and my husband and animals. There's something else at work here.

After I get the bone off and slapped into the designated "bone" can that stands at one end of the table, lined with a heavy-duty garbage bag, I move on to the top round, a circle of flesh, about as big as a hubcap. It's part of the steer's buttock, basically, thick on one side, near to where it once clung to the aitch, thinning at the edges, as the muscle peters out toward the base of the shank. I start at this thin edge, pulling up at the muscle and flicking at the filaments underneath, until the meat rolls off. I trim away a bit of the hardened outer layer of fat and remove the cap, another, smaller circle of meat that sits atop the round like, well, a cap.

I've pulled well ahead of Jesse, which is not surprising. He doesn't get a lot of cutting practice, and I've been working here three or four days a week, ten hours a day, for three months now. Not all of that time is spent at the table, of course—there's the Cryovac machine to be worked, wholesale orders to be compiled, coolers and freezers to reorganize, and of course a fair amount of sitting around shooting the shit—but I've clocked enough time to have picked up a good bit of speed. We've descended back into silence now, all of us working intently, no noise but the music on the iPod (we've switched to early Madonna), the slap of meat on wood or into plastic luggers, the clatter of bones into the can. I pull out the big leg bone, peel the cylindrical eye round off the side of the trapezoidal bottom round. Pull out the thick, veined wedge of fat in the center with its trove of glutinous glands, roll out the conical knuckle. All these (but for the fat wedge, which is thrown away) will be bagged pretty much as is. I have to trim the silver skin off one sloping side of the bottom round. Aaron may have me tie it to cook for the roast beef he will (closely) supervise me making. Aaron's method for roasting beef for the front counter always varies slightly. At the moment, it goes just about like this:

AARON'S ROAST BEEF

> 7 pounds bottom round, trimmed of silver skin, fat cap
> left on
> Salt and pepper
> 3 tablespoons vegetable oil
> 1 onion, sliced into ½-inch rounds
> 4 cloves garlic, lightly crushed
> 6 two-inch marrow bones
> 3 tablespoons butter, sliced into thin pats

Preheat the oven to 300°F.

Tie the round with butcher's twine into a neat, even rectangle, or have your butcher do it for you. Season the roast generously with salt and pepper on all sides.

In a large ovenproof roasting pan, heat the oil on the stove over high heat until it's reached that Beckettian "almost smoking" point. Sear the roast on all sides, taking particular care that the fat side reaches a good, crusty brown. Take the roast from the pan and set aside on a plate, then turn off the heat under the pan. Add the onion and garlic, briefly browning them using the residual heat, before setting the marrow bones in among the vegetables, arranging them into a rack. Rest the roast on top of the bones, fat side up. Arrange the pats of butter on top. Set the roasting pan into the oven and cook for about an hour and a half, basting every fifteen minutes or so—you want as much of the rich juices that melt out of the bones to be absorbed into the meat as possible.

The roast is done when a meat thermometer inserted into the center reads 130°F. Remove it from the oven and let it rest until it comes to room temperature, then slice thin for sandwich meat. Makes enough roast beef sandwiches to feed a small army.

Oh, and: after you've finished, smear the marrow from the middle of the bones on some bread, sprinkle with a bit of salt, and you have an ambrosial snack.

I'll do that a little later on. For now I have to remove tough sinews from the end of the knuckle, and from the upper shank muscles, which will go into the grind. I work away. The lyrics in my nostalgic head aren't the ones playing on the iPod, but those that often linger up there, from an Old 97's rockabilly tune I once referred to, half-jokingly, as D's theme song: *I don't want to get you all worked up. Except secretly I do. I'd be lyin' if I said I didn't have designs on you.*

I enjoy our bursts of talk at the table, which then sink back into an industrious quiet. The rhythm of it feels like real work with comfortable companions. But at the end of the day, as soon as I take off my leather sheepherder's hat, wash my hands and knives, scrape and salt the table, this peace is already leaving. When I walk out the door, the need will come down on me again like an anvil.

"Jules, come have a drink. Mother's Milk. It's local. We have half a keg back there we need to get through."

So I sit around with Jesse and Aaron and Josh and drink the beer, darker than I usually take it, and bitter. We talk about this and that, nothing important, mustaches and presidential hopefuls. Juan has a glass poured too, but he can't sit yet. He has dishes to wash, a band saw and grinder to break down and clean. Miles to go before he sleeps. As I do, in my own little way.

"So, Jules. Did you know that butchers in Paris have their own entire language?"

"What are you talking about?"

"Well, it's slang. Like pig latin. It's called *louchébem*. They, like, switch around syllables. It's so they can talk smack about the customers."

Josh is straightening out his long red hair with his fingers and rebraiding it. "Do they have a word for 'Bite me, douche bag'?"

"I'll look it up."

I ask, thinking ruefully of how, I know, my evening is going to go, "Do they have a word for 'crazy lady'?"

"Almost certainly. Hmm. I feel a nickname coming on..."

I could ask out any one of these guys, whose company I enjoy so much, for another drink around the corner. But I don't. I leave after the one beer. We lock up; I walk alone to my car.

There's no place that's really safe, other than the shop, these days. I'm just climbing into the Outback when my phone rings. "I need to ask you a question. Are you seeing him still?"

"What? No! No—I—I haven't even talked to him. He's not—" I can't tell Eric the truth. Can't tell him, *He's not speaking to me and it's killing me.* "Where is this coming from?"

"You know what? Forget it. I wouldn't believe you, whatever you said. I don't want to know."

"I haven't *done* anythi—I'm sorry. I'm sorry."

Eric and I haven't had sex in months. And though D is gone, hasn't exchanged a word with me in weeks, despite or because of the desperate, pleading texts that our horrid at-last-real breakup didn't succeed in deterring me from, still he's there, of course, living in our apartment. Eric doesn't touch me. And I can't touch him either. The truth is that Eric's love, his very dearness, is excruciating to me, a constant stabbing. If we were to sleep together now— sleep together as in sex, of course; we still sleep in the same bed every night I am home—he would see that too clearly. It would kill him. I know because it's nearly killing me. It's a horrible thing to admit even just to myself. It gnaws at my bones.

But I crave, I do, and I can't yet seem to shut it down; it's like plunging around a dark basement, pawing the walls desperately for the light switch and finding nothing but clammy bricks and cobwebs. And it's not just about D. Oh, maybe it is. It's so hard to know. Because, yes, I dream of being welcomed back into his bed, of reconciliation, but that's becoming too painful to dream upon. And when it hurts that much, it's time for a little cure-the-headache-by-slamming-the-fingers-in-the-cutlery-drawer treatment.

Lots of people like indulging in a bit of light submission. It's not necessarily such a big deal. I was always interested, in an academic sort of way. It just always felt so... well, goofy, in practice. In Eric's and my little experiments. I figured it was one of those desires that works out better in the mind's eye. And then D came along.

"Come home with me."

I remember the first time, when I knew it was certain. We were standing in front of a deli at the corner of 12th and University Place, on a November afternoon in 2004. We'd had our friendly lunch, which had grown into something else. But this was where we should have parted ways; I'd already been away from home too long.

"I'll come tomorrow. I will. But I can't today. I have to walk the dog." I tried weakly to pull out of his arms, but his hands remained firmly clasped behind the small of my back.

"You'll change your mind if you don't come now. Come now."

I was flushed and breathless, ready. D may have protested that time was of the essence, that I was a grown woman who needed persuading, who was capable of changing her mind, but in truth he'd known, from the moment he kissed me there on that corner while we waited for the Walk sign, that he would get me back to his Murray Hill apartment for the first time that day, and with a minimum of fuss. He didn't even bother to conceal the shine of certainty in his eyes.

All my young life, when push had come to shove, I'd been the one to pick what or whom I wanted, and to make sure I got it.

Steamroller Julie. It's how I got my husband, how I got my new career. But now I was being the one wanted, taken, had. I was helpless against that assurance. Liked the helplessness.

"Okay. But I have to get back soon. One hour. That's all."

"Perfect. Come on."

He's like that, seems to suffer no trace of uncertainty, nary a moral twinge. For the two months before Eric found out about the affair, D felt no compunction about anything. He readily attended dinner parties to which I readily invited him, readily exchanged footsies and covert glances, readily even spent the night on the couch so he could have a wee-hours make-out session and then breakfast with us the next morning, comfortably digging into his eggs Benedict at a booth with his lover and her unknowing husband. (His *lover!* How I relished rolling the word around in my mind, writing it in a covert e-mail or text—though always with ironic quotation marks—even tasting it on my tongue, though I would never speak it above a whisper, and then only to myself.)

"Come on. Come to me."

"I'm on my way."

I was finally doing something I ought to have felt ashamed of, and for the first time in a long time, no obscure guilt squeezed my heart at all. I was giddy. Wanton. I had a *lover*.

"At last you came." D answered the door naked.

"As soon as I could."

He slammed me up against the wall, screwed me in the foyer before he managed to get my clothes off. Carried me—me, a big girl, not light and lithe—past his roommates' closed doors (I chose to believe they weren't home)—to his bedroom. Threw me onto the bed, knelt to unzip my black high-heeled boots. Raised his eyebrows in an expression both ironic and genuinely, excitingly lustful. "Rowr…"

"Oh, please. I'm wearing stupid argyle socks." Eric's socks, actually.

"But look at that reveal," he said, indicating the shoes' red leather lining. "R-*owwr*."

Hours later, when I arose to dress and leave, he pulled me back to bed, yanked me by the ankle as I crawled his bedroom floor looking for my underwear, a lost boot, a broken necklace. He slapped my ass, bit me, hard, left bruises all over my body that I had to take care to hide, dark and mottled and as distinct in shape as the bites taken out of surfboards by sharks. He had figured me out.

Not that I made it difficult. Under D's influence, I opened up like a grinning harlot flower. The first time he slapped me across the face, after all, I was bound in trusses I'd given him. But the thing was, it wasn't so much the slap itself; it was the gleam in his eye as he delivered it, the utter confidence that he'd guessed right. The sting on my cheek made me gasp, but his sureness was what freed me.

I am, empirically speaking, a successful person. But all the things that should have made me feel sure and independent hadn't. It was D who gave that to me. It was when he smilingly roughed me up that I finally felt fierce, strong—emancipated.

But now he's gone, and it turns out my freedom was only probationary. The grinding guilt has returned. My guts twist with it.

Eric calls again just as I've turned off 213, south of Rosendale, onto the twisting road to Rifton. "Look, I'm sorry about what I said before."

"It's okay. I'm sorry if you think I've done something wrong." I can't keep a small trill of resentment out of my voice. And that's not entirely a bad thing; resentment is nice for covering up the remorse.

"No, you didn't do anything, I know. I'm sorry. I guess I just get a little crazy with you up there all the time. Robert misses you."

For the last couple of months I've been staying up here in my rented apartment three or four nights a week. I've always had great faith in the healing power of geography. Absence makes the heart, and whatnot.

"I wish you could be okay with this. I want to do this, the butchery, and I'm going to, and there's nothing wrong with that, and it has nothing to do with you or us." I'm getting emotional now, a bit self-righteous. Protesting a tad too much.

"Honey, I want to be understanding here. But you're right. I don't get it. I'm trying."

"Okay. I'm sorry. Can you just—"

"Yes. I'm fine. I'll be okay. I just miss you and..."

"I know. I'm sorry. Look, I think I'm going to cut out here in a minute." His voice is growing sparser and quiet on the line. "Good night. I love you, I really do."

"I know. I love you too."

When I'm alone in the chilly apartment at night, a bare kitchen, small living room, bedroom painted white and blue, I cook up my dinner, a steak or a sausage or a chop. I open my first bottle of wine. These are the last pieces of the simple, jigsaw-puzzle part of my day. It is nine p.m., I'm tired in that stoned sort of way that means I'll not be asleep for some hours yet. My wrist throbs vaguely. Piling several pillows against the wall for a backrest, I make sure my wineglass is full, pull up my laptop, insert a DVD.

"What's a stevedore?"

It doesn't matter what that line means in context. Or rather, it matters very, very much to Eric and me, but you don't need to know what makes the line so priceless, why I can repeat it, out of the blue and for no particular reason, and Eric is right there with me. What matters is that this unlikely TV show, *Buffy the Vampire Slayer,* canceled years ago, forms a singular touchstone of our private marriage-language. Watching it feels like coming home to him. And tonight, after our tense, aborted conversation, it feels almost like an act of apology, of fidelity. I am entirely Eric's Julie while watching *Buffy,* one of the few bits of pop culture that doesn't instantly bring D—who is both a cineaste and a *South Park* fan—to the forefront of my mind. I watch three episodes.

By then it's after eleven. I shut down the computer, set it on my bedside table by the now half-empty second bottle of Syrah, switch off the table lamp, and settle down, pulling the sheets fitfully up over my shoulder. But I can tell immediately it's going to be no use. The laptop comes out again; I sign into my instant message account. Thank God, Gwen is online.

> Julie: Hey. What's up? You're not still at work, are you?
> Gwen: No, thank Christ. Over at Matt's.

After years of bad luck, Gwen seems to have found a boyfriend who suits her. Being Gwen, of course, she's still stormy and annoyed at times, but they go on trips together and visit each other's families, and he buys her clothes and fixes her computer, and by all accounts they have all kinds of sex. I try very hard not to be bitter.

> Gwen: What's up with you?
> Julie: I'm upstate. Feeling rather like shit.
> Gwen: Sick?
> Julie: No. Just the usual thing. D. I'd flushed him out for a few
>   hours there, but once I try going to sleep…
> Gwen: Oh, Julie. When are you going to let the douche bag go?
> Julie: I just don't understand. Why does he hate me so much?
> Gwen: I've already spelled this out. He. Is. A. Douche. Bag.... I
>   want to punch him in the face.
> Julie: That would be great.
> Gwen: You know, I just saw Match Point, finally. The Scarlett
>   Johansson character is like you and D combined. You're
>   the drunken hysterical part, and he's the part that needs
>   killing.
> Julie: Hi-LAR-ious. Of course I'd take him back in a minute,
>   though.
> Gwen: Now I want to punch you in the face.
> Julie: Thanks.
> Gwen: Listen, honey. I've got to go—Matt and I are going
>   to… well… I gotta go.
> Julie: Understood.
> Gwen: I love you. Take care.
> Julie: Thanks. Love you too.

Dammit. That wasn't enough. I pour myself another glass to dose myself that little bit closer to sleep, then trawl the Internet awhile, looking for a certain something. For the particular kind of photos and cheap videos that distract for a time—women bound and helpless and begging, men withholding, commanding, sure. There's a certain brainless eroticism to this sort of thing, for me. At least my body responds, even if my mind soon feels jaded and in need of a scrubbing. I try to focus on outlandish scenarios, images of exotic, tawdry humiliation. But my brain just bats these bits and pieces lazily about like a bored cat, then wanders inexorably back to its more accustomed, but more dangerous, feeding grounds.

A cold, sardonic face, that unbeautiful one with its cool eyes and wide Rolling Stones lips I've by now memorized. The pebbly cyst still to be felt in a left earlobe, a closed-up hole from teenage rock-god years. A way of taking off clothes, deliberate, so different from my own impatient stripping. A matter-of-fact yank at my thighs, pulling me toward those lips, a way of giving that feels like something's being taken, like I'm being emptied out. A voice, low, amused, with a guttural purr to it that makes my breath catch.

Before D broke it off, we occasionally indulged in phone sex, an easy way to make use of brief periods alone, when we'd worked ourselves up but couldn't manage to schedule a tryst. We never talked dirty during these phone sessions. Instead we made a game out of hearing each other, trying to time ourselves to each other. This was a much more challenging game for me than for D, basically because I'm a shitty poker player. No matter how stealthy I tried to be, I'd always throw him a moan, an "oh fuck," the ragged, stuttering little gasp he knew meant I was there at the edge. Whereas I had nothing to go on but the tiny catch in the breath, the quickening of that wet slapping sound that barely reached the receiver, the occasional shudder repressed behind a bitten lip. And in the end, we sometimes cheated. He would speak, for the first time since we murmured our hellos. Whispering, urgent but measured, almost angry, a demand more than a question. *Tell me when. Now?*

"Yes, please, please now..." His name comes out as a sob, the memory of those sounds on the other end of a phone line making my muscles tighten and spasm. The tendons of my wrist and index finger ping painfully, and then I cry myself to sleep. But at least I get there, my hand squeezed between my thighs not for pleasure, just for comfort, as a small child might do.

The next morning I get up again with puffy eyes and lips purple with wine, a few hiccups of sadness still left to jump out of my throat. But I shower and change into a pair of jeans and one of the black Fleisher's T-shirts (YOU CAN'T BEAT OUR MEAT!) I wear to the shop every day, and by the time I go outside into the nippy fall air and climb into my Outback I am feeling calmer. Usually, I'd be headed to the shop for a day of getting scraped up and telling dirty jokes and cutting beef. Today, though, I have an elsewhere to be. I've got an appointment with a pig.

6

Off the Hoof

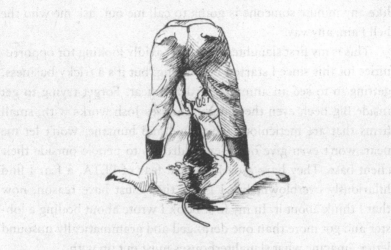

IT IS A brilliant late November day, the sky a heartbreaking blue over the nearby ridge of the Shawagunks. The morning sun glints off the bright tossing leaves of the trees that line the edge of this green field I have walked down a short muddy track to reach, following a ragtag crowd. Kids in their twenties mostly, CIA students. A wooden-gated corral stands in the field, within it five pigs, chasing one another around and snuffling happily in the muck. When people approach the corral, to coo or snap pictures, the pigs come up to the gate, ears pricked and heads high. A few yards away, an old Austrian man in coveralls is loading a small-gauge rifle.

Aaron turned me on to this gig; every fall the CIA arranges to have its students witness and participate in a pig slaughter, done the old-fashioned way. The event is headed up by one of the senior instructors, a man named Hans, who, it is rumored by Aaron, once won the European Master Butcher Competition. (I wonder if there really is such a thing. I like to think the winner gets a belt.)

He told me when and where to go; eight a.m., a side road on the way up to the Mohonk Mountain House, a gorgeous if slightly *Shining*-esque old historic resort. Aaron has to be at the shop and so, to his emphatic regret, can't come along, but says, "You *have* to go. You have to see Hans at work. He's an artist."

I wish he were here. I know no one, and I feel like an impostor, like any minute someone is going to call me out, ask me who the hell I am, anyway.

This is my first slaughter. I've been avidly looking for opportunities for this since I started butchering, but it's a tricky business, getting in to see an animal killed for meat. Forget trying to get inside Big Beef; even the slaughterhouses Josh works with, small firms that are meticulously hygienic and humane, won't let me near, won't even give out their addresses to people outside their client base. They have a pathological fear of PETA, a fear I find hilariously overblown, but I guess they must have reason, now that I think about it. In my first book I wrote about boiling a lobster and got more than one deranged and grammatically unsound letter; imagine what slaughterhouses must put up with.

I spend a few moments leaning with one foot on the wooden fence, contemplating these animals who are about to be dead, whose flesh I may very literally wind up eating. (The farmer providing the animals for today's spectacle is one of Josh's suppliers.) I've always had a bit of a thing for pigs, actually. And not just the cute Chinese potbellied variety, though, God, I want one of those. I like hogs. I like that they're both filthy and smart, like that they can be vicious but are also known to appreciate a good scratch behind the ears from time to time. A pig is kind of my power animal. Honestly, it's a shame they taste so damned good, but of course that's part of my connection to them.

Other people are gathered around as well, on either side of me, presumably thinking the same sorts of thoughts. Being kids, and culinary students, and friends and/or rivals, their talk contains quite a bit of evasive bravado, inclining toward one-upmanship, outdoing one another in knowledge or nonchalance. But I don't believe them. There is a tang in the air, a palpable anticipation, and not just of a lesson in a culinary art. We are about to witness, many of us for the first time, a violent death—a murder, if you define murder as the deliberate killing of an innocent being. And we are all nervous and excited and a little bit thrilled about it.

At a call from someone or other, the crowd (there are probably about thirty of us) begins to gather around a livestock trailer a bit away from the corral, which has two more hogs inside, separated from each other by a metal grating running down the middle. The bed of the trailer is strewn with straw. Hans, a gun in one hand and a metal bowl of chow in the other, opens the gate at the back end of the trailer to get to the first animal, who doesn't retreat at his approach. When he puts the bowl down on the floor, the hog trots right up to it and immediately digs in. Hans puts the rifle to its forehead.

When the gun goes off, it sounds like a champagne cork popping. The theory, which I'm not entirely sure I buy, is that the hog's skull is so thick that the small-caliber shot does no more than stun it; it's the pick immediately afterward, thrust into its carotid artery, that kills it.

Hans shoves in the pick and hauls the animal out onto the grass with one movement. The circle of curious onlookers, who have gathered close to catch sight of the shooting, hop back.

So this is where the phrase *bleeding like a stuck pig* comes from. The creature's legs work furiously as blood jets from its throat. The force of its jerking spins it around in circles like a spasmodic breakdancer. All in eerie silence. There's no terrified squealing, what we're watching is not conscious suffering, it's just the innate need of any living being to hang on to life. Like watching a patient who, though brain-dead, nevertheless fights hungrily for breath when taken off the respirator. As it struggles, the hog smears itself in its own blood, which continues to flow out torrentially and sinks into the deep grass, absorbed by the ground like water.

It takes maybe a minute for the animal to come to stillness, though it seems much longer. Hans loops a rope around the animal's rear legs, cinches it tight. He points to two students in the crowd, gestures at the rope. "Take it over there."

Two boys grab hold of the rope and drag the dead hog over to a spot where an old porcelain bathtub has been sunk into the ground. (Men outnumber women in this group by probably three to one.)

Two ropes are laid out across the tub on either end of it. When the students give the body a shove, it drops heavily, in the way of dead things, into the tub, on top of the ropes, so they're now looped under it, one at the shoulder, the other near the rear legs. As the rest of us gather around, a couple more volunteers start scooping bucketfuls of boiling water from a vat about the size of a smallish hot tub sitting atop a big woodstove and pouring the water out into the bathtub until the hog is half-submerged. At Hans's direction, four guys take hold of the ropes' ends on either side of the tub and pull them back and forth, tug-of-war style, so that the body is turned over and over. By the time the water has stopped steaming, the pig's coarse hair has started coming loose, floating, and the ropes have worn away two long, bald areas, the skin beneath poached white and soft. It takes four people to pull the body back out of the tub and onto a piece of worn plywood.

When Hans asks for more volunteers, half a dozen people step eagerly forward, but I am not one of them. I tell myself it's because I should let the tuition-paying students, those who are here legitimately, get the experience, but the truth is that somewhere deep inside I don't want to be a party to this slaughter, that I feel somehow less culpable as an observer than as a participant. Nonsense, of course.

Volunteers kneel on the ground all around the hog, with cup-shaped rubber scrapers in hand. As they rub off all the hair, great soggy clumps shedding into growing piles shifting about in the breeze, the body shudders, fat rippling under its skin like an overweight jogger, legs sawing back and forth as if it's still alive and struggling to get away. But once all the hair is off, the work of five minutes, as the hog lies there, pale and bloated, it is already more meat than animal.

The body is carried to a nearby shed with a little covered, concrete-floored patio. A chain threaded through a pulley attached to a wooden beam overhead is looped around the hog's rear legs, and two broad-backed boys tug on the other end to lift it up off the ground until it's hanging free.

The next part is where slaughter meets butchery, where everything starts looking very familiar to me. After making a couple of hissing passes across the honing steel with his knife, an unshowy thing not much larger than what I use in the shop, Hans without flourish slices the hog open from stem to stern. Then he reaches inside, scoops out its pallid entrails, and pours them into a large bucket. The liver is cut out, the heart that so recently worked efficiently enough to pump all the creature's blood from its neck in a matter of seconds, the stomach, the lungs together with the windpipe, all the way up through the animal's throat, ending in the blue tongue cut loose from the floor of the mouth with a swipe. He cuts the head smoothly off and sets it to one side. What remains, the emptied body, the edges of its sliced belly hanging open like a set of curtains, is more or less exactly what I see at Fleisher's.

The CIA does teach butchery, but not extensively. Most students get about seven classes in meat processing, only some of which include hands-on practice, so what is now, after three months, completely familiar to me holds great fascination for them. After the hog has been halved with a quick pass of a butcher's saw, they take turns leaning in to get a look at the sides, pointing out the spareribs, contemplating where the Boston butt comes from. (The shoulder, I could have told them but don't; it's the same muscle as what's called a "chuck roast" in beef.) I back away to let them get close. It's over for me. The hog has gone from contentedly grunting farm animal to nothing I haven't seen before, in under ten minutes.

Hans is already loading up his rifle again.

I make myself watch the "processing" of one more animal. When Hans enters the second hog's pen, it won't stand up, just lies resolutely, chin between hooves, looking up at him. It doesn't seem panicked, but it looks so much like Robert the Dog when I come home to find he's been in the garbage can that I can't help thinking it must have figured out that something bad is afoot.

Part of me thinks I should stay longer, stick it out—they have half a dozen more animals to go through—but instead I head back down the track toward my car, which is parked at the side of the road. I've seen my slaughter; two were enough for me.

I head back to the shop, a half-hour drive through the beautiful morning, and get to the shop before it opens. As I walk through the door, Josh says, "Back from the killing fields. You scarred for life? It's rough, right?"

I fake a look of trauma. "Pretty intense."

But the truth isn't so simple. I think mostly I'm disturbed because I'm not so disturbed at all. I just saw this creature killed and gutted, and I'm more or less fine with it.

As I'm tying on my apron, Aaron comes up to me with an unidentifiable something on the end of a fork.

"Try this."

"What is it?"

"Just eat it."

"Is it something disgusting?"

"No." He cocks an eyebrow. "But I wouldn't tell you if it was."

I open my mouth and close my eyes, obedient, as he pops the something in. I chew.

"Not half-bad. What is it?"

Aaron grins. "It's heart."

"Heart?"

"Grilled beef heart. You like it?"

"I do. Sorry, you're going to have to try harder to wig me out."

Aaron makes a *who, me?* face. "I'm not trying to wig you out. I'm trying to educate you. Educate!"

"Uh-huh."

"Hey, Julie?" Jessica is dressed up more than usual, in fitted jeans tucked into leather boots and a nice black top with a draping cowl neck. Her hair is not in its usual frizzy updo, but down and smoothly styled. I think she's wearing makeup. She doesn't look particularly happy, though.

"What's the occasion?"

"I'm going out to one of the restaurants we supply in a couple of hours. Josh...can't make it. Or won't. So do you want to come? It's a great place, and I'm betting there'll be free dinner in it for you."

"Absolutely!" I swallow my gobbet of heart.

The drive from Kingston to the restaurant will take about an hour and a half. It would be a little less if Josh the speed demon were driving in his itty-bitty Mini, but tonight it's just going to be Jessica and me in their big red van. I unfold the mirror on the sun visor and take a peek. "Good God, I'm a mess."

"Eh, you look fine."

"Um, thanks, but I really, really don't." I've got no clothes with me at the shop but the jeans and Fleisher's T-shirt I'm wearing. My hair is mussed and pressed sweatily against my skull, my face is bare of makeup and flushed with my day's exertions. I stink. I run my fingers through my hair a few times, but soon give up and settle back into my seat as Jessica pulls into the traffic circle that spits us out at the New York Thruway toll plaza.

"So I've heard a lot about this place, but I'm like the last person alive not to have been. Even Eric went, with his ex-girlfriend."

"Ex-girlfriend? But I thought you two have been together since basically birth?"

"Yeah....Um."

Jessica glances over at me. *"Ahh."*

I grimace sheepishly. I've been so good up to now. But I suppose some of everything that's so constantly roiling inside was bound to slip out sometime. I'm relieved, to tell the truth. Suppressing the urge to blather is exhausting. "Yeah. It's been an interesting few years."

Once the floodgates of female conversation open up, shutting them down again is not really an option. Before we've driven half an hour, I've explained both Eric's indiscretions and my own, bemoaned the loss of my lover, and admitted to my preference for a bit of the rough and tumble.

"Wow. If Josh slept with someone...I don't think I could take it. I can barely stand him sometimes as it is."

"Yeah, what's going on with you two lately? I mean, if I can ask? Jesse said there was something of a blowup yesterday." Josh and Jessica make no efforts to disguise their disagreements from colleagues. They've been known to rail at each other, right by the cutting table, yelling and snorting with ire, then march off in opposite directions, muttering in disgust, while the rest of us are left standing around in the clearing dust. Afterward, when the tension recedes, Josh refers to it as "Mom and Dad fighting in front of the kids."

Jessica rolls her eyes. "Oy. I'm telling you, husbands and wives working together....I try to get him to concentrate on something he doesn't want to deal with, and he just flies off the handle. Made this big damned fuss about being too swamped to come out with us tonight, as if I'm inconveniencing him." It's nearly dark now, high clouds fading to purple. Jessica flicks the turn indicator for the Tarrytown exit.

"Well, I am amazed that you two can fight like that. Eric and I practically *never* actually fight. Even during the worst of it—"

"Is that good?"

"I don't know. It's *easier*. Though there was this one time when he sleepwalked in the middle of the night and when I woke up the next morning he'd taken all the knives out of my knife block and lined them neatly up on the kitchen counter—"

Jessica cuts a glance over at me. "Okay, that's psychotic."

"Oh, I think he was just feeling guilty because he'd broken one of my knives, stabbing it into a cutting board—"

"Which he did why?"

"Oh, he was angry. I bring it out in him, I guess. I sometimes think I ruined him. He was just a gentle soul when I found him."

"You do realize that's crazy, right?"

"I guess."

We're pulling up onto a gravel drive leading to the back door of a rambling stone building. It looks like the restaurant's staff entrance. "Well, every marriage is its own special hell, sometimes, right?" We get out, slamming the van's doors shut. The air smells faintly of animal dung. I'm conscious all over again of my hat hair and my meat-spattered shoes and T-shirt.

And she just walks right in the door. It's the sort of thing I would never do—barge right into a bustling place full of people busy doing important jobs to find the person I want. I am more of a linger-at-the-doorway-looking-cowed girl. But I follow her through the narrow, terra-cotta tiled halls to an open doorway.

"Hey, Dan. You got a minute?"

The chef is a thin man, with full lips, a high forehead, and a long nose. Large, dark eyes. He gives Jessica a slow smile. "Absolutely." He holds out a hand with long fingers, meeting her eyes in that way that particular people do, then turns to me.

"This is Julie. She's an apprentice at the shop."

"It's a pleasure." He shakes my hand as well, and meets my eyes too. "Pull up a chair, why don't you both?"

We do. Introductions over, Dan turns all his attention to Jessica. I simply sit, trying to look both attentive and small, as the two of them talk slaughterhouses and budgets and FDA approvals. The conversation lasts for maybe twenty minutes; I entertain myself sometimes by watching the hordes of restaurant workers in their chef's checks bustling to and from the bright kitchen outside the office, and sometimes by watching Dan talk to Jessica. I know his style, recognize it all too intimately—the eye contact, unwavering then broken, the fingers playing along the edges of objects on his desk, the low chuckle that's just amused enough. I am a sucker for such performances, but it seems to have no effect on Jessica. She laughs her honking laugh only when Dan says something to merit it, she merrily twinkles or playfully smack-talks without a trace of self-consciousness or strategy. I'm envious of her.

"I need to get back into the fray out here. But thanks for coming. You're staying for something to eat, right?"

"That'd be great, thanks."

"All right. We'll throw a little something together for you."

Jessica rolls her eyes as the hostess walks us out of the kitchen into the dining room, where I stand out like a bedraggled Amazon in the honeyed light.

"What?"

"Him 'throwing a little something together.' You'll see."

And so I do. For the next two and a half hours, Jessica and I eat our way through untold courses of wonderful, precious food—teeny tiny bulbs of fennel on sticks, pork chops so little they kind of freak us out (was this pig yet out of the womb?), paper-thin slices of apple. Two hours later, I will honestly not be able to remember all of what I've eaten. I'm a champion eater, but this has even me feeling defeated. But there is a moment that makes the marathon worthwhile. The pig bonbon.

It's tiny, a perfectly shaped one-inch square. It is announced to us as pig heart, but it doesn't look like the heart Aaron popped into my mouth earlier today, like a slice of dark meat. No, it seems to have a creamy texture, like a pâté. The square is sandwiched between two impossibly thin, crisp wafers of dark chocolate. Jessica and I are dubious. We pick up the squares and pop them into our mouths at the same time.

Have you ever had a food-related orgasm? It's much like the traditional variety—uncontrollable, accompanied by unseemly moans, somewhat embarrassing to experience in public places. Upon letting the pig-heart bonbons melt on our tongues, Jessica and I achieve simultaneous ones.

"Holy Christ..."

"Oh my *fuck!*"

Jessica throws her head back. I growl and beat my open palms on the tabletop. Our eyes meet and it's magic.

Five seconds later, still a little flushed, we have our heads together and are mapping out strategy. Because once you've had your first pig-heart bonbon, you can spend the rest of your life trying to get more.

"So it can't just be heart in there. The texture is too smooth. I'd think some liver in there, and cream..."

"Right. But still very meaty and dark. And then the wafers or cookies or whatever were so thin and crisp, almost like just a crisp chocolate candy coating."

"But only just the tiniest bit of sweetness..."

The ride home is quiet, both of us trying to stave off the soporific effects of fifteen courses of macho-host food. I lean my head against the cool glass of the window, stare absently out. "You know, I wonder if he would even have liked that meal. Wonder if he would have noticed it."

"Who? Eric? Or, no...whatsisname, the other guy?"

"Yeah. He never seemed to really care about food. Actually, he never seemed to really care about anything I cared about. It was always this fucking polite interest."

"Well, that doesn't sound fun."

"But it was always such a thrill when he really appreciated something. I remember I showed him this film short I like one time, and he loved it."

"That's big of him," Jess sneers. I shrug. "Would Eric have liked it? Would he like pig-heart bonbons?"

"Are you kidding? He'd have gone bananas. He'd have made himself sick on all that food."

"Well. You share things with the people who want you to share them. Who get it. Otherwise, where's the fun?"

"I guess."

By the time Jessica drops me off at my apartment in Rifton it is nearly midnight. "Thanks for the dinner and the ride and everything."

"Thanks for being my wingman. I'll see you tomorrow. You want a ride, since you left your car at the shop?"

"That'd be great, if it's okay."

"Great, I'll see you tomorrow."

"Great." I slide out of the van, start to slam the door shut, then pause. "Oh, and…this is weird, maybe, but could you not mention all the stuff we talked about tonight? I kind of don't want it being known around the shop."

"I won't if you won't." Jessica waves, then pulls a U-turn and heads back the way we've just come. I fumble for my keys in my pocket.

Not there. I open up my purse, fumble there. Nothing. Wait a minute, wait a minute…How can this *be?* I go through everything again. Still nothing. I don't get it, I just don't—

Blinding insight. My key ring. I gave it to Josh so he could move my car out of the day-only parking lot. My key ring, you know, the one with my keys on it.

It is remarkable how many times this has happened to me. In the two-plus years since things started with D, I have locked myself out probably half a dozen times. One of the times, I tried to climb through the second-story window of our Queens apartment by standing on two stacked milk crates. The resulting bruise to my hip when I smashed to the pavement was so enormous and dark that not even Eric, with his fevered, angry imagination, could think to attribute it to rough lovemaking with another man. I'm pretty sure there is a fairly complex system of guilt and self-punishment at the bottom of all this.

I have a downstairs neighbor, but repeated knockings and doorbell ringings do nothing but awake a yappy dog. Giving up that tack, I walk around the house, looking for some mode of entry. I find a rickety ladder that gives onto the eaves, and having picked my way up it, I see I can get to my kitchen window from there.

Too bad it's locked tight. I tug and tug and tug, but it's useless. I think about breaking it, even, but I can't get out of my head the horrid vision of somehow slashing my wrists to the bone on the shards, and I can't go through with it. Meanwhile, my fear that I'll awaken my neighbors and that they'll shoot me before I can explain what's happening has faded, and I've stopped tiptoeing.

I even stomp a little. But not a single light blazes on, not a voice speaks. The dog doesn't even bark anymore.

I sit down on the roof. It's getting cold. Quite cold. I pull my BlackBerry out of my coat pocket, and I am surprised to see that I have a stairstep or two of service, though the battery is nearly dead. It's twelve thirty. I scroll through my address book, punch Call when I get to *ballnchain*. Get voicemail. "So guess where I am? I dare you to guess. I'm on the roof of my apartment. Locked out. And—oh, hey, look—it's beginning to snow. I'm not sure what I can ask you to do about any of this, but if you get this give me a call?"

I pull up another number from my address book, a West Coast area code. It rings only once before going to voicemail. I know D's awake; he never goes to sleep before two or three in the morning. His voice is no longer even on the message; it's just an automated voice telling me the person I'm calling is unavailable. I murmur a few words into the phone, sounding tearier, and probably drunker, than I actually am, about being locked out, on a roof, cold and tired and so lonesome for him. I know he will not call back, of course, though every time I find myself in one of these sorts of situations, I think, *Is* this *the circumstance that will move him?*

Eric calls back when I'm halfway down the teetering ladder. I sigh. His timing is always so inconvenient.

"Hey, babe, why don't you just go to a hotel?"

"I don't have a car. Left it at the shop. Now you're cutting out. My phone's about to die. Fuck."

"Okay, look. I'm going to call you a cab. What's your address again?"

"How are you going to call a cab?" I'm now standing in the street in front of my house, in a glittering circle of snow lit up by the streetlight, scuffing petulantly at the thin but increasing accumulation. Not a car passes, and there's not a soul out.

"They have this amazing thing called the Internet? I'll find a company, call you back. If you don't hear from me—"

"I won't. Phone's dying, I said."

"Okay. Well, I'm ordering you a cab. Call me when you get to a motel. I love you."

I hang up without saying good-bye, as if this entire debacle is his fault.

The cab is over an hour late; he's had to come all the way from Kingston. "Hey there," he asks as I climb in, "get stuck?"

"Locked out."

"Jeez. So where you headed?"

"Isn't there a hotel over toward New Paltz? By the thruway?"

"Motel 87, yeah. We can do that."

"Great," I say, lying back against the seat in utter exhaustion. "That would be perfect."

So this place is just about what you'd expect from a thruway-side motel, murky yellow light in the bathroom and graying carpets. But there's a bed, and heat. By the time I unlock the door to my room and fall onto the bed, it's after two. I pick up the phone receiver, call my husband. When he answers, I can tell he's been sleeping.

"It's me. I'm all tucked away."

"Good, baby."

"Thank you. I'll call you in the morning."

"Okay..." He's got that breathy, drifting tone he gets when he's not really awake at all. "Sleep tight, babe."

"You too."

I manage to get my clothes off, but not my contacts. I sleep with them in, naked under the sleazy coverlet. When I wake up the next morning, I shower, finally washing off my carnivorous smell with motel soap and no shampoo. Then I call Jessica.

"So a funny thing happened last night after you dropped me off..." I go through the whole story in as little detail as possible.

"You idiot. Why didn't you call me? You could have slept at our house."

"I didn't want you to have to turn back so late at night." In truth, it had not occurred to me to call her. Why hadn't it occurred to me to call her? Why did it only ever occur to me to call those same two faraway men, rather than the nearby woman who could most plausibly have helped?

"Well, that's incredibly dumb. You're at Motel 87, right? Off Exit 18?"

"That's the one. I'm so sorry."

"It's totally fine. I'll be there at around nine."

"Thanks, Jessica."

"Not a problem. I'll see you in a bit."

I'm back in the store by ten that morning, breaking down lambs. My hair still isn't clean. I'm wearing all the same clothes I had on yesterday, tired to the bone. The cutting is all that's keeping me standing.

7

Opus Nauseous

AARON IS BREAKING a pork loin down into chops for the case, and I'm at the table peeling off spareribs when he calls over to me, "Hey, Jules, you want to practice on the band saw?"

The band saw is a machine about seven feet tall, with a thin, serrated metal blade stretched taut, vertically, the serrations facing forward, at the juncture of a stable metal surface and a sliding plate, all of it at about counter height. "Um..." I'm still a little nervous around the thing; power tools and I are not necessarily friends. But I can't let myself wimp out around Aaron, so I say, "Sure."

Not for the first time, he walks me through some basics. Unplugs the machine, then opens up compartments at top and bottom, points out how the blade is actually a large band of flexible metal, threaded around two wheels. When the blade is removed to be washed every day, it can be spread out into a circle so large I could stand inside it with arms and legs spread wide like Leonardo da Vinci's Vitruvian Man. Aaron shows me how the blade locks in and out, how to tighten knobs and click levers to make sure everything is safely in place.

(Aaron is nothing if not a completist. His demonstrations on breaking down a cut of meat, making the perfect roast beef, or using the sharpening stone are dizzyingly detailed. He has been known to correct my stance for stirring soup in front of the stove.)

Once he's checked everything, and made absolutely sure I've committed to memory each detail of the machine's workings and the entire process for breaking the saw down and putting it back together (which of course I haven't), he walks me to the side, plugs the machine back in, and points to a big red button at the upper left corner of the apparatus.

"So when you pull this red button here, the blade starts going around. You stand like this, at the side here. *Never* stand in front of the blade—something happens, you catch on a bone or it goes faster than you're expecting, you fall in, it's all over. So you stand to the side, right?"

"Right."

"Now, get yourself up against the sliding edge here. Really push your hips against it. Anchor yourself." He has the short end of a rack of pork loin chops wedged against the metal lip of the sliding plate. "Make sure whatever you're cutting is resting in the most stable way possible, with the flattest part of the meat down." He demonstrates, rolling the rack back and forth, up onto the tip of the rib bone. "If you cut it this way, balanced on end like this? It's gonna catch on the blade, roll over, your hand is going to go flying, and something is going to wind up getting cut off. So—flat, like this."

With the machine still off, he shows me how he can use the pressure of his hips to move the plate from front to back, holding firmly onto the meat at a respectful distance from the blade, lining up with it to slice right between the ribs and through the backbone. "Leaning away all the time, smooth movements, not too fast or too slow. And when you want to stop, just push the red button down again. Got it?"

"Got it." Not entirely sure that I do.

"Okay, give it a try."

"Um. Okay. A little scared." But as he moves aside, I take his place at the edge of the machine, press the tips of my pelvis bone to the lip of the plate, take hold of the rack and press it down flat.

"Don't be scared. Respect. *Respect* the band saw."

"Done." I take a breath, pull the button out. The saw starts up with a whine, and I start cutting. In a matter of moments I've cut off half a dozen chops. The smell of singed bone is sharp in the air. My fingers are getting awfully close to the blade. I don't have the guts to cut the last few. I push the button and let the saw whir to a stop. Aaron cuts the remainder, demonstrating a far more casual attitude toward the machine than he has tried to inculcate in me. But I guess when you're teacher you can take shortcuts.

Aaron really fancies the idea of having an apprentice. And I, unreformed honor student that I am, fancy being one. One thing I think both of us enjoy best, though it goes unacknowledged, are his poker-faced attempts to gross me out, and my resistance to each attempt, iron-stomached and staunch. The pigs' heads that come in a cardboard box with the rest of the usable offal every time we receive a few sides of pork provide him with various opportunities to break my resolve. The first time we get some, he pulls them out of the boxes and lines them up on the table.

(Josh, of course, cannot resist holding one of the heads up to his face like a mask, just because. I take his picture.)

"All right, we're going to cut out the cheeks."

I do not blink. "No problem."

Pigs' cheeks are just like our cheeks, fleshy rounds. Feel along on your own face, if you like, as I describe: cutting from the hinge of the jawbone, dig the knife up under the ridge of the cheekbone, down to the arc of the upper teeth, curving around just short of the corner of the mouth, and back under, following the jawline up again to the hinge. You're left with a palm-sized clump of meat and fat, not exactly round, which Josh can sell to restaurants in the city because pork cheeks, as it turns out, are some of the most luscious things imaginable. If you can ever get your hands on some, you can prepare them just so:

BRAISED PORK CHEEKS

  2 tablespoons vegetable oil
  1 tablespoon butter
  4 pork cheeks
  2 medium onions, coarsely chopped
  6 peeled garlic cloves
  6 plum tomatoes, coarsely chopped
  2 sprigs fresh rosemary or 1 teaspoon dried
  2 sprigs fresh thyme or 1 teaspoon dried
  2 bay leaves
  Salt and pepper to taste
  2 cups dry red wine

Preheat the oven to 325°F.

Heat the oil and butter to "almost smoking" in a heatproof casserole over medium-high heat. Brown the cheeks on both sides and set aside. Toss in the onions and garlic and sauté until they begin to color a light gold. Add the tomatoes and seasonings and cook, stirring, until the tomatoes have begun to give off liquid, a couple of minutes. Add the cheeks back to the casserole and pour in the wine. Bring to a boil, cover, and place in the oven. Cook for three hours or so, until meltingly tender. Serves four.

Bring to the table alongside polenta or egg noodles. Don't tell your more squeamish guests exactly what it is they're eating.

Aaron demonstrates how to cut out the cheeks the first time, and then I unhesitatingly pick up a knife and set to. I've found since working here that I have a surprisingly strong stomach for this stuff, compared to most folks who come into the shop, even some of the folks who work here. But one thing does worry me. So the next time Josh walks by, I wave him over, making sure Aaron is out of earshot.

"So, is it possible that I could, you know, cut through into, like, into the brain? Seems like brain is something I want to avoid. Or, I don't know, the eye?"

Josh stares consideringly down at the head. I show him how it seems to me that when I'm cutting at the top end of the cheek I'm getting awfully close to some sensitive areas.

"I don't think you could do that." He doesn't sound entirely certain.

The shop is full of customers; it's afternoon on a Friday, always a rush time. Josh looks over his shoulder at the bustling line. We're not an apologetic bunch at Fleisher's, but at the same time, we do try to have a little concern for our clientele, some of whom can be a tad squeamish. Jessica can't even count how many complaints they've had from scandalized mothers who've been at a loss to explain to their small children the sight of men in white coats walking from the truck parked out front through the shop doors with whole, skinned lambs hoisted over their shoulders, eyes wide, teeth bared, and tongues lolling. (The lambs, not the men.)

"If you do, though, this is what you do." He says this with uncharacteristic understatement, nearly whispering. "Slowly put down your knife, take off your apron, go to the bathroom, and puke.

"That's what I'd do."

But I don't ever cut through into the brain, and pretty soon I'm de-cheeking pig heads like a champ. It's actually work I enjoy, in a perverse way. I like grabbing the heads by the ears and pulling them around to face me. Like exposing the sharp teeth, getting a glimpse of what the jawbone looks like beneath the flesh. Like the neat packages of meat I wind up with.

"Good job," Aaron says. I might be imagining it, but I think I can see the wheels turning as he tries to decide what to throw at me next. "Cut off the ears too. We'll smoke them for dog treats."

"No problem." They come off with two quick saws of the knife, exposing the white tubes of the ear canals.

"Good." He walks into the kitchen as I move on to more pedestrian work, bagging livers and kidneys for the freezer, breaking down some of the sides, which I still can't do in anything remotely like one minute, twenty-five seconds, but have gotten pretty comfortable with. Shoulder off loin, loin and belly separated, loin off round, all the pieces piled into a repurposed grocery cart to be rolled back to the cooler, looking pleasingly grotesque, a psychotic's dream of a shopping trip.

A while later Aaron returns, and I can see by the glint in his eye, belying the businesslike set of his face, that he's come up with a new challenge.

"Okay, Jules. Just talked to Josh. We're going to make headcheese."

"No problem."

Now, in my opinion, *headcheese* is maybe the most unfortunate misnomer in the culinary world. For while some people might get a little queasy over the definition—the meat picked off the boiled head of a pig, shredded, seasoned, and set in aspic—it certainly is less disgusting than the images conjured by putting the words *head* and *cheese* in such close proximity. I already know this, and figure I can handle whatever is coming, since it will involve no unidentifiable pale curdy substances from inside a pig's skull. "What do we do?"

"First we have to brine these heads for a week. There are some big white plastic buckets in the back by the sink. Go get a couple, and I'll tell you how to make the brine."

So, following Aaron's directions, I mix up a combination of water, salt, cider vinegar, and spices in the buckets. When I grab the first head to dunk into it, though, it becomes quickly obvious that they are not going to fit.

"Well, we'll cut them in half on the saw. You can do that, right?"

"Sure."

"There's a trick to it." Of course there is. "I'll show you." Aaron takes a head over to the saw, stands *in front* of the saw blade (I thought we weren't supposed to stand in front!), balances the head on the ridge of its snout (*not* the steadiest, flattest way to hold it) with the mouth facing toward him, and leans forward (leans forward!) to open it up, pointing out to me the sharp front teeth at the front of the ridged palate.

"These teeth are actually harder than the steel saw. So you have to stop before you get there and slide it back, then finish the job with a cleaver. You could break the saw blade on those teeth, and if that thing comes loose, snapping around like a whip? It's all over."

I carefully do not react to the stunning images he has brought to mind. "Gotcha."

"Okay. Go ahead. I'll watch you do the first one."

I'm just about to pull the button to get the saw going when Josh comes up, aghast. "What *the hell* are you doing? If you cut through there, you'll expose the brain. It'll contaminate the brine."

"Jules is going to remove them," replies Aaron without a hint in his voice that he is taking any pleasure at all in the imminent prospect of having the apprentice scooping out pig brains.

Josh's eyebrows shoot up nearly to his hairline as he says, "O-*kaaay*" in a high-pitched singsong thrumming with skepticism.

So the saw comes on and, gripping the head by the exposed cheekbones, leaning in, determinedly refusing to entertain notions of somehow stumbling forward and slicing my own face in half, I carefully run the thing through the whirring blade, up through the chin, to just short of where I imagine the lower set of front teeth to be, and back away from the blade again, pushing the red button to stop the dangerous spinning. Grabbing hold of either side of the slice I've just made, I pull the skull down and apart into two halves, joined by the bit of front palate and lip still uncut.

"Done."

It's actually a pretty impressive sight, this head split in half, exposing the shape of the inside of the mouth, the row of teeth, the impressively thick bone of the skull (no, I was definitely never going to cut through that accidentally while removing a cheek, and I finally believe Hans's assertion about the small-gauge bullet being in no danger of penetrating this bone), and the two halves of the brain, surprisingly small, nestled pale and moist like oysters in their shells. Before Aaron can prompt me, I scoop each half out with cupped fingers. "And done."

Jesse's looking on, fascinated and a bit appalled. "Wow."

I just hold the brains out to Aaron. "Do you want to keep these for anything?"

"You can throw them away," he says nonchalantly. I do, tossing them, equally nonchalantly, into the trash. All this nonchalance is, I will say, partly put on, but neither am I particularly disgusted by what I've just done. The brains were tidy things, looking just as brains should look.

"See? Easy as that. Now you'll just cut through the front bit with a cleaver." He moves the nearly bisected head over to the table next to the band saw to show me. "When you swing the cleaver, always keep your other hand behind your back. Don't want your hand anywhere near." Aaron doesn't say, but I think he's at least a little impressed with me. At least he damned well ought to be.

I get through the four heads we have, sawing and scooping and cleaving. I'm not very good with this last, just as I've never been good at hitting a baseball with a bat or a billiard ball with a cue. The idea of a cleaver is that it's about blunt force rather than razor sharpness. It is for hacking, for breaking through bone. Swing it hard from above your head down to the point that needs separating, an action that requires both strength and precision. I generally can manage only one of these attributes at once, if that. With my right hand tucked self-consciously behind my back—the instinct is to hold the meat down with it, but Aaron is right, my aim is far too wild to risk getting my hand anywhere near my swing—I cleave. Takes a couple of tries. First I am too timid, then I am off the mark. Luckily, a few messy, asymmetric chop marks make no difference in this case. I load the heads into the buckets of brine, put on the covers, and label them with the date, written in Sharpie marker, on a length of masking tape. They will sit in the corner of the cooler for a week or so, unmolested.

For that week Aaron comes up with no particular challenges to my intestinal fortitude. He feeds me a bit of raw beef fresh from the grinder, both of us popping a pinch into our mouths at the same time. "It tastes sweet, right?"

It does. "Yeah. It's good."

He cooks up a steak "black and blue"—very briefly over very high heat so that the outside is charred dark, the interior still cold.

"Just the way I like it," I say. I'm not even lying, exactly. Exaggerating perhaps, but maybe not even that.

Then it comes time for Headcheese, Stage II. First thing on a Tuesday morning, Aaron lifts the pigs' heads from where they've been brining. The flesh is now pale and bloated and smells somewhat unsavorily sour. In the biggest stockpot in the kitchen—a remarkably large object, probably two and a half feet in diameter and tall enough that, when it's set on the stove, I have to stand on tiptoe to peer in—we bring several gallons of pork stock to a simmer, then slip the heads in, until the pot is filled to the brim with gruesomely grinning, fleshy half skulls, eyes still in their sockets, cloudy now and shriveled, bobbing in the rich broth. There they quietly bubble away throughout the day; in the evening Aaron fishes them out to cool on large trays overnight.

The next day we pick through the trays, the meat now falling easily off the bone. We lift out jawbones and skulls, and also the ridged hard palates, stray teeth, knobs of cartilage, shrunken eyeballs.

The eyeballs give me a little trouble, I have to admit. But I'll be damned if I'll show it. I industriously run my fingers through the remains of the heads while Aaron strains the broth through a cheesecloth and boils it down some more until it is gelatinous, sufficient to, once cold, hold the meat I've picked clean in suspension.

By the time the headcheese has been made up, the shop has already sold all the chops and roasts and pig's-ear dog treats culled from the last four hogs Josh bought, and he's due for another delivery. This time when the pork sides come in, along with their accompanying cardboard boxes full of extra bits, I start right in on unwrapping the heads, pulling them out of the boxes by the ears, slapping them down on the table, and cutting off the cheeks. There's an order in from the city that needs to get filled right away, in time for the next morning's delivery. Aaron is beside me at the table working on his side-breaking time. ("Breaking sixty seconds today, Josh!")

I'm halfway done with my third head when my knife slips into a little pocket of something soft, and an unexpected ooze bursts forth, something approximately the color and consistency of guacamole, leaving an avocado smear on my knife as I pull it away. For a moment, I just stare in puzzlement.

"I...um...what's...um?"

Aaron glances over and freezes as if he's just seen a wild animal readying to pounce. In a slow, even voice, he says, "Throw the head away now. Go wash your knife and your hands."

I belatedly emit what I think could actually be called a squeak, dropping my knife to the table with a clatter. "What is it?"

"It's a...an infected gland, or.... Just throw it away."

I do. Hurry back to the sink and scrub both my knife and my hands with scalding, soapy water, unable to repress a whole series of convulsive shudders.

Aaron's already laughing at me when I return to the table. "You shrieked like a little girl, Jules."

"Oh, please. You were freaked too." There's a tone to his teasing that I like, though. He's covering up his disgust by poking fun at mine.

"'Eek!'"

"Shut up."

8
Meathead Holiday

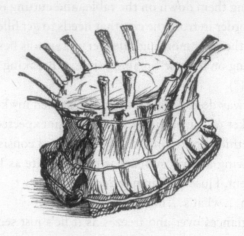

"WHAT A PRETTY little whore you are."

"Shut up." I stand in this unattractive stranger's foyer with my hands against the wall, skirt hitched, and legs spread, staring at a grimy layer of paint. "Just do it. Now. Whatever you want."

I've finally gone over the deep end, I think as I hear a condom wrapper being ripped open behind me. After some months of dickering, I've made good on a sad fantasy I've been distracting myself with since D stopped speaking to me. It's not about pleasure or comfort or desire. It's about contempt, for myself, and for any man stupid enough to want me. Contempt feels like relief.

The man rips my panties down and goes about his nasty, brutish, and short business. He mutters filthy, stupid nothings into my ear with hot breath. I squeeze my eyes shut, concentrate on D. With what different, breathtaking force he once would throw me against a wall, pull up my skirt. When all my need became too much for him, when he needed to just shut me up. How better everything was between us afterward.

It's over in three minutes. In five I'm back out on the street, my guts aching and my BlackBerry in a trembling hand.

I don't know what to do. Just had the worst sex in the world with a total stranger to try to get you out of my head. It didn't work. I know you want nothing to do with me, but I need help. Please. XxxxoHH-j

That night, I'm back home with Eric, chopping pancetta for a pasta dinner. The knife doesn't shake in my hand, I am capable of smiles and conversation that, if not closely observed, seem natural. But the tremor is not gone, it's just gone underground, making my eyeballs jiggle in their sockets. When my BlackBerry trills on the kitchen table, my breath goes and I nearly knock the cutting board off the counter when I reach for the phone. But it's only Gwen calling. "Hey."

"Hey yourself." Gwen's voice is queer, with both a twist of tension and an unusual drip of concern. "I just wanted to call to see how you're doing."

"Um...I'm fine." I didn't tell Gwen about my experience this afternoon; didn't tell anyone but D. "Why do you ask?"

"Oh, no particular reason. I just...just thought maybe I should check in. See if you're holding up. We haven't talked in a while."

I glance up at Eric. He's across the room on the couch watching Jim Lehrer, sipping from his wineglass. I take a gulp from my own and reply as casually as possible, "Oh thanks, I'm doing good. Eric and I are just putting together some dinner. You want to come over? Just spaghetti."

"Ah. No, thanks. But soon, for sure. You'll be on IM tomorrow?"

"Sure." I'm pretty sure now what she knows and how she knows it. I just don't know what that means.

"Okay. We'll talk then. And—I love you, Julie."

"Um, I love you too."

"Have a good night. Be good to yourself."

"Okay. 'Night."

When I lower my phone to press the End Call button, I notice that my hand is quivering again. Of course, with the butchery, my hand is often tired these days. Eric looks up from the TV. "That Gwen? What did she want?"

"Just checking in. We'll have her over to dinner in a few days, probably. You want some more wine?" I ask as I pour some for myself. I walk toward him and empty the last of the bottle into his waiting glass.

I HAVE gotten quite good at tying roasts, which pleases me immensely. Is there a single action that more quintessentially evokes butchering? It is both delicate and, sometimes, painful. The twine can bite into fingers, cut off circulation, but the swirling motions as I quickly make the knot and pull it tight are graceful and feminine.

As the holidays approach I'm getting more and more practice with tying, as people begin ordering fancy roasts for their celebratory dinners. Thanksgiving is supposed to be the single craziest time of the year, a line out the door, many of the customers cranky and worried, waiting to pick up their heritage turkeys or some pâté for their cocktail hours or bacon for their brussels sprouts. Every year, apparently, the Fleisher's crew makes something of a celebration of the ordeal. Everyone dresses up as some goofy thing or another. Jessica hands out plastic glasses of beer. This year Hailey, the heartbreakingly young new hire they have at the counter, lovely and tiny and endlessly sweet—dubbed Schmailey by Josh—will be the one who rings up orders and calms the restless beasts lying in the hearts of anxious cooks on overdrive. I wish I could be there for that.

Instead, Eric and I wind up spending the holiday in Dijon, France, of all places, with his father and stepmother. Eric is running the Beaujolais marathon. He was never a runner before, but since our marriage has fallen into such spectacular shambles he has suddenly taken up the sport. He's already run the New York

City Marathon and is determined to get more under his belt. On the day of the race we meet him at the finish, at the top of a rather punishing hill in the center of the town of Beaujolais, along a medieval cobblestone street.

"How'd it go?" I ask, giving him a kiss on his sweaty cheek.

"Good! Sort of silly." He plops down on a chair at the sidewalk café table his stepmother and I have staked out near the finish line. "The Beaujolais marathon is not the place to work on breaking any records. We were literally running down stairs into wine cellars."

"You're kidding!" Jo Ann's tone is, as usual, effusive. Delicious delight with the magical oddity of the universe is her favorite emotion.

"I didn't drink the wine, which I sort of regret."

"They were passing out wine at a marathon?"

"Oh yes."

Eric always looks remarkably not-at-death's-door after these races, though for the rest of the day his brain function is not what it usually is. He seems to be built for endurance. I honestly think the running is helping him keep his sanity—whatever sanity either of us has managed to maintain.

"So, I got this, though." He holds up the shiny silver cup hanging by a sash around his neck. "What is it, anyway?"

"I think it's a *tastevin*. Like, a pretentious sommelier's cup."

"There are unpretentious sommelier's cups?"

"Good point."

We stay at a beautiful country inn, an ancient old house with light-filled rooms and a classically snooty Gallic proprietress. Eric and I love it. Yet I'm with him and his parents at every moment. I feel very alone and very crowded in at the same time. I think Eric feels the same way; catching a look at his face when he doesn't know I'm watching, I see eyes somehow both dull and wet. It seems sometimes that we aren't so angry with each other anymore, that we shouldn't be, with D and Eric's lover both out of the picture. But I wonder if he still longs for the woman he broke it off with. Whoever she was, I certainly know how the comforts of simple romance tempt.

When I find a café with Internet access, I send another in an endless wash of e-mails. It's as involuntary an action as sneezing.

I keep thinking how much fun you and I would have here, lounging about all indolent and shit.... This is me pretending that one day soon you're going to start talking to me, and we'll get together and this whole thing will be this funny story we tell.... xohxohxoh

I try not to expect and indeed receive no response.

Thanksgiving dinner is a multicourse lunch at a Michelin-starred restaurant in a small village. I'm distracted. I don't remember afterward what we ate. At least I'm spared the afternoon of football, the part of Thanksgiving I dread. The origins of my deep-seated phobia surrounding all spectator sports are obscure, but the result is that I can barely be in the same room with a TV blasting statistics and plays. It's one of Eric's and my few absolute incompatibilities. This year he scurries out to find Internet service every few hours to check on the scores, an arrangement I am content with.

In the evenings Eric and I wander the cold and damp streets of Dijon, a somber town, but with a sort of understated melancholy that feeds all too well into our mood. I've taken up smoking again after having (mostly) quit for some time. France seems the place for it.

"I have to say, it suits you. Very sexy."

Though Eric essentially disapproves of my habit, he's also something of an enabler. I think he likes the look of a woman smoking, just as he likes the look of a woman with a martini glass in her hand. It fits his noir sensibility. In any case, he might say I'm sexy, but I just smirk skeptically, and he follows up with a sad, affectionate smile. We're acting out parts, and we know it.

"Oh, wow. Look at those."

In a shop window two mannequins are draped with two men's scarves, dramatically and abstractly floral, one pattern orange and crimson and gray, another sky blue and sea green and gray.

"The blue would look gorgeous on you." And the red would suit D to a tee. "Would you wear that?"

"It's kind of out there. I like it, though. But, um, I'm not buying a three-hundred-dollar scarf."

"That's pretty crazy, it's true."

Later, I return alone. I finger the exquisitely soft weave of the two scarves longingly. Can I buy two three-hundred-dollar scarves? How insane is that? Finally I whisper "Screw it," pick one, and carry it to the counter.

"The red is an excellent choice," the handsome young man behind the counter says, in English, as he begins to wrap the scarf in tissue paper.

"Thanks," I reply, not saying what I think, which is, *Actually, it's the worst of choices.*

The Monday after we return from France, I pull my first actual, for-real stalking. I easily convince myself it's only fair, after I've tried for so long to reach him in all the more usual, less invasive ways. I warn him ahead of time, via text, that I'll be there, with a gift. I wait for an hour and a half outside the door of the building where he works. When he finally comes out, my face melts into a soppy smile that I can't prevent at the sight of him. But he merely grimaces as if in pain and keeps walking, allowing by a single impatient jerk of his head that I may follow. We walk together in silence a moment, downtown. He's wearing a leather jacket I've never seen before, as well as the familiar crimson knit cap I was thinking of when I bought the scarf.

"What do you want?" Still walking. Not looking at me. His anger is coming off him like the basal grumble of an idling semi truck; I feel its vibrations in my chest. I've never seen him truly angry before. It terrifies me, makes me stammer and blush.

"I just—I don't know. I just—all of a sudden this silence. You seem to hate me, and I don't understand why. I just thought, if maybe I could understand what happened, I'd be able to feel better."

"Well, what do *you* think happened?"

This is how D argues. Teasing out answers, giving none of his own. I think of it as his Socratic method. It makes me feel like a schoolgirl with scabs on her knees, but I've never been able to alter the line of an argument with him so that it turns out any other way.

"I don't know. It couldn't be the horrible anonymous sex. The silence was the *reason* for the horrible anonymous sex."

"You had horrible anonymous sex, and then you *told* me about it. Why would you do that?"

"I just—"

"Why would I want to be in a relationship like that?"

"I—" I am shocked into speechlessness. I could never have guessed at such a reaction, from D—unhurtable, impenetrable D. For a vertiginous moment I'm almost thrilled.

We come to a standstill at the south end of Union Square, across 14th Street from the Whole Foods, at the crosswalk. The holiday craft fair that takes over the square from Thanksgiving until Christmas is being erected; to get out of the way of pedestrians we back up against a wall of brightly painted plywood. "Look, I'm not really mad." He's talking so quietly I have to lean in to hear him. I want to touch the smooth leather of his lapel so badly, it's like fighting gravity.

"Yes, you are." I stand a moment, hideously unable to speak. Strings cinch tight around my throbbing heart.

"Did Gwen call you?"

I nod quickly, looking hopefully into his eyes, beautiful eyes even when angry, for forgiveness or concern. "Yes…she didn't say anything about…she was just checking on me."

"Good." He won't meet my eyes, stares at his feet. "I wanted to make sure you were okay."

"I…I'm…thank you."

"I just can't—" I can't catch all his words. I hear him say something about being "unable to reciprocate," a phrase I immediately latch onto as possibly horrible, but also maybe hopeful. I can work with *unable to reciprocate*. I can make it easier for him to reciprocate, I can do without reciprocation! But I don't dare say anything, and then he says, "I have to get some lunch and go back to work."

I nod vigorously, obediently. "Yes. Go. Eat."

"I want to hug you, but…" His words descend again into indecipherability under the roar of traffic.

"I'm sorry…what did you say?"

"I want to hug you, but I don't think I should!" Snappish.

"Oh. Okay. All right."

"I've got to go."

"Yes. Okay." I try to press the bag with his scarf inside into his hand, but he just gives me one last, faintly incredulous glance, and turns to walk away.

I manage to keep from collapsing to the pavement in tears for approximately half a block. Wind up sobbing at the feet of the Gandhi statue near the corner of 15th and Union Square West. So classic. I ought to have my own *New Yorker* cartoon.

HAVING MISSED Thanksgiving at Fleisher's, I must make up the time, for myself and for Josh. I'll be working right up until Christmas Eve. My parents and brother are coming from Texas for the holiday so I can both spend time with them and log in the necessary hours at the shop. They've rented a cottage just up the road from my small apartment. We're going to make pork crown roast for Christmas Day dinner; I'm going to cut and tie it myself.

But it's not quite time for that. For now, I'm just tying a bottom round for Aaron. I bring the cone-shaped spool of butcher's string to the table. I place the oblong muscle, which I've released from its Cryovac bag with a slash of my knife, on the table so that the short end of the rectangular cut of meat is facing me. I unwind a couple of feet of twine and slide it under the round, then loop up over the meat from the back to the front. Holding the twine taut along the top of the round with my right hand, with my left thumb and forefinger I loop the other end, the one snaking out from under the meat, over and under it. I perform the same twirling movement with thumb and forefinger a second time, over the upper length of string, down through the loop I've just made between my first knot and the incipient second. Then with my left hand pinching the two-loop knot, I gently, evenly, pull the string through it, until it tightens. I don't pull too quickly or the knot will catch before it's cinched tight around the meat. Once the string has done its job of gathering the meat in a bit, not too much, I make one final twirl of thumb and forefinger, an overhand knot, and tighten, to reinforce. Then I cut through the string, freeing it from the spool, leaving at the forward end a neat knot, two white, slightly unraveling bits of string sticking out like a young girl's pigtails.

All this is the work of about ten seconds. Which is not terribly fast. I'm more precise—or perhaps, to be honest, more hesitant—than I am speedy.

The next loop of string goes around the length of the meat as well but perpendicular to the first, so that the string never slides under the round. Getting the angle on the loop in this direction was at first a little tricky, but I've gotten pretty used to it. I still have to tilt my head to the side to get my bearings. Again, I don't pull the string too tight; if there's too much pressure now, the twine could snap by the time I finish.

Next I lift the round off the table, turn it ninety degrees, and set it back down. I'm going to be tying circles of string up and down the whole length of the roast, about an inch and a half apart. In the end, the little bulges of meat between the loops of taut string will make the roast look segmented, like a little flesh caterpillar. An image that we will not be sharing with the customers. I start in the middle, scooting the twine up along the underside of the meat to the center. Loop, loop, cinch, loop, cinch, cut. From there I move out. One circle to the left of center, one to the right. If I had started from one end and worked to the other, it would be like squeezing a toothpaste tube from the bottom, correct form for toothpaste but not for beef. I want a regular cylinder when I'm done, which will cook evenly, not a squashed roast, tiny at one end, bulging to bursting at the other.

When I finish the roast I furtively eye the clock. Two minutes. I cannot yet tie a roast in twice the time Josh and Aaron can break down a side of pork. (Josh recently edged out Aaron's score of fifty-eight seconds by two seconds. Stopwatches are now involved, and precompetition stretches.)

Josh walks by, always walking by on his way to someplace else. "Julie, that's *perfect*. You are my god."

"Uh-huh." That would seem high praise, except that Josh uses that particular phrase about five times a day. Still, it *is* rather lovely. I fancy that I tie the prettiest roasts in the shop, though I would never say so. I carry it back to the kitchen along with several marrow bones—that is, sections from the middle of the shank bone, cut on the band saw into two-inch rounds. I rub the roast generously with the salt and pepper and brown it over high heat on the stovetop before arranging it on top of the bones and sticking it into the oven.

Then I wash my hands and loiter for a moment over a cup of coffee. Juan's trying out a new chicken and lamb sausage, "Moroccan-style." He's fried up some of his latest batch before stuffing it into the casings. On a kelly green plate sits a small pile of cooked ground meat, a slowly cooling pool of grease. I nibble.

"Mmm. Juan, what's in this? Good!"

Juan shrugs. "Dried apricots, garlic, cilantro, turmeric, ginger… I don't know. It's missing something, I think."

"Yeah?"

Juan shrugs again and rubs his chin. He is beginning to grow a goatee for the Great Facial Hair Face-off that Aaron has got scheduled for the spring. We both take another taste of the sausage and stare together at the plate intently. Then he nods. "Just a little more cinnamon, I think."

"Jules?" Aaron gestures me over to the table. He's holding a rack of lamb's ribs loosely in one hand. "You set the timer?"

"Yeah. One hour, twenty minutes, right?"

"At what temperature?" Pop-quiz style, he asks.

"Three hundred."

"And what do you want the thermometer to read?"

"One forty?"

Aaron cocks his head and just stares at me for a moment, going, "Aaaahhhh..." I know by now—well, I'm pretty sure—that this is his "tweaking" noise, what he does when he's thinking about adjustments. Or then again he could be lightly chastising me for having remembered wrong. Which would be annoying but not unlikely, as he's always tweaking. It can be hard to keep up with the changes. "Let's try for one thirty. It's going to continue to cook after it's come out of the oven, as it rests."

" 'You're like a textbook with arms. I *know* this.' "

"What?"

"It's from *Buff*—. Nothing. Just riffing, sorry."

"Don't forget to baste. We want all those juices from the marrow to soak into the meat."

"Yup."

"Okay. So now." He slaps the ribs onto the table. "Now you're going to practice for your Christmas crown roast bonanza. You're going to make what's called a 'half crown.' Usually with a crown roast, you use both racks of ribs, but this time you'll just use one."

("Racks of ribs"—yet another of the many unbearably euphemistic terms in butchery, suggesting that the bloody cage that once held in this dainty creature's innards can be transformed into a neat something to hang your hat on.)

"I'll talk you through it." He pushes the ribs toward me. "You're going to separate out the ribs. Band saw."

First he shows me how to chine the rack, using the rotating blade to shave off the chunky edge of the spine, get rid of excess bone. Then he tells me to lay the rack out flat, resting on the broad curve of the ribs, hold one end of the rack firmly in each hand, and run the blade just into the vertebrae at the junctures between the ribs, without cutting too much into the eyes of the chops. I don't worry about standing in front of the blade anymore, don't think about cutting off my hand or sending a bone flying into someone's face. Well, not too much. *Respect the band saw,* after all. Within a minute or less I've got it done. The rack is still in one piece, but the backbone has been split between each rib, which makes the whole long piece as flexible as an accordion.

"Now you're going to French the ends of the rib bones."

I do not look cross-eyed at Aaron when he says this, because I know that he doesn't mean *that* kind of Frenching. "Frenching," to butchers, is the action of cleaning and exposing the bones of a rib roast, which will, in the end, stick up from the bound meat in a proud circle. Aaron demonstrates with the first rib. He begins by scoring all four sides of the bone with a knife; the tough film adhering bone to flesh has to be compromised. From the place he's scored to the end of the rib, he slices through the meat on either side. Then, where the rib has been scored, he loops around a length of twine, up through the intercostal meat, and ties it with a butcher's knot. Cinches it tight, then wraps the string around his palm a couple of times and pulls sharply toward himself, along the length of the bone. All that meat comes off in a clump, leaving the bone perfectly smooth and dry. "Simple." He scoops up the meat scraps and throws them into a lugger of lamb meat that will go into Juan's second batch of sausages. "Now you try."

All doesn't go quite so easily for me. I score the bone, make slices in the meat, get the twine up tight around the rib, yank and yank. Still the string hangs up on those stubborn gobbets. What's more, each time I yank, the string pulls tighter around my hand and digs in, cutting two furrows, at the base of my pinky and in the meat of my thumb. These are soon oozing blood. I'll be damned if I'm going to say anything about it, but it does hurt, and I know I'm hesitating, afraid of hurting myself more.

And then I break the string. "Shit," I mutter, I hope too quietly for Aaron to hear. He's now a few feet away, leaving me to my own devices. I pull off the string embedded in the flesh of my hand, snip the now-impotent circle of twine from the meaty rib, then walk as quickly as I inconspicuously can, and grab a couple of Band-Aids, which I slap on. On my way back to the table I reach into a bin below the counter and find a cutting glove. We rarely use these bulky things in the shop (if a bit of latex gets in the way of your cutting skills, imagine what a thick layer of braided stainless steel will do), but now I pull on the glove and set out to try again. Aaron has noticed my brief absence, or heard my cursing, or has just espied my glove. He doesn't say anything, but now he's watching. Making me nervous.

I knot another length of string around the rib. I yank. Nothing. "Dammit."

"Use inertia. Start with the string stretched away from you. Then give it one hard pull toward you, along the line of the bone. Like this." He takes the twine from me.

"I can do—"

"Calm down. I'm not going to do it. I'm just going to show you." With the string gripped in his fist he pantomimes the motion, starting with his arm straight out, past the far edge of the rack. Then, slowly, he moves his arm in, elbow into his side. "But instead of pulling the string just horizontally, pull it up a little so that you're pulling the string right along the upward curve of the rib. Otherwise, you're fighting the bone as well as the meat. That's why the twine breaks."

"Ah. Okay. I get it." I grab the string back from him. Yank.

Yank.

Yank.

On the fourth try, the meat finally comes away. And the Frenched bone is perfect, white and bare. I did it!

"Oh my God."

"Now you've got it."

"I don't think I've ever done anything so satisfying in my entire life."

"Let's not get carried away."

"Okay, you're right. I can think of one or two things. But with my clothes on? In a butcher shop? This is pretty much it."

Well, it never gets that good again. The next bone is too thick for the twine technique. The string snaps once, twice, three times a lady.

Josh waits until Aaron's gone back into the kitchen, then says, "Don't listen to that dumb-ass. Just use your knife like everybody else in the world does." And so the rest of the rack I clean the dull, slow way, scraping, scraping, struggling not entirely successfully to get off every last shred. It's not glamorous. But when I stand the rack on its end, bend it into a circle, and tie it tight with another skin-biting pull of the twine, like a tug at a Southern belle's corset, the crown roast is a thing of beauty, emphatically female. "Eye candy," Aaron calls it, setting it in the case. It looks rather sluttish there, nestled amid the more pedestrian pork chops; I feel almost as exposed as a Frenched bone, just looking at it, as if anyone walking in could reach certain conclusions about the person who made it.

"Jules, you been basting?"

"Shit. Right. Sorry."

I want to see who winds up buying my sexy little she-roast, but when it goes I'm in the back, scooping marrow out of the bones that until moments ago had served as the rack for the roast beef, and spreading it on toast.

"HEY. HOW'S THE MEAT?"

"It's good. I'm freaking exhausted. Driving home—I mean, to Rifton. My connection might cut out here in a minute."

"Okay. I miss you."

"I miss you too."

During our separation, when I had my Yorkville sublet, I made it my own. Bought a brightly colored futon, a new big-screen television. Brought a couple of plates, a few pots and pans, from Queens. My kitchen was tiny, tinier even than the one in which I'd cooked through five hundred and twenty-four Julia Child recipes a couple of years before. Which is saying something. But I didn't mind, because it was mine. I had two small windows that looked out into the ailanthus-green row of overgrown garden patches that filled the center of the town-house-lined block. I could look into other people's windows, watch the woman who meticulously made her bed in bra and slip every morning, the more erratic goings-on of a family of four in their breakfast nook. I had snapshots of Eric, the pets, my family, that one my father took so long ago of D, small reminders of my history and my connections to the world. But the tiny apartment was just for me.

Eric didn't have that. Eric had our old, hideous apartment, which in my four-month absence quickly acquired a male mustiness. Overripe bananas languished, not only in the kitchen, but also on side tables and in his briefcase. Kitty litter got ground into the rugs. A crack mysteriously appeared in the picture window in the living room—not the spiderweb left by a piece of gravel kicked up by a semi rumbling down Jackson Avenue, but rather a long, straight fissure right down the center of the pane. It ran along the same axis as a ridge in the linoleum floor stretching the length of the loft; a flaw in the foundation, we guessed, perhaps also responsible for the unnerving way that the stairs down to the street seemed to be pulling apart, gaping at the juncture of the risers.

I'm holding my phone to my ear as I talk to Eric, in defiance of legality and driver safety. "You got plans tonight?"

"You know. Clean the house. Beer. *Battlestar Galactica*. What about you? You having dinner with Josh and Jess?"

"Nuh-uh. Steak. Wine. Sleep."

Worse than the detritus and the disrepair, though, for Eric, was the inescapable flood of memory. We have always been pack rats, both of us, and we've lived together for ten years. Our apartment is crammed to the gills with all the stuff of our lives. Books and photo albums and furniture and art and more books. He couldn't get away from it. While I sat serenely in my monk's cell, he was in a place with no spot for his eyes to rest on that didn't remind him of what it was that was cracking apart.

"Can you hear me now, honey?"

"Barely... You're cutting out."

"Okay. I'll try to call you later tonight."

"Okay, babe. I'll see you in a couple of days."

And now I'm doing it to him again. We are not separated, technically. But I'm still running away.

"I love you."

"I love you t—" And the connection is lost.

CHRISTMAS IS just a few days away now. The plan is to meet at the shop in the afternoon—my parents and brother in one rental car driven up from JFK, Eric in another with Robert the Dog. I'll give them the big tour of the shop. Then, taking off together in our three cars like a flock of fossil-fuel-guzzling geese, we will head back to their rental cottage. We'll be together, and I will cook with my mother and wrap presents with Eric on the floor of my apartment and play-wrestle with my brother and do the crossword with my dad and rub my dog's belly, and we will decorate a tree, and I will let myself be part of a family again.

Until then, I wallow in my solitariness. I don't do constructive things with it. Sometimes I simply stare out the windows. Or indulge in crying jags. I resort to a bit of stalking, which I convince myself, as stalkers probably always do, is actually charming and, ultimately, irresistible. The scarf I've been holding onto for nearly a month now, I pack in a box. I buy a large candy cane and attach to it a piece of white cloth, meant—adorably, I think—to resemble a flag of truce or surrender. I contemplate with all seriousness, as if there were a rational choice, where to mail this little care package. D's work? His apartment? His mother's house? I wind up reasoning—as absurd as the word *reason* might seem, applied here—that the last choice makes the most sense. I mail it to Massachusetts from the tiny Rifton post office on my way to work one morning. Swallow a lurch of shame and fear, and also of wild hope and anticipation, as it leaves my hands.

Josh and Jessica, being Jewish, don't go in so much for all the Christmas hoopla, and they insist that Thanksgiving is a much bigger day for them, businesswise. Still, after a bit of a lull between holidays, things are picking up.

Josh, with major assists from Aaron, Juan, and Tom, is constantly working to perfect his pâté and chopped liver and double-smoked bacon, his roast turkey and smoked pork chops, and an endless array of sausages—bratwurst, sweet Italian, chorizo, merguez, chicken Thai. Each batch a little different until he gets it right. With Colin, the enormous redheaded CIA grad and ex-navy guy who Josh has recently hired as an extra cutter—and with whom I have instantly bonded over our shared love of Willie Nelson and Hank Williams III—I have cleaned out a closet in the back. We've hung dowels, and now sausages dry there, fat salamis and skinny "jerky sticks," always some new experiment. And they are all snapped up by customers, especially now, during the season of cocktail parties. I roll eye rounds in seasoning and pack them in rock salt, then take them out a week later, brown and dry. I brush off the salt and tie them the way Tom has shown me, with one long piece of butcher's twine, ending with a loop on the end. They go in the curing closet, from whence they'll eventually emerge as bresaola. I taste liverwurst with a spoon, straight from the chopper that Josh is so proud of, a big steel bowl on a rolling stand, with blades like a circular fan, only terrifyingly sharp. They turn meat to a sticky pink puree in a matter of seconds. We ponder whether the liverwurst needs more salt. We decide yes.

JOSH'S LIVERWURST

Josh, of course, makes his liverwurst in vast quantities, but if you have a food processor you can replicate it on a smaller scale, about three pounds' worth, at home.

> 1 pound pork liver, cut into several pieces
> 2 pounds pork belly, cut into several pieces
> ½ teaspoon marjoram
> ½ teaspoon sage
> ½ teaspoon white pepper
> ¼ teaspoon nutmeg

¼ teaspoon ground ginger
4 tablespoons finely chopped onion
Pinch onion flakes
2 teaspoons salt

Preheat the oven to 350°F. Lay out the pork liver and belly on a roasting pan and cook in the oven until the meat and offal are rare to medium rare—the liver should still ooze just a bit of blood, the meat should be cooked through but still good and pink, the juices not entirely clear. Let cool just slightly, perhaps five minutes.

Place the belly meat and liver in the food processor along with all the remaining ingredients. Puree on high speed until the mixture is completely smooth, stopping now and then to scrape down the sides of the food processor.

Let come to room temperature, then cover and chill.

I break down whole lambs. I take off the heads first (Juan will sometimes take one home with him; someday I need to ask what he does with them). Then the back legs come off the creatures (and they are very much still creatures, skinned and cleaned and with their feet cut off, but utterly recognizable). To do this I simply balance them on their backs with their rear legs sticking out past the edge of the table. I slice through from the edge of the slit belly down to the backbone, just above the hip on either side. Then, reaching into the cavity, I press down on the backbone, anchoring it to the table, while with my other hand I grab the lamb's ankles or whatever you call them on a lamb and pull sharply down, splitting the backbone with a satisfying crack.

Occasionally Josh waltzes with a lamb. Its head back, eyes lidless, looking like a ghoulish debutante in a hideous swoon.

I cut and cut and cut. Rounds, shoulders, ribs, loins. I bone out hams and peel out skirts and break through joints and cut, cut, cut. Hours at the table, on my feet. My back gets sore, my eyes blear. My fingers freeze. And my wrist. My wrist.

"Julie, have you eaten lunch?"

"Not really hungry."

"Julie, would you take a fucking break already?"

"I'm good."

Josh finally puts his foot down. He stands in front of me and whispers. "Julie. Put the motherfucking knife down, or I'm not letting you near the table again." Then a roar: "Eat a damn sandwich!"

So I reluctantly take off my apron and hat, pick up one of the sandwiches Josh has brought in a big white bag from the deli next door. (Josh is constantly buying lunch for his employees—sandwiches or Chinese food or barbecue. That is when he isn't corralling Aaron into cooking a "family meal." I find it so far above and beyond as to make me somewhat uncomfortable, like when he gives me piles of meat and refuses to let me pay. For what he's allowing me, *I* should be buying *him* lunch.) I sit at the battered round table in the rear of the shop, unwrap my lunch, and munch halfheartedly, drinking from a huge plastic glass of water. I've not had any all day, and realize, once I stop for air, that I'm parched. I also realize that every bit of me aches. I feel like I could close my eyes and sleep here in this straight-backed chair. It is such a shame that I don't feel like this at night in my lonely room.

Aaron plops down in another seat. In addition to his sandwich, he has some chicken soup he's ladled up from the big pot burbling away on the stove.

"How you doing, Jules? Got the thousand-yard stare going there."

I know it. I can feel the strange intensity with which I'm poring over a tile of linoleum a few feet away. "Ehn." I chew slowly.

"It's only three thirty! We got miles to go!"

"I know, I know. I'll be fine. I am fine. God, this sandwich is good."

"What kind did you get?"

"No idea." I look down at my sandwich, stare at it for an inordinately long while. Time feels like taffy. I can hear that my conversation is strange, pocked with odd pauses. "Something white. Turkey."

"Yeah, that reminds me, we gotta bone out those turkeys. They've been thawing in the cooler a few days. Should be unfrozen."

"Boning out turkeys, huh? Sounds..." I try to come up with the word. "Hard."

"Every day you learn something new." He rises to get seconds on soup. The black-and-white of his chef's checks make my eyeballs quiver a little in their sockets as he walks by. When he comes back, as he sits down he says, "And tomorrow we make your crown roast."

"Oh. Yeah. Cool."

"Hey, Aaron, can I take my break now?" Jesse is ambling back from the counter, his fingers already reaching to his waist for his apron strings.

"Give me five minutes, Jesse." Aaron dumps his dishes in the kitchen sink, then strides to the back door. He'll now roll himself a cigarette and sit on the metal back stairs in the brick alley behind the store to smoke it. "Three minutes."

Jesse looks to the front of the shop, where Hailey is helping the only customer. A brief respite. He just stands there for a minute, staring out over the counter to the front door. "I am fucking *exhausted*."

When he glances over at me, I'm gazing sort of more at his chest than his face, half-dazed, not saying anything but nodding absently like a bobblehead doll some minutes after having been bobbled.

"But then you're right there with me."

"...yeah."

It seems like far less than three minutes later that the big emergency door in the back bangs shut and Aaron has returned, as chipper and bright-eyed as ever. "Turkey time!"

BONING TURKEYS is not exactly an overnight trip to Paris on the Orient Express, but neither is it such a terrible ordeal. I remember the first time I boned a whole duck. It was a terrorizing experience, but incredibly satisfying once correctly done. The turkeys are like that, only bigger and less delicate and therefore less frightening. Start by slicing down the length of the backbone, then just work down the rib cage toward the breastbone, keeping your knife edge in against the bone rather than out so you don't cut into the meat or, more important, through the skin. For the leg, work the meat off the thighbone, which you leave attached to the carcass, then separate the thighbone from the drumstick, at the joint. Once you've loosened the meat from the drumstick, you can just poke up from the bottom end and pull the bone clean out, like taking a shirt off over your head, turning it inside out in the process. The wing comes off in basically the same way, though it's a bit tougher to wiggle out. Do the same on the other side, until the skeleton is connected to the flesh only at the thin ridge of cartilage running down the center of the breast. This is the only slightly tricky part, because the skin is thin here, and you don't want to tear it— especially if you're working for Aaron, who prides himself a stickler for such niceties. A bit of care will generally get you through with no harm done. And that's that. Bones in one bin for making stock, flesh cleaned up a bit (as anyone who's ever celebrated an Oktoberfest knows, turkey legs have some heavy-duty sinews, so you have to get those out), and you're done. Simple.

Except. It turns out that these particular turkeys, leftovers from the Thanksgiving rush that have been languishing in the freezer ever since, are not, despite several days out of the freezer and in the cooler, what you'd call entirely thawed. Colin and I stand side by side, trying to get into the birds. Some are simply too rock-hard to cut. Others we can work with, but within seconds our hands are frozen to the bone. I have to take frequent hand-shaking breaks, flopping wildly around to get the blood circulating, a mixed blessing, since blood turns the frosty ache to burning needles. "Jesus good God Christ. Yowch."

Colin is running his hands under hot water, wincing in a much more manly, understated way than I am. He tosses me a pair of latex gloves from the cardboard box that sits behind the counter. "Desperate times…"

And the gloves do help, some, with the cold. But there are so many turkeys to get through—about a dozen, I judge, looking at the overflowing bin—and all so very, very cold. And about three birds in, the inevitable happens. The tip of my knife slips, splits latex and then thumb flesh. And I don't notice until I pull my hand out of the bird to warm it up. "Dammit." Colin just looks up and gives me a sympathetic grimace. Gloves in the trash, it's back to the kitchen sink and first-aid box for me.

For some reason, different animals cause differing amounts of pain and infection. Pork is the worst; a scrape against a bone immediately turns an angry, itching red. It stings like crazy when you wash it, and the mark of it remains, often for weeks. Beef, on the other hand, never seems to cause me problems at all. Turkeys are somewhere in the middle. I squeeze the cut, rather a deep one, to try to stop the bleeding. It doesn't really want to stop, though. I find myself shifting in a slightly panicky way from one foot to the other. Though my brain does a fair job of handling cuts with gritty composure, my body still recoils at the sight of my own blood. I tend to get dizzy, my heart races. I do my best to suppress these shameful physical indications of squeamishness. Squeamishness is weakness. So I take a couple of huffed breaths, will myself to stop dancing about like a child who needs to pee. When the blood finally slows, I dab it with oregano oil—it does seem to prevent infection, hippie shit or not—and wrap it tight in a Band-Aid. Immediately have to replace it when blood soaks through it in seconds. Squeeze some more. Decide to sit down. This is not a major thing, of course—nothing at all really. I just need to sit.

Josh has a story about the early days of the store, when he was just learning butchery himself. Other than remembering some time spent, when he was a child, in his grandfather's kosher shop, Josh hadn't really any experience in the craft before he and Jessica made the quixotic leap to open a butcher shop in Kingston, New York. They didn't decide to open Fleisher's because they were big carnivores. On the contrary, Josh had been a vegan for seventeen years, and continued to practice this insanity for six months after the shop opened, until Jess finally laid down the law. "I cannot be the only person at this shop responsible for knowing what meat tastes like." (Josh is now, needless to say, a passionate convert; he wears a shirt that says, BACON—THE GATEWAY MEAT.) No, they decided to open Fleisher's because, basically, they're hippies. Well, nouvelle hippies. Meat hippies. Which is an infinitely cooler thing. Meat hippies do things like write dissertations on pornography and travel throughout India alone (Jessica) and work as a bike messenger in the early nineties in Manhattan and possess child-hood friends who grow marijuana in Vermont legally (Josh). They are willing to lose their shirts, if necessary, to open butcher shops selling nothing but hormone-free, grass- and grain-fed, humanely raised, local meat, but they're frank in their hope that it will instead make them rich. They venture into ghettos to deliver free meat to old men on food stamps with chronic iron deficiencies, and they give coats and cars to their strapped employees. They hold Humvee drivers and sanctimonious vegetarians in equal con-tempt. They are passionate and outspoken and strong and skepti-cal and foulmouthed and hopeful. They're the kind of people I want to be.

Anyway. When Fleisher's first opened in 2004, it was just Josh and Jessica, breaking down meat and trying like hell to sell it. Josh enlisted Tom to teach him, and between Tom's mentorship and much practice he caught on quickly. He was an experienced line cook, so knew at least a little about meat, and maybe those butcher genes got passed along as well. But much of the time he was alone in the shop with mountains of meat, cutting for hours on end. And Josh swears to me that he once managed to stab a knife straight through the back of his hand into the table. I really don't quite know that I believe this, first of all because Josh has been known to exaggerate on occasion, and second because I just can't picture what he could be doing that would result in that particular outcome. But he insists it happened, and insists that he pulled it out of the table and drove himself to the hospital, bleeding buckets.

So this little accident of mine definitely goes in the category of "no big deal." I remind myself of that and man up. The bleeding does, eventually, mostly, stop. I bandage it again, and this time it stays bandaged.

It always takes a bit of a push to get myself back to the table after a cut. I linger over a cup of coffee, go to the bathroom, fiddle with the iPod. But I can't leave Colin alone with those damned frozen birds any longer, and so at last I head back in. Within another hour or so we've got them all done, except of course for the ones that are still frozen solid.

"You finished?" Aaron has this way of sort of appearing out of nowhere, like a grade-school teacher with eyes in the back of his head. "Okay, now we're going to make roulades out of them to roast for the case." He takes one of the boned turkeys, now just an ungainly flap of meat, an uneven mess of pink flesh on one side, yellow goose-pimply skin on the other, and seasons the pink side generously with salt and pepper. Then he demonstrates how to roll it up into a fat baguette, at a diagonal, so that the white meat of the breast and dark meat of the legs are evenly distributed, tucking in any loose, untidy bits. The roulade seems disconcertingly floppy, and I can see that Aaron is having a spot of trouble wrangling it together. He has to try a couple of times before he gets it into a shape he finds acceptable. Then he ties it, just as I tied the round roast earlier: one loop vertically along the loaf's length, another horizontally, then lots of short loops across to form a long, skinny, perfect golden column of turkey.

It takes him about fifteen minutes, all in all. Which I figure translates for me into three quarters of an hour, easy.

And I'm right, for the first one, anyway. It turns out that making turkey roulades is the sort of thing that the phrase "herding cats" was invented for. Getting the thing rolled up, for starters, is like handling a passive resister. Some hunk of leg or dangling shred of wing is always slipping out of hand, flouting my efforts to make it conform to the status quo of cylindricality.

Once I do get it rolled up into some semblance of Aaron's example, it is a tricky business keeping it there as I slide the string beneath it and try to tie. I tighten too much the first few times, and the cylinder gets pulled into a squishy U shape, or the loop of twine just slips right off, knotting itself up in the process. I don't tighten enough, and the string comes right off when I adjust the turkey to apply the second loop. Finally I get the pressure right, and get the first two securely on. I start the short loops up and down the length of the thing. Again, squishiness is a factor. I'm not working with one muscle as I was with the round, a muscle with its own logic and shape. I'm forcing a gruesome mess of chopped and torn flesh into a logic of my (or Aaron's) own.

It's frustrating, improvisational work, a constant nudging and encouraging of meat to make it go where you want it. Turkey is stickier than beef or pork, too, coats the twine in a sheen of slick goo that makes the knots catch unexpectedly before they're tight enough. Lots of twine goes to waste, down the mouth of the garbage can; I try to hide this evidence of my failure from Aaron, nudging bones on top to mask the frayed bits of string.

But when I do finally get everything tucked and secured and even, there's a different kind of feeling of accomplishment. I'm not a sculptor who's found the face that was already there in the marble. I'm a trainer who's broken a wild stallion, neutered it and rendered it safe for children to ride in circles around a dusty ring at summer camp.

After the first roulade, it gets easier. I adjust my prodigious tying skills to this new challenge, and soon I'm churning them out at near-Aaron speeds. (Perhaps, in truth, even faster. I don't like to confess even to myself how competitive I've become, and how inordinately proud of my little accomplishments. I guess even women are subject to testosterone poisoning.)

"That's pretty good-looking," Colin says.

"Thanks."

"Way better than mine."

"Oh, whatever." I'm glad he said it. I was feeling guilty for noticing, not without a certain glee, that in fact mine do look a little better than his.

"You know, I was thinking," Colin muses, as his thick fingers perform the delicate knotwork. "I think every time I read the word *butchery* from now on, it's going to piss me off."

"How so?"

"Well, you know, I read a lot of history. You know, military history. And I'll come across sentences about 'butchery on the battlefield,' like *butchery* means something is bloody and messy and, I don't know, unskilled. And it offends me a little, frankly. Because butchery is just the opposite of that."

I am coming to love Colin. "I know just what you mean."

"A thing of beauty, Jules," Aaron says, arriving at the table to retrieve two of the roulades. "Bag the rest of them when you're done. We'll stick 'em in the freezer for later on."

"Yup." I whip out six more of the roulades before the day is out. Celebrate with a Mother's Milk. And an ice pack for my left wrist.

I KNOW that Fleisher's is a magical place, of course. But after several months of day-in, day-out work there, the magic becomes a sort of background glow, a happiness I don't have to think about.

Sometimes when we're walking Robert the Dog, some stranger will stop and exclaim, "My *God,* that's a big dog!" And I look at him and suddenly I'm seeing him all over again, and I think, *My* God, *he really is, isn't he?* That's what it's like bringing new people into the shop. What I've come to take for granted is passing strange to newcomers. Just the case, bursting with bright heaps of meat, brisket and ground lamb and racks of pork chops and sausage and liverwurst, is a source of wonder. When I pull open the door of the cooler in back by its great chrome latch, let visitors peer in at the sides of pork hanging like clothes in a crowded closet, I myself see it anew—a perverse take on *The Lion, the Witch and the Wardrobe*. I find myself thinking again something I thought on my first day here, that should I dare to press through all that closely packed flesh, I would not be surprised to find some odd, thrilling new world on the other side.

"This is...amazing."

"That's good, right?" It's always hard to know how Mom is going to react to things, even though over the years enough familial energy has been put into figuring it out to power a midsized city.

"I've never seen anything like it. It's...yes. It's good."

She, Dad, and my brother follow me through to the back of the shop. I explain about the salami closet and the sausage stuffer and all the prepared foods made in the shop, the soup and roast turkey and pâté and chicken potpie. Aaron and Colin are at the table, and Josh and Jessica are both assisting Hailey and Jesse at the counter because the crowd there is building up. Juan is bagging ground beef for wholesale orders in the city, ten-pound Cryovac bags he can now fill pretty reliably on gut instinct, using the scale only to double-check. (Anyone who's ever worked a meat counter knows the oddly triumphant surge that comes with putting the meat on the scale and having it hit exactly the desired weight on the first try. It's happened to me once or twice, and I always feel like ticker tape should start falling from the ceiling and party horns should blow in celebration. For Juan, though, it's a regular occurrence.) Though everyone is busy, they all accept with equanimity the horde of meat-tourists trundling through the place. There are smiles and introductions all around. This is one way you can distinguish between Fleisher's and your classic old-school butcher shop. There is a distinct lack of curtness.

"Your daughter rocks," Josh tells my mom. "She is so fucking cool."

"Oh!" My mother is not offended by the language Josh uses, to be sure, but she is just a tad taken aback by his enthusiasm. "I know she is."

"You see this?" He forces me to make a muscle-boy curl and squeezes my biceps. "Hard as a rock."

"Oh, please." But although he exaggerates by a good long way, I allow myself to feel flattered. Under most circumstances, to be seen by my mother like this, with my greasy skin and hat-head hair and flushed face showing its tendency toward rosacea under no makeup and baggy T-shirt under white apron making me look even more like a sausage than usual, would have left me feeling distinctly uncomfortable, even ashamed. But here in the shop, I find I don't worry so much.

"This," I say, opening up the front cooler and pointing at the large, untidy parcel, wrapped badly by me in butcher paper, with my name written on it in black Sharpie, "is our Christmas dinner. I'm going to tie it up this afternoon. It is going to be gorgeous. I promise."

I'm not in fact entirely certain on this front, but Aaron has assured me it will be a piece of cake. Well, we shall see. There's still too much work left to be done at the shop for me to leave with my family. Once they head out with Eric—who's been waiting outside with patient Robert—to find their cottage, I will set to work.

There are two racks of pork wrapped in that white paper— twelve rib chops in all, about fifteen pounds of meat and bone. I've now learned how to do a crown roast, but this is happening on a scale some degree of magnitude beyond that of the dainty lamb half-crown I made before. Chining, the first step, is something I've not yet become entirely at ease with; I let Aaron walk me through it again. Unlike other, more straightforward uses of the giant scary band saw, with chining you have to improvise as you go, adjusting the line of the cut as you see fit, rather than just anchoring the meat to the table and buzzing through. I tend not to cut it as close as I really ought to do, out of hesitancy. Then I hold the rack by the ends and, just as with the lamb, cut through the vertebrae between each rib, without cutting too deeply into the eye of meat behind them, to give the rack the flexibility it will need if I'm to shape it into one half of a pork doughnut.

Next I have to French those rib ends. This I'm confident I know how to do, so I get out the spindle of twine, the cutting glove, and my knife.

By the end of twelve ribs, forty minutes later, I've gotten to be a fair hand at the Frenching. (Yeah, I admit, that really still just sounds dirty to me.) I often break the string as I tie and yank— even with the glove, my palm is red and pinched from the string's bite—and more often than not I've allowed the gobbets of inter-costal meat I pull off to fall to the floor rather than onto the table, from where it would then go into the luggers for grind. But pull it off I've learned to do, and I have to resort to scraping shreds messily with my knife on only two or three of the thicker bones. All that's left is for me to tie the two racks together into a crown. I force each of them into a semicircle and, while Aaron helps me by holding them in place, I tie them together. Same concept as before: loop around the corset of ribs; hold the twine taut with right hand while looping over, under, and through with the left. Slide knot down, just a bit, then over, under, and through again. Give the end of the twine a firm, even pull, pinching the knot in the left hand, until the waist of the crown roast is tightly cinched. For a moment or two it's touch and go as the racks try to make a break out of the circular shape Aaron is forcing them into. He holds firm, though, and I pull hard and tight, and in a matter of seconds it's done. The crown is about the same circumference as a garbage can lid, the white rib bones splayed atop it, the eyes of the chops plumped out below like a muffin top over too-tight jeans, if muffin tops were to be considered lusciously attractive. Gorgeous.

But there's no time to appreciate my handiwork now. "Congratulations, Jules."

"Thanks."

"Now wrap it up and put it back in the cooler. Wipe down the table, so we can get some beef out here." (You can't cut beef and pork at the same time on the same surface. Josh says it causes cross-contamination and is illegal. I don't really understand this, nor do I buy it entirely, but them's the rules. I just work here.) "No rest for the weary, chop chop. See what I did there? 'Chop chop'?"

"You're very clever."

We spend the rest of the afternoon frantically trying to keep the case full as a steady crowd of customers parades through the shop, chattering holiday cheer and anxiety. I need to leave and get back to my family, help my folks get settled in and give Eric a respite from Robert Duty—not such arduous work, since Robert mostly just lies around three feet away from wherever you are, occasionally farting or asking for a tummy rub, but Eric has been shouldering far more than his fair share of it lately, and it can get to be a psychological burden, the single-parent routine. But there's no chance I'm getting away, between wholesale orders and the demand for Christmas beef. It's nearly eight before we've gotten everything stowed and ready for tomorrow, the day before Christmas Eve. I dash to the car parked two blocks away in the free lot. I have two rotisserie chickens in hand for our dinner.

Mom is already ensconced in the kitchen of their rental cottage when I pull into the driveway, has thrown together a green salad and is sitting at the dining room table, Tanqueray and juice in hand, poring over a cookbook to nail down the grocery list for our several planned blowout meals. (Mom and I have gotten better over the years at not making ourselves sick with exhaustion when cooking for family holidays. We no longer make appetizer soups with homemade breadsticks, six side dishes to go with the brined turkey, and five desserts, for a Thanksgiving dinner for six people. But we still tend to go a little loony.) Eric is outside on the back porch with Robert, who's not allowed inside, and Dad and my brother already have the jigsaw puzzle out. "I brought chickens. We can just throw them in the oven for a few minutes to warm up."

"The corn bread is baking in there right now at four hundred degrees. I decided to go ahead and put that together so it can sit out tonight, so it'll be stale enough for the dressing for the roast. But it'll be out in a few minutes."

"Okay. What can I do?" I pop a bottle of red wine, pour a healthy glass. I have to catch up; it's a little late for my first drink of the night.

"Well, you can help me figure out the menu. I wanted to make that cranberry tart we did that Thanksgiving in Virginia, the *Martha* one, but I can't find it."

"Okay, hold on. Let me check on Eric and Rob."

"Sure." And then, as I walk by her on my way to the back door: "Wow. You *really* smell like meat."

"I get that a lot."

Eric is sitting on a cane chair in the dimness, bundled up in his coat and reading Dashiell Hammett by the square of yellow light streaming through the windows of the kitchen door. Robert lies on the floor beside his water bowl, looking typically melancholy with his chin resting between his paws. He manages an upward gaze and three thumps of his tail in greeting. "Hey, babe. How's it going out here?"

"Good. Fine." I ruffle his hair and he sort of bounces the side of his head against my hip.

"You want a drink?"

"Sure."

"Wine? Vodka tonic? Weller?" (Weller being my father's preferred brand of whiskey, which he carries with him on the plane when he comes up north, since it's tough to find here.)

"Mmm! Weller, please!"

"Just a sec."

I get him his drink, a couple of generous slugs in a red plastic cup. "You know, we can't spend the whole holiday with one or the other of us sitting out in the cold with our dog."

"No dogs allowed in the house. And I'm not leaving him alone at your place while we're all here. It's Christmas."

"He doesn't know it's Christmas. Anyway, I think we should just let him in."

"Don't want to get your mom in trouble with the landlady."

"It's not like he's going to shit all over the place or get on the furniture or anything."

"But all the hair." He reaches down to rub Robert's proffered belly—Eric is a much more devoted belly-rubber than I am, a much more doting parent—and, indeed, a poof of floating pale fuzz rises up. I sigh. I'm a pretty obedient girl, as I've by now made clear, but sometimes Eric makes me look like a regular Johnny Rotten.

Standing on a Greenwich Village sidewalk outside a trattoria on a mild fall evening, waiting to be seated. Leaning against a gate, nuzzling and snuffling and smiling those too-intimate-for-public smiles and generally telegraphing all too clearly that this is a couple who will be having sex within a matter of hours. We're interrupted by a slightly sheepish middle-aged woman I've never seen before. "Excuse me.... Are you Julie Powell?"

"Um...yes. Hi." So this happens, only very occasionally. Someone who's read my book and has somehow managed to recognize me. Generally it's pretty thrilling. But the problem is that that first book is about, among other things, the sweet certainty of my love for my sainted husband and the particular perfection of our union. It wasn't a lie, what I wrote. But things are not so simple anymore. It may be that they never were, that I just ignored the complications. In any case, I have either way made a mess of a relationship that people I don't even know look to as a paragon of the genre, and being spotted making out with some strange man in front of a Mario Batali restaurant strikes me as a dread occurrence. My mind races as the woman chats about my book, how she loved it and gave it to her best friend, and asks what am I doing now? Maybe she won't even address D.

But of course she does. She sticks her hand out to him, saying, "And you must be the long-suffering—"

*Smoothly, instantly, D takes the woman's hand in a firm grip
with a broad, shit-eating grin that could not be more unlike my
husband's sweet, self-conscious, lopsided smile. "Eric. One and
the same."*

*I almost laugh in dizzy relief, right in the woman's face. I must
look completely dazed, with hectic eyes and a plastered-on smile.
D's no wild-eyed rebel, doesn't race hot rods or start fistfights in
bars or snort lines off strippers' asses (...much...that I know of).
But he has a way of, with just a sly smile, a tiny lie, making me
feel gleefully wild. I am trembling; I can't wait to get him home.*

This entire heaving memory has washed over me and receded
(leaving me drained and sodden, as these memories always do) by
the time Eric has straightened up and brushed the dog hair off his
pants.

"Well," I say, allowing the overwhelming longing to morph,
unfairly, into irritation, "We have to figure something out. We
can't do this the entire time."

"All right, all right." He picks up instantly on my annoyance, of
course, knows how my moods turn on a dime, more lately, but really
always. Once, when he was feeling generous, he called me *moody
and beautiful*. He's not feeling generous now, and why should he?
"Maybe we can put him in the stairwell down to the basement.
Block the doorway with some chairs or that bench or something."

"Okay. Yeah. Let's do that." I hate it when I snap at Eric, even
when he deserves it but especially when he doesn't, and not just
because it's not nice to snap. My mother carps in just the same
way, and I despise hearing that tone come from my own throat.
Again, not only because I feel defensive on my father's behalf
when my mother digs into him, though I do. It's also because I feel
in her, when she takes these unwarranted swipes, hints of a too-
familiar, bone-deep unhappiness, or discontent.

I am instantly affable again, apologetic. "That's a good idea."

"Julie? You coming? I really need your input on this."

"Yeah, Mom, we'll be right in. We're going to move Rob into
the basement stairwell. That'll be okay, don't you think?"

We move Rob over. He plods along with that familiar look of resignation with which he always suffers unexpected changes to his circumstances. By then Mom's taken out the corn bread to cool on a trivet, turned down the oven, and put the tinfoil-wrapped chickens inside. It's almost nine. As I sit across the table from Mom to help her decide if we want to make the green beans with shallots or the brussels sprouts with pecans and garlic, and whether the apple pie with lard crust we sometimes make is too much trouble to do in this small kitchen, I suddenly feel the weight of my exhaustion. My feet throb, and my back. As I pick up a pen to write the shopping list out on the back of an envelope—"Ow! Shit!" The pen clatters from numb fingers as I grasp my wrist, within which something or other has just popped painfully.

"What the hell is wrong with you?"

"Jesus." Shaking my hand out, wiggling my stiff fingers. The initial stab has already dissipated, but there's an alarming thrumming like a piano wire vibrating from my fingers up to my elbow. "My hand has decided it's done, I think."

"Let me see." I hold out both hands to my mother, who takes them in hers and compares them, turning them to see the insides of my wrists. There is nothing subtle about it now, my left wrist is clearly thicker than the other, and of a slightly different color, paler. When Mom presses her thumb down at my pulse point, my middle two fingers spasm, jerking twitchily in toward my palm, and I wince.

"Honey, this is carpal tunnel."

I shrug. "Well, not sure what to do about that."

"Well, what you should do is not do what you're doing any-more until it's better. But of course you're not going to do that."

"Nope."

She gets up and goes over to the refrigerator, digs some ice out of the open bag in the freezer, and dumps it into a Ziploc bag. (Our family always has plenty of ice wherever we go. It's part of the shopping list that we automatically tick off whenever we first pull into a new town: orange juice, mixed nuts, and ice, followed by a trip to the liquor store for gin, Jack Daniel's for Dad if he hasn't brought his Weller, Tanqueray for Mom, vodka or red wine for Eric and me.) "Well, keep it iced at least. I had to have surgery for this, you know. This is no little thing."

"Okay, okay." So I do. I keep the ice on it throughout dinner. Mom is enthusiastic about the chicken, and she's right, it's spectacular, the aroma exquisite, the spice mix rubbed into its skin a blend perfected by Juan, a closely held secret, which I am determined to wrangle out of him one day.

After we eat, my brother, Dad, Eric, and Mom sit on the floor around the coffee table peering at twenty-five hundred tiny puzzle pieces. The image on this year's annual puzzle is a vintage Polynesian postcard, which seems simple enough, but the water and all the Gauguinesque shadows are a bitch. I've never had quite the endurance for puzzling that the rest of my family—especially my brother and Eric—has, and besides, my wrist has now sunk into a deep sulk and snaps at me whenever I try to do anything so ambitious as pinch a small piece of colored cardboard between thumb and forefinger. So instead I lie back on the couch staring at the pages of the open book resting on my tented knees, sipping my fourth or fifth glass of wine, until my eyelids start drifting rather determinedly downward and then I'm jerking awake to the sensation of my glass listing dangerously in my hand. That's my cue: time for bed. I set the glass—emptied, luckily, down my gullet rather than onto the upholstery of the couch in my parents' vacation rental—in the sink. Stepping away, I bump painfully into the corner of the counter. "I think we should head to bed."

We say our good-nights desultorily. We're all in our evening doldrums by now; I was not the only one drifting on the couch.

As we head out into the chill air, I realize that Eric is gripping my upper arm too tightly, which makes me angry, even though I could use the support when I stumble on the uneven ground. "What?"

He jerks hard on my arm as if he's the only thing keeping me from slipping to the icy pavement. Robert walks alongside us, oblivious, occasionally scooping up a mouthful of snow. "Why do you have to get so sloppy?"

"What did I do? What? Why do you get so mean?"

"Forget it. Never mind. Let's just get you home."

We manage the cold quarter mile back to my apartment, climb the dark stairs, and tumble into bed, after Eric forces a big glass of water and a couple of aspirin on me.

But once the booze has worn off, the pain comes back. By three a.m. I am wide awake. To riff on a Kris Kristofferson song, there's no way to hold my hand that doesn't hurt. My thoughts flit back and forth among the throbbing ache, obsessive mental butchering reenactments, and preoccupation with the generalized physical longing that is pretty much my home position. By the time seven a.m. comes around, and Robert has begun stretching and yawning for his walk, my eyes are itchy and red, my stomach has gone sour with sleeplessness. And my wrist still hurts like anything. I get up feeling as creaky and old as hell. A short walk around in the frosty morning with the dog, a Diet Pepsi from the supply I keep in the fridge, a hot shower; I didn't bathe last evening, spent the whole night in my meat schmutz. It's gotten so I don't even notice it anymore, certainly not after a few glasses of wine. I wonder if Eric has gotten used to it or if he's just too polite to say anything. Then I'm ready to go.

Eric barely manages a "See you tonight, babe" when I kiss his shoulder good-bye.

"So, WHAT the fuck is wrong with you?"

My knife has slipped from my hand to the floor, barely missing my leg on its way down. I'm muttering under my breath as I massage my left palm with my right thumb.

"It's nothing. My hand...my hand is just a little screwed up. I'll get over it."

Josh grabs my hand. "Let me see."

Again I'm submitting to inspection, again my wrist is being turned back and forth under peering eyes.

"Dude, your hand's fucked up."

"A little," I admit. "It's okay. It was fine for a while. I'm just getting a little tired."

"Well, then sit the fuck down and rest, brain trust."

"I'm almost done with this—"

Jessica, who always overhears, has come over and is looking at my wrist too. "Has this been going on long? Have you tried massage? Acupuncture really works, too."

"I haven't tried anything. It'll be fine."

"Well, if you wind up suing us for workers' comp—"

"Oh, please, I'm not going to *sue* you."

"No, I know, but you know what I'm saying. Sit. Have some soup. Get some ice on that."

Josh very nearly throws me into a chair. "No way you're working anymore today."

"It's fine. Look, it's not even two, and you guys are going to need help with the—"

"You think you're going to win this argument?" Josh flutters his blue eyes at me. "How *cute*."

Sighing, I submit to Josh and Jessica's smart-assed version of solicitude. I get my mug of soup, sit at the table in back, will the feeling to return to my crippled limb. But they're right, everybody's right. My hand has given notice.

"Look, you oughta go spend the day with the fam anyway. Decorate trees, drink nog, do what you people do."

Resistance, I now realize, is futile. Besides, maybe Josh is right. I should not be hiding on Christmas Eve eve.

Wait. Not hiding. Working. *I shouldn't be working,* is what I meant.

"Oh, fine. Fine. So you guys coming by for dinner tomorrow?"

"Got nothing better to do, sure. What should we bring?"

"Oh, the usual. Booze. Snacking accessories."

"Sounds good. And Steph and Matt coming with? That cool?" Stephanie and Matt are old friends of Josh and Jess, a couple who own a house up here and come from the city every weekend. Since I'm usually up during the week, our schedules thus completely opposed, I have met them only once or twice.

"Sure. More the merrier. Jesse already said he's coming for sure." I've invited everyone in the shop. I've already posted a map and directions, scrawled out on a big sheet of butcher paper in red Sharpie and stuck up on the wall with masking tape. "And what about you, Juan?" I call, raising my voice to reach the kitchen. "You in?"

"What?"

"My house? Tomorrow?"

Juan wipes his hands on a white terry-cloth towel. He's elbow-deep in dishes. "I'll try."

"You can get a ride with us," Josh offers.

"Or me," adds Jesse from the counter. "Your place is right on my way."

"Yeah, okay. I'll try. Thanks."

I HEAD back to my apartment with my enormous paper-wrapped pork roast and six pounds of lamb stew meat. Rob meets me at the top of the stairs with his usual casual interest, but a "Hello?" reveals that Eric isn't around. No doubt helping my folks with groceries, tree shopping, or some such. I've left him a text or two, but haven't heard back. I wedge my meat into the refrigerator with some difficulty, fill a bag with ice, and lie down for a bit. Robert the Dog pulls himself heavily up onto the bed at my feet, as he always does when it gets cold. I should really make him get down, but I don't.

"Julie? You here?"

When I open my eyes again with some alarm, the room has gone dim with evening. Of course the sun is setting early these days, but I must have slept, I don't know, three hours at least. My ice pack has melted into a Ziploc of cool water. I sit up with a guilty start, much as I do the mornings after I black out and can't quite recall how the night before ended or if I did something stupid like drunk-dial my ex-lover or get into some teary fight with my husband. "I'm here, yeah."

Eric walks into the bedroom, bundled up in his coat. "You sleeping? We didn't know where you were."

"Sorry. I texted you."

"Ah. I let my phone run down. Crap service up here anyway."

"Yeah, I figured." Rob and I both climb out of bed, both of us creakily. My wrist is still pinging away.

"Well, we got the tree. And stuff for cooking. Talking about just going out tonight."

"Going out? Where?"

"I thought you'd have some suggestions."

"There is fuck-all around here. You can barely get pizza delivered."

"We'll figure something out. Anyway, we should go down to the cottage. Tree decorating and nog."

"Yup, yup, yup..." I'm still in my meat clothes, sticky, stinking T-shirt and jeans. "I don't guess I have time to take a shower. What time is it?"

"Go ahead and take one if you want. It's five thirty. We'll have to figure out a dinner plan, I guess." Eric's squatting to give Robert his belly rub. Utterly unfairly, I am sometimes annoyed by the attention Eric offers our dog. I try to transform it into affectionate exasperation. "You spoil that dog—"

"Everybody needs a good belly rub. Don't they need a belly rub? Don't they need a belly rub?" His nose is up against Robert's, play-growling as the dog snorts blissfully.

"Should we feed him here or there?"

"I'll feed him. You getting into the shower?"

"Nah. Oh, yeah. I guess. Blar."

Eric stands at last and brushes the dog hair off his jeans. "Where did that come from, 'blar'? You say that all the time. It's weird."

God, marriage is a strange thing. Everything clear, nothing said.

"I don't know. Just picked it up somewhere."

I know exactly why Eric is asking me this. He knows I know. My vaguely defiant tone is the closest we will get to a discussion of the fact that he thinks I picked it up from D. (Which I didn't, as it happens, but all new vocabulary not part of the official marriage jargon is immediately suspect.)

"Well, I'll feed this one. Shower will make you feel better, maybe."

"Maybe." I strip down, throw the dirty clothes in the general direction of the duffel bag I live out of when I'm up here. We have always been casually naked around each other, slept in the nude, wandered the house without a stitch on. Long ago, I used to think it was a mark of our sexy, adult coupledom. Now I fear we're just completely immune to the sight of each other's bare skin. I don't even merit a second glance; Eric heads to the kitchen, Robert following with pricked-up ears, while I go into the bathroom.

It takes the water forever to get warm.

DINNER IS some pasta with store-bought sauce we dig up in the pantry. The tree is a funky-looking thing with bald spots and a crooked trunk, just the way we like it in our family. Mom has decided she doesn't want to get pine needles all over the carpet—not sure why we didn't think of this before—so we wind up putting the tree on the front porch, adorning it with the lights, tinsel, and the sparse decorations I've brought up from where they usually live in our storage unit in the city. We huddle around in our coats, squeezing between the branches and the side of the house to get the decorations hung. When it's done it's rather lovely, if odd. Ten minutes later as we're sitting down to dinner it blows down in the wind, and Dad and my brother spend another twenty minutes securing it to the porch beams and handrail with twine.

Christmas Eve Day is, as usual with my mom and me, spent in

the kitchen. While the boys—Dad, my brother, Eric, and Robert—toss around a football in the front yard, I roast poblano peppers over the gas flame of the stove, brown lamb stew meat in bacon fat and olive oil. Mom toasts pecans in the oven, crumbles up the corn bread that needs to be thoroughly dry by tomorrow for the crown roast's stuffing. I hold ice to my wrist, which again kept me awake through the night. I stared at the ceiling, listening to Eric's and Rob's contrapuntal snores, as tears leaked down into my ears for no particular, immediate reason.

Jesse is the first guest to arrive, by quite a few hours.

"Hey, I like your tree! I haven't had a Christmas tree for years."

"Yeah, well, we'll just be lucky if it doesn't blow down again. Where's Juan?"

"He wasn't answering his phone."

If I'm honest, I hadn't really expected him to come, but it's still a disappointment. I've not expressed this to anyone, but I'd gotten sort of set on having everyone from Fleisher's there. "Ah well, come on in. Want something to drink? We got wine, eggnog, booze of all description...water?"

"Eggnog sounds great. And some water too, actually."

"Come on in. We're still cooking, of course."

"Of course."

Jesse is just exactly like he is at the shop—a little slow-moving, quiet, engaging. He offers to help, and within minutes my mother has him tearing up slices of bread and they are chatting about gerrymandering and the Democrats' chances for the 2008 election.

By nightfall the rest of the gang—Josh and Jessica with Stephanie and Matt, and another of their friends, Jordan—has found us, after a bit of searching and a nasty incident involving a U-turn gone wrong on a patch of ice and a resultant churned-up mess of mud on a stranger's front lawn. The lamb chili stew and some mulled wine are both bubbling away on the stove, filling the cottage with their aromas. Robert is behind the bench out on the stairwell, and the small house is so full of people that there is always someone to give him pats, until eventually, after enough drinks and the persuasions of a bunch of people who are not so keenly aware as everyone in my family is of the landlady's "no pets" rule, and of, in general, all the dangerous ways there are to step on other people's toes and take up more than his fair share of space in the world, he's released to roam the house.

The stew is delicious and potently spicy. It is a dish that Mom and I make often, though generally only for family or Texas expats, as most of my New York friends are sensitive to heat—but I knew this crowd could take it, and they can.

"This is fantastic, Kay," Jessica tells my mom, and the sentiment is echoed by a chorus of agreement so effusive as to fall on my family's ears, we who are so chary of compliments, as obscurely insincere. I know that insincere is the last thing these people are, and, as exquisitely sensitive as I am to the tiny vibrations of mood and secret thought of every member of my family, most especially my mother, I can't relax for knowing that she doesn't quite see this. My brother, never a spurting fountain of conversation, has gone almost perfectly silent and, while attentive to the flow of talk, has that tiny half smile and the slightly shaded eyes that tell me he's got his bullshit meter out and is scanning the beach, listening for that telltale quickening tick. My mother has a version of the same shadow in her eyes—they are so alike, my mother and brother— though she never stops talking. My mother is a woman who could converse with a goat, who is found universally charming even when she's thinking mean thoughts, which she does from time to time. Her failure to respond to Josh and Jessica, Stephanie and Matt and Jordan, as instantly and warmly as I have, irritates me.

But after all, these five are old friends; they bring their entire history into the house with them, a history that makes them ebullient together, loud and bursting with inside jokes and stories that then have to be explained. It makes the cottage feel more crowded than it is. As much as I've been looking forward to this meal, to introducing my butchering family to my blood kin, I can understand why the fit is a little awkward, why my polite, sardonic, retiring relatives are a little bowled over by this walking circus of a group. And on Christmas Eve, designated "family time." It is making my mom prickly, I can feel it, though of course she would never betray that to guests. Later, when I ask her opinion of them, it will turn out, as I suspected, that Jesse is the only one she's entirely one hundred percent on. Of Josh and Jessica she will say, "They're very nice. And I like anybody who likes you as much as they obviously do. They are a little, well, New Yorky." She doesn't even realize what it is that "New Yorky" implies. I will be embarrassed, and angry, and will start to argue, then let it slide because what's the point, really, except that having my mother not love what and who I love, just as much as I love them, disturbs me more than it should.

Shortly after D moves back to New York, before he's gotten me into bed but after I've begun to suspect that that's where it's heading, if I'm not careful, my parents come to town for a visit. As usual, theater, expensive meals, and lots of booze are the prime activities on the menu. I've bought us tickets to see Mary-Louise Parker in a revival of Reckless, *and I made us reservations for after at L'Impero. We wind up with an extra ticket. And so I invite D. Natural enough, I tell myself. Officially speaking, he is now Eric's and my friend.*

Of course what I'm doing is presenting him for approval. And the jury is definitely out on that. Hell, he even sets my bullshit meter ticking, like he's walking around with a scoop of yellowcake in his coat.

"I can't stand Scorsese." (My mother often makes pronouncements like this. She can work herself into a rage at any mention of, say, Nicole Kidman—"She looks like a lab rat!"—for years on end, and then all of a sudden the actress will be good in something or get dumped by her insane cyborg first husband, and all of a sudden Mom will not only do a complete one-eighty, but will also claim to never have felt any way but positively about the lovely girl. It's rather charming, actually, and something of a family joke, these violently held opinions, hilarious except when one

finds oneself in a screaming match about Bill Murray or getting a
frying pan thrown at one's head over a fine point of evolutionary
theory.)

"Sure you can."

"No, I really hate him. Taxi Driver? Fucking Goodfellas?
Overrated, macho crap."

"Did you see Alice Doesn't Live Here Anymore?"

Bull's-eye.

"Oh, I love that one. Kris when he was young.... That's Scorsese?"

And he's got her. Later he'll tell me that with one glance at her,
and at my grizzled, tall, deeply Texan father, he instantly knew
she would be a Kristofferson fan.

As it turns out, I will never mention D's name to her again;
once he and I start sleeping together I won't be able to trust myself
to. But at this moment I can see he plays her as effortlessly as he
plays me. My mother and I recognize that he's both dangerous
and silly, self-congratulatory and slightly irritating, but some-
how, mysteriously, irresistible. Furtively, I'm happy—as if my
mother is giving me her approval for what I've halfway decided to
do. A year later I'll find myself thrilled all over again when, after
briefly meeting D's mother, he says to me, "My mother loves you.
'I really like that girl,' she said." It irks me that I, a thirty-three-
year-old woman, still need a parental permission slip to go on my
emotional field trips.

So Christmas Day is better, because we can get back to our
usual routines of being family together—cooking, sitting in
corners reading, doing jigsaw puzzles, and sipping celebratory
daytime alcohol. We open our presents in the morning after re-
erecting the tree that blew down again in the night. Mom and Dad
have laid out the stockings for Eric, my brother, and me along
with the presents "Santa brought"—i.e., the ones they didn't want
to wrap—just as they have every year since I was born. By noon
we're hitting the eggnog again, and the boys are bowed over the
puzzle while Mom and I season the roast and start to put together
the side dishes.

"Isn't it pretty? I made this!" I say of my beautiful crown roast, like a kindergartener presenting a prized tempera paint master-piece. I make a joke of being childishly proud to cover up being childishly proud.

"It's gorgeous, Julie. I'm amazed you did that."

"Oh, it's not that hard." Of course I am immensely pleased.

The roast involves nothing more than several hours of cooking, some prodding with the meat thermometer I remembered to borrow from the shop, and a bit of anxiety. I'm worried about overcooking my beautiful creation, and I'm worried about undercooking it. I try to resist getting snippy, but when I go to the bathroom I make the mistake, the terrible, masochistic, impulsive, habitual mistake, of texting D. I wish him a merry Christmas, cinch myself tight into the cozy fantasy of his answering, of his thanking me for the beau-tiful scarf he will wear though he knows he shouldn't because it is beautiful and his mother loves it and it goes so well with his favor-ite crimson winter cap. And then, though the pork smells fantastic, I can't decide when it's done. The bones are darkening and unctu-ous fat is pooling below the rack and the temperature seems right, but aren't those juices running awfully pink? and Eric is looking at me with suspicion, picking up my strange vibrations, and I'm feeling my lungs being crushed, I'm panicking because I have this responsibility to everyone, to be happy and good and make a great crown roast and I really don't know what call I should make on the damned thing, I'm going to ruin it, and suddenly there are tears, and my wrist cramps in a wrenching spasm and the meat ther-mometer slips, clattering, from my fingers.

"Julie, what is wrong with you?" My mother, like everyone else, recognizes these tantrums, though she is mystified as to their cause.

"I...I don't know what to do about...about the...about all of it. I'm ruining Christmas dinner. I am a thirty-three-year-old butcher who can't read a fucking meat thermometer."

Everyone has his own technique for dealing with these fits of mine.

Mom snaps at me until I go from angry to teary and contrite, then strokes my hands and peers into my eyes soulfully. "I don't know why you do this to yourself, but you always have."

Eric takes me by the shoulders, gazes at me with something very close to terror, and speaks with quiet intensity. "Julie. Calm down. Please. Calm. Down."

My brother rolls his eyes and walks away.

But I like my dad's way best. He grabs me in a headlock and rubs my hair with his big knuckles, the male version of my own. "Oh, Jules," he says, giggling, "you're so crazy."

That cheers me, somehow loosens the binds, and for a while I can breathe again, not worry about having to take care of everything and everyone, every secret thought and perceived vibration.

I overcooked the roast. But my family doesn't seem to notice, or at least they are very kind in their praise; sensitive to my feelings, no doubt, after my recent breakdown. And it is still delicious, even if the texture is off; while Fleisher's pork is good enough that you don't need to cook it so much, it is also, with its loads of lovely fat, better able to cope with overcooking than your standard supermarket variety. We eat far more than we need to, and then Mom slices up the pie we decided to go ahead and make and doles it out. Dad leans back in his chair and puts his napkin on his head, which is just something he does after big dinners; we don't even think about it anymore. "Well, dears, this was all wonderful. I'm going to have to go vomit now."

"Yeah, sweetie, it was really good," says Eric, squeezing my hand and leaning over to kiss me. I smile, and feel a sort of pang, think for a moment about my BlackBerry that has not buzzed all night, will never buzz again, not for the reasons I want it to. Why is it that Eric's compliments, his approval and love, constantly offered, don't seem so real to me as a single word, any small acknowledgment of my existence, from D? It's unfair and cruel, and I kiss Eric more tenderly than I have in months, in private apology.

That night, as I lie in bed gripping my wrist, I remember

something I haven't thought of in years. When I was a girl, I went to the same camp every summer for seven years. In all that time, it was my mother who wrote me letters, two or more a week, faithfully, sending along little care packages, books and games and cassette tapes. With one exception. On August 8, 1988, my father wrote the only letter he would send me in seven years. In the body of the letter he said he just couldn't help himself, because of the date, 8/8/88.

I treasure that, the random, occasional ways that my father has always shown his affection. He hardly ever tells me that he loves me; he doesn't need to. I know it. He doesn't have to tell me of his love for anything precious inside me. Instead he proves I'm precious by every now and then bequeathing to me something he delights in. An observation, a favorite book, a movie, a bird sighting at the feeder outside his window. It fills me with warmth. I don't want any more. I wouldn't know what to do with more. I like my expressions of love meted out. Earned.

My eyes widen in the darkness, and my breath catches. I turn my head to look at my BlackBerry, sitting by the side of the bed like a stone. I stare at it, feeling the dull throb in my wrist and waiting, until somewhere in the early hours I at last am asleep.

9

Too Close for Comfort Food

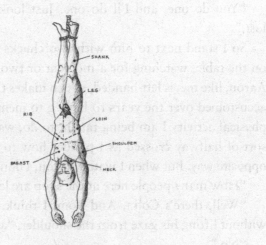

EVERY STEER THAT comes into the shop arrives broken into eight pieces, called "primals." The best way to picture these primals is to use your own body as a sort of guide. First, hang yourself by a hook upside down, gut yourself, take off your head, and cut yourself in half vertically. The next cut you'll make—just at the wide fan of the shoulder blade—will take off one of your chuck shoulder primals. An arm, a shoulder, and half of your neck and chest. Next to come off are your rib sections—all but the very top of your rib cage. Then cut off your loin sections, making the cut right at your tailbone. What you've got left hanging is your two legs and buttocks. These are what are called "rounds." Butchery-wise, I've pretty much got breaking down rounds, well, down.

Chuck shoulders, though, are a whole other problem. This is the biggest primal on the animal, and full of funkily shaped bones, knobby vertebrae, which, unlike the loin and rib sections, have to be removed to get to the meat. And then there's the blade bone, an epic battle just in itself. Someday, maybe, I hope, I will be able to break down a shoulder in fifteen minutes, and that is when I'll know I'm a real butcher. For now it takes me, I shit you not, close to an hour and a half.

"Hey, I'm sorry, Aaron, can you walk me through some of this? I should have this down, I know..."

"You do one, and I'll do one. Just look over when you get lost."

So I stand next to him with two chucks laid out side by side on the table, watching for a moment or two before I get started. Aaron, like me, is left-handed, which makes this easier. I've grown accustomed over the years to having to mentally flip around any physical activity I am being taught to do, watching with my eyes sort of halfway crossed as I picture how to make it work in the opposite way. But when I watch Aaron, I don't have to do that.

"How many people here at the shop are left-handed?"

"Well, there's Colin. And Tom, I think....Hailey," he calls, without lifting his gaze from the shoulder, "are you a lefty?"

"No."

"Aww. That's too bad. You seem like you might be part of the team."

Hailey screws up her face at him in mock annoyance. At least I think it's mock.

"Jules, can you name all seven left-handed U.S. presidents?" Aaron in one of his quiz modes.

"Um, hmm." Pulling my chuck shoulder toward me, inside of the chest cavity facing up, the top of the neck pointing away. I start with the easy part, cutting out the rope, a cylinder of meat nestled into the spine, rising up into the neck. It's just like taking out the tenderloin, except less stressful because the meat is more or less worthless, going straight into grind or perhaps set aside by one of the cutters to take home; we all love cheap meat that also happens to be tasty, and the rope makes excellent stew meat. "Let's see. Clinton, I know. And Bush—"

"Which Bush?"

"The elder, of course. C'mon. Like that moron could be a lefty? Reagan."

"You got three."

"Ford...Truman?" Having tossed the rope aside, I've put down my knife and picked up the butcher's saw. I cut through the rib bones on either end, both right up close to the spine, where the rope used to be, and right up against the breastbone, which (if you want to picture this on yourself again) is where the two sides of your rib cage came together in front in a wedge of cartilage when you were still whole. On the other side of that cartilage is a big hunk of yellowed fat where breasts would be if steer had the same kind of breasts we do. The sawing is the slightest bit tricky. Because the arm and shoulder are tucked up under there, the whole piece doesn't lie flat, but tips toward you, with the far, top end of the rack of ribs higher than the bottom part. This angle is not ideal, since you don't want to saw deeply into the flesh below the ribs. You have to sort of squat and come at the ribs from below so that by the time you get through the bottom rib you haven't delved deep into the muscle at the top end.

"That's right."

"That's all I've got."

Aaron straightens up and, still grippling his knife, sticks out first his thumb and then his index finger. "Hoover, Garfield."

"Not a universally stellar lot, it must be said." I've taken knife back in hand, in a pistol grip, and am cutting down right over the upper edge of the top rib until I hit a thick white layer of fat. Down the slices I've made on either side of the ribs, I rake my knife to find that same obvious line of fat. "Did you know Barack Obama is left-handed?"

"What is the deal with you people?" Jesse pipes up. It's a slow February day, he's lackadaisically wiping down the counters just for something to do. "As if a shared demographic of deadly accidents and heightened suicide rates is something to be proud of."

"Heeey," says Aaron. "We're brilliant! We're creative! We're tortured!"

I don't say anything, but I'm smiling down into my meat.

"Heeey. I thought you were left-handed."

I'm sitting across from D at a diner on the Upper East Side. He's got a forkful of omelet halfway to his mouth, in his right hand. But can that be? I distinctly remember the moment, a couple of weeks back, when I'd noticed he was a fellow traveler. I was tied up at the time, as it were, and had my mind on other things, so I didn't mention it, but I'd certainly filed it under the category of Fun Facts to Know and Tell.

He understands immediately where I've gotten the idea, and gives me one of his little half leers. "No, I only do one thing with my left hand."

And now comes the fun part. This is actually one of my favorite things to do—not even just in butchery terms, but in general. I mean, I can think of a few things that top it. But in much the same way as knowing a trick in a computer game, where the power nugget is hidden or where you have to jump with triple speed at just the right moment to escape the ravening what-have-you, taking off this section of ribs feels like engaging in a privileged, secret shortcut. Take the meat hook in your right hand (if you're a lefty) and thrust it down through the meat over and under the top rib, so that the hooked end comes up between it and the second rib down. Then just pull. The seam separating the ribs from the fat below is thick and lusty, and comes apart with a gratifyingly sticky noise, no knife required, except maybe at the very end. Set the ribs aside. You can slice these with the band saw into short ribs, if you like; sometimes we do and sometimes we don't. We generally have more short ribs than we can sell, and the ones made from this end are not quite so meaty as the ones that come from lower down, in the rib section. But I'll probably set a few aside to bring home with me when I head back to the city tonight. I like taking meat that isn't costing Josh much money.

Once you get off the ribs, you reveal the brisket, treasured by Texans for barbecue and Jews for pastrami and Passover pot roast. This is also not difficult to remove, though the first step, stripping off the cartilage-lined forward end of the rib cage, isn't exactly a barrel of monkeys. The bone dissolves into cartilage, which is easily sliced into. You'd think this would make it simple, but what it means in effect is that it's easy, when scraping your knife down underneath the knobby arc to loosen it from the meat below, to inadvertently leave some inedible white bits embedded in the brisket, which you'll then have to shave off.

Next stick your knife in just below the armpit (it's not called an armpit on a steer, I don't imagine, but for the sake of the imagery), under the brisket muscle, and drag it horizontally toward the spine. Then make another, vertical cut from there straight down the middle of where the ribs once lay, down to the next tier of fat. Then the brisket, too, can be peeled loose with a good tug of the meat hook. Beneath that is a fatty layer in which is buried a small, long muscle that most butchers disregard but that Josh has us roll out. He will later cut it into two-inch round pieces, roll each one in a strip of house-made bacon, and sell them as "faux fillets" for eight bucks a pound.

Now we get to the pain-in-the-ass bit.

The irritating thing about a shoulder is that after all the work it takes to break it down—and I haven't remotely gotten to the tough part yet—most of the meat is, while exceedingly tasty, not worth a great deal. Chuck eye, shank, brisket—all are fatty, cheap cuts that need to be cooked a long time in a slow oven until they melt into fall-apart tenderness. The one exception, and it is a bitch of one, is the clod. This piece lies atop the shoulder blade, adhering tightly to that triangle of bone that looks nothing like any other bone in the body—a widening expanse of gray, shaped like a shovel's blade, to which the meat ferociously fuses. The clod is quite valuable, not so much for the retail market as for wholesale; trendy New York chefs buy it and slice it into steaks, roast it whole, even grind it for those high-end, thirty-buck hamburgers they all feel like they have to have on their menu these days. And they want it entire, a wide triangle of beef unmarred by errant knife strokes. So this is where it gets really tricky. I stand, just staring down at the shoulder for a moment. "Okay, Aaron? This is where I need some help."

"Flip the whole piece over, first of all. So the foreleg is on top." The thing is damned heavy, and cumbersome. It takes some doing to turn it. Once I do, Aaron reaches over and palpates the fat and meat with his thumb. "Feel right here," he says. Sure enough, there is a distinct thin run of bone slicing straight through the flesh like a shark's fin through water—the ridge of the shoulder blade, set at a ninety-degree angle to the bone's flat wedge, which widens and thins out into cartilage toward the side of the cut facing toward us. The ridge runs from the blade's upper point, where it meets the shank, down to nearly the bottom of the triangle, where it shrinks to nothing as the bone peters out into cartilage.

"Start there, with that," says Aaron. Then he gestures with his knife, indicating a triangular shape from along that line up to the joint and then over, along the length of the shank bone. "This is the money cut. So don't screw it up."

"You do realize, right, that I've had three different people show me how to cut out the clod, some of them several times, and every single time, I swear to God, they've done it differently?"

"That's good! If you learn different ways to approach it, you'll figure out how the thing really works. There's a logic to it. Figure it out, and you'll be able to butcher any animal on your own. You can butcher people once you figure this out."

"Whatever. I like rote learning."

"Go ahead. You'll remember as you go."

I start by exposing the top edge of the blade bone, moving down carefully so the knife doesn't meander off track. All the way up to the joint and then over, along the line of the shank. I've now outlined the edges of the clod, what I'm to pull out. I dip my knife back into the cut I've made to the ridge top and work my way, so carefully, down, along the right side of it. From the lower edge of the chuck, facing me, up to the joint, I meticulously loosen meat from bone.

Now, if I were Aaron, I would hook my left forearm under the upper tip of the clod, hold the blade bone down to the table with my right palm, and rip the muscle off in one manly swoop, cleanly breaking the tight bond, leaving the blade bone bare, the muscle untorn. The sheen of the silvery layer that fused the two together would come away with the meat, rendering the surface of the clod smooth and dry, as if covered in wax paper. It's one of those little miracles of butchery, the expert tearing out of a shoulder clod.

I, however, am no Aaron. I give it a try—a wrenching pull, as I clasp the meat to my chest—but I haven't the strength, or maybe I just don't have the nerve to use it. The clod comes up a few inches, then catches, hung up, threatening to rip. Still applying upward pressure so I can see into the crevice I've started to open, I stick my fingers in there and push with a windshield-wiper back-and-forth motion against the tight edge of that fusion, feeling for the points that are resisting. With my fingertips, I urge them to give. A knife would be quicker, but far messier. I want to do this right.

"How you doin' there?"

"Okay. I'd rather be slow than destructive."

"All a balance, Jules. All a balance."

"How very Zen of you."

Laboriously I pull up, then dig in, pull up and dig in, working the muscle loose bit by painful bit. It's half an hour before I get the thing mostly up, so that only the cartilaginous hypotenuse of the blade bone is still attached to the meat. I hold up the clod with my right hand, and with my left I fumble about for my knife without looking, which (if I thought about it for two seconds I would realize) is seriously stupid but is something I've become very used to doing. Once I have it in hand I use it to break that last connection—a small bit of cheating I can live with. The bone beneath is as smooth and gray as an overcast sky.

"Christ," I whisper as I at last drop the clod onto the table. I'm sweating.

"What's your time on that? Got four more chucks back there to do."

"I'm working on it, I'm *working* on it." Out of the corner of my mouth, Indiana Jones style. Grumbling playfully so as not to grumble in earnest.

The other bad thing about chuck shoulders is that once you've gotten the clod off, a satisfying but exhausting achievement, there's still a ton left to do, most of it tedious. The neck bone, complicatedly buried in the meat, has to come off to get at the chuck eye. Inevitably a lot of flesh will come off with it, which later will have to be trimmed away, shred by shred, in among all the knobs and crannies of the vertebrae, which, you will find yourself thinking, are just entirely too fussy and clearly designed by nature as a sort of posthumous "fuck you" from steer to butcher.

Rolling out the chuck eye is sort of fun, as all cuts with a good, sticky, easy-to-follow seam are, but then I have to crack off the shank, breaking into a *really* tricky joint that it sometimes seems I will never be able to penetrate. Once I do, and push down hard, there is that lovely pop as the joint opens, then the obscene slow drip of clear synovial fluid. But the meat of the leg, once pulled off the bone, is threaded through with thick sinews that must be shaved out. The rest of the meat—and there is still a lot of it—just goes into the grinder. But before that happens, the remaining bones have to be pulled out, and a thick chunk of fat buried between muscles, which you might think you could just carelessly chop up, has to be removed, as it is riddled with glands. The glands are fascinating to look at, shiny, rubbery nuggets, gray or deep burgundy or occasionally green, but they are things you definitely do *not* want popping up in your hamburger.

Finally, finally, I finish. It's taken me a solid hour. Aaron has broken down three in that time. "Good Lord."

"There's one more back there," Aaron says, grunting a little as he pulls his clod loose. "Want me to go get it for you?"

"No, I can handle it." In truth I'm not sure that I can. Chuck shoulders weigh about a hundred fifty pounds, and they're awkward, with no convenient way to get a solid hold on them. But I have just taken more than an hour to break one down, and I'm not about to ask for any coddling at this point. I head back to the cooler.

Sometimes the chucks are hanging off hooks from bars, which makes getting a grip on them marginally easier, but I'm not in luck today, for this one is sitting on one of the Metro shelves, at just about thigh level. Conscientiously bending my knees, I squat in front of it, force my arms under the shank on one side and under the backbone on the other, and start to lift.

It's a close thing. I very nearly make it, nearly get the weight of the thing balanced just right. But at the last minute, just as I'm about to straighten my knees, it goes wrong, I topple, fall onto my back, and the chuck is now protected from the floor by my hips, on which it's heavily resting.

Crap.

I will have to call for help, of course. But for a long while, I don't. I lie there, my bones grinding into the floor, contemplating the laughable fate of dying under a mountain of beef. The funniest part is, this is really not such an unfamiliar position I find myself in.

"Er…Juan?" No one will hear me back here behind this insulated steel door unless I shout. Juan is the person I am least embarrassed to have to ask for help, he is completely without the supercilious gene, and besides, we have a shared history of cooler accidents. Some months ago, I was in here with him, helping him arrange an alarming surfeit of meat. Four thick steel rods rested on the top shelves of two Metro units pushed up against either wall, and on them were hung side after side after side of pork, beef shoulders and rounds, lamb. It was a deeply overcrowded walk-in closet of flesh. Juan, being both smaller and stronger than I, was three rows deep in the stuff, pushing bodies around, when a harsh, shrieking crack made us both glance up at the rods overhead. We assumed that they were beginning to give under the weight. But it was worse than that. The Metro—industrial shelving units designed to bear thousands of pounds—was bending, sinking, swaybacked under the rods like it was melting. "Um, maybe you should—" But Juan was already scurrying out from under the meat curtains that were starting to shift ominously. He got out seconds before the things started giving way, pork and beef tumbling down with slow, collapsing groans. It was an awe-inspiring sight, like watching a tall ship sinking after a disastrous naval engagement, masts smashing one by one, hull wrenching apart, splintering.

"What the *hell* is going on in there?" We heard Jessica bellow. But until she swung open the door, we didn't answer, just stared at the destruction, the completeness of it, not yet even beginning to contemplate how we would go about picking up the pieces. "Well, you got out from under, at least."

"Wow."

"Yeah." I ogled the devastation. Almost reveled in it. What now?

"Wow."

So, yeah, Juan and I have shared a moment. He's the one to call. "Juan? A little help?"

By the time Juan gets me out from under the chuck, racks of ribs, peeled off the shoulders, are beginning to pile up next to the band saw. I'm no longer afraid of the saw. In fact, I rather enjoy it, the efficiency of it and the noise, the electric smell of singed bone. Without being asked I begin to saw the racks into two-inch strips, across the bones, for short ribs.

Of course, there are many, many things I love to eat. Liver, as I believe I've mentioned. The occasional Skittle or Cheeto, sad to say, does tempt.

But short ribs are perhaps my very favorite thing to eat. Maybe along with oxtail. Now, there's favorite, and favorite, of course. An exquisitely aged strip steak, of the kind Josh and Jess sell at Fleisher's—from a beast raised on grass and just a bit of good grain, living a life as pleasant as a steer's life can be, aged for three weeks until the flesh is buttery and the meaty flavor is con-centrated to an almost unbearable degree—is a rare pleasure (at twenty-five bucks a pound it ought to be rare, anyway), sexy and indulgent and rather like being in bed with a man who does things just right, without being asked.

But short ribs contain a different kind of intimacy. A clandestine close-to-the-bone-ness. And so much fun because they're sort of a secret. I mean, of course if you eat in the best of restaurants, you will see that short ribs have popped up all over the place in recent years, so it's not as if these fatty, unctuous, glorious squares of bone and fat are my secret alone. Chefs and cooks and butchers, the tribe of people invested in the selling of meat and the feeding of people for money or love, all adore short ribs. We love them because they're cheap, and because cooking them, while an investment in time, is the simplest thing you can do for the greatest reward. Bought for little more than a song, then simply left alone in an oven to braise for hours in wine or stock or beer, they come out glorious, the sort of food that leaves one feeling nourished not only in the gut but in the mind. You will feel as afloat as you do on a glass of good wine—not Margaux '66 divine, just *good* wine, the wine you need on that particular happy, cold night. And whether you're a chef trying to get your patrons to enjoy themselves and pay as much as possible for the privilege, at the least cost to you, or a woman who wants her friends and family to eat well, feel good, and be impressed for not much effort, short ribs are the way to go.

A Nice, Simple Way to Make Short Ribs

4 pounds short ribs

Salt and pepper to taste

2 teaspoons crumbled dried rosemary

3 tablespoons bacon fat

3 cloves garlic, lightly crushed

1 small onion, cut into half rings

1 cup dry red wine

1 cup beef stock

Preheat the oven to 325°F.

Pat dry the ribs and trim off excess fat. I'm not a big fan of trimming fat off meat, as a general rule, but I think in this case it's permissible and possibly even advisable. Once you've done this to your satisfaction, season generously with salt, pepper, and rosemary.

Warm the bacon fat over medium-high heat in an ovenproof stockpot until almost smoking. Quickly brown the ribs on all sides, working in batches, setting them aside on a plate once done. After all the ribs are browned, pour off all but three tablespoons of the fat in the pan and throw in the garlic and onion, stirring a couple of minutes until the garlic is fragrant and the onion is beginning to turn golden. Add the wine and stock, which will hiss and almost instantly come to a boil. Return the ribs, along with any juices that have collected on the plate, to the pot.

Cover and place in the hot oven. Cook until the meat falls very easily from the bone, at least two hours. Serve four to six of your friends, with the pan juices and a big scoop of mashed potatoes.

And oxtails? Oxtails are even more of a secret than that. It's the name that camouflages them so well. Oxtail. That is just five kinds of unpleasant. And it also happens to be exactly accurate. Oxtails come out of the box that each steer is delivered with, containing all the extra bits Josh might want to use. There's the liver, and the heart, which is also delicious, and not scary at all, once you've gotten yourself around all the metaphors and imagery. A heart is just a muscle, after all, which is something I should remember more often. The tongue. The sweetbreads, occasionally, if we're lucky. (Sweetbreads—another instance of necessary euphemism—are actually thymus glands and are a pain in the ass to remove, generally not worth it unless you're working with a large number of slaughtered animals at a time.) And the tail. Which looks just like a tail. A little more than a foot long, two or three inches in diameter at the base, tapering to a point, threaded through with the last bones of the vertebrae, getting smaller all the time.

To prepare the oxtails for the case, ready to cook and eat, you cut between each vertebra, which is a fun thing to do because it's so much easier than you'd think. At this point, each is joined to the next by cartilage that is simple to cut through with a boning knife once you find the right spot. And although the bones are getting narrower and narrower in diameter, they're all the same length, so once you've found the first point of breach, it's child's play to guess where the next will come. It makes me feel powerful and smart and, yes, a little sexy to cut up oxtails. When I'm done, I am left with about ten cylinders of meat and bone, all the same height, the thickest of them lush rosettes of meat with bright white centers, the smallest ones no larger than a fingertip, almost entirely white, hardly any meat to them at all. Arranged on a plate for the case, they seem to naturally fit together into a whorling, floral circle, the most beautiful thing on display. And yet no one buys them. They are my secret. I take them home and cook them for myself. And for Eric, of course.

I've spent a lot of time thinking about D, about the desolation I feel without him. I wake up with him in my head, go to sleep with him still there, drink and drink to try to make him go away. Even the butchery, that blessed distraction, that way I can take a knife and do something new, break something apart to make something else beautiful, understand something, a body, its parts, the logic of it—even that chases the memory of my old lover, the longing for him, to the far edges of my mind, but not away. He's always there when I quit for the day, wash up, drive back to the city or to my small rental apartment. Retreating into the dark with my iPod for company (all the songs reminding me of him) is like watching a fire dying in the wilderness at night, the creeping thing getting closer, hovering at the edge of the light.

I've thought a lot about that. And yet, sometimes I think I've thought almost not at all about my marriage of ten years, about the man I've known and loved since I was eighteen years old, a child, unformed. About the man who formed me, not like a sculptor, not like a person of intention and power, but like a sapling taking root too closely to its sister, so that they grew and slowly grew until, so many years later, you'd think they were one tree, their branches so entwined, their bark overlapping, their trunks joined. Now that they are essentially one thing, to kill one would be to kill them both. I haven't let myself think much about that. Eric would say—does say—that the reason for this is that I have no room in my besotted, childish mind for him anymore. That D has overtaken me, seduced me, made me small, and that my love for him, my yearning, is all I feel anymore. There's some truth to this version. But there's also a gigantic hole in it.

D does consume me, still. When one has eaten a beautiful dry-aged steak, one remembers it, longs for it. That longing doesn't stop. At least, it hasn't yet, and doesn't feel like it's going anywhere.

But that's not the reason I've not been writing about Eric. The thing is this. Longing, love, lust, all those L words—that's easy to write about. I can think about the way D fucked me, or the way his hair felt silky under my fingers, or that mole on the inside of his index finger, or that tiny lump in his earlobe—and I'm there. I'm living it again. I'm remembering something I had and don't have anymore, something I don't have to imagine doing without because I'm doing without it. I may cry afterward, from the loss, but there's pleasure in it as well.

But to think about Eric, now, after these years of pain, is to contemplate something incomprehensible to me. Separation.

Of course I've thought about it. We both have. We've even done it. But because I've spoken the words, because I've lived without him for a period of time, doesn't mean I understand it. Eric's right, I don't think about our marriage that much, not in the way I think about being in bed with D. But it's for the same reason I don't ponder my veins, or the floor of my room. I don't ponder because I don't even see the world without it. It's too big, or buried too deep, with edges that thin out to nothingness, binding itself to everything else. It's embedded in my dark, precious flesh.

Gwen speaks, sympathetically, of a "clean break." She sees the pain we have been putting ourselves through, and she doesn't get it. Why we inflict such torture. Why we still stand like boxers who can't throw the punches anymore but have the unconquerable advantage of not being able to fall down. "A clean break." (*Divorce,* a word I won't permit, can't even take seriously.) As if we were just cracking open a joint. As if we could just apply enough pressure, push hard enough, and come loose from each other with a satisfying pop and a slow, clean drip. She, our closest friend, doesn't quite realize that we're one thing, Eric and I. Not the "one flesh" bullshit of the wedding ceremony. But one bone. You can't snap a bone in two with a delicious pop. You have to hack, saw, destroy.

When I cut up the rib bones to take home for a slow-cooked Sunday supper, the band saw makes a buzzing roar and the pleasant smell of scorched bone drifts to my nostrils. They will make a warming stew for a chilly night. I bag them up, along with my oxtails, say my good-byes, and head home, two hours back to the city. On the way there, my thoughts are predictably filled with D. Part of me imagines driving to his apartment, knocking, making him let me in. But I don't. I drive home, where my universe awaits, to make oxtail soup.

All this, the short ribs and sex and Fleisher's and D, these are things that, heartbreaking though it might be to contemplate, I can imagine doing without. I can't imagine that about Eric. Which means, in a strange way, that I can't really see him.

But I'm getting there, coming closer. Or maybe I can feel his absence getting closer. Another thing edging in with the shrinking reach of the campfire's circle of light. That possibility. And that scares me. It seems horrible that in order to see my dear husband I have to be able to picture my world without him. But maybe I shouldn't be so afraid. Dreaming it doesn't have to make it so. I can think of a life without short ribs, but that doesn't mean I have to live it.

Maybe, just maybe, seeing us for what we are, both together and apart, will make our dark worlds a little less scary.

10
The Dying Art

EVERYTHING HAS SUNK into gray, still, icy winter. Nothing seems to move—not me, not Eric, not this paralyzing need and sorrow. Even the butcher shop has become routine, a pleasant enough routine, just as my marriage has become a pleasant routine, usually, marred only by the occasional late-night crying session or insinuating comment.

Out of the blue, one day, while I'm stocking the freezer in the front of the shop—quart-sized containers of duck stock, packages of dog food patties, locally made yogurt—I get that back-pocket buzz.

So are you fucking somebody? Just wondering.

I go red, self-consciously turn my face to the open freezer door while I rack my brain to think of what I've done now. Other than Jessica and, I suspect, Josh, none of the gang up here knows much of anything about any of this, and I don't want them to now. I type with my back turned to the meat counter.

What?!! No! Why?

I just figured. . . . Whatever. Do what you have to do.

I'm not DOING anything!

And I'm not. There was a time not so long ago when I was, when I tried to dull the ache with a handful of anonymous encounters, rough and unpleasant. But it didn't work; I only wound up being both hurt and bored. Bored automatically by any other men who wanted me, their panting, the resentful sense of obligation their want made me feel, their lack of imagination and intelligence— evident in both their copious spelling errors and the eagerness with which they wanted to fuck me. Because they gave me their attention for such a pittance, they weren't worthy to give it.

All of this is just the tiny tip of the lethal iceberg of all I can't bear to talk to Eric about, even though he knows it, or some of it, anyway. The fear I feel at the prospect of simply speaking is akin to the terror of being physically beaten, though my gentle-hearted husband would never in a million years do such a thing. I bear the sorrow of not being able to talk to my best friend because it hurts less than imagining the stark fear of talking to him.

Sometimes, though, it surfaces, briefly, in the middle of sleep-less nights of tossing. Four a.m. always the dark hour.

"I hate that you love that asshole!"

I told Jessica that we never fight, and that is mostly the truth. I hesitate to even call these late-night outbursts "fights," because that suggests a mutuality, or common field of battle. What it is instead is the shedding of the patchwork of defenses Eric has built up to be able to live with me in peace every day. His eyes fly open; he is suddenly awake. He sighs loudly, tosses, mutters. I am instantly as wide-awake as he, but I keep my eyes studiously closed, try mightily to keep my breath even and slow, as if he'll not unleash his anger on me if I play possum convincingly enough. The more he tosses, the more still I become. And sometimes it works. Sometimes, on lucky early mornings, he drifts back to sleep by around six thirty or seven without having said anything more than a grunted "Oh, Julie" that I can pretend to have slept through. Other nights, he grabs me suddenly, by the shoulders, shakes me. And he makes the one declaration he has spent the last hours working over in his mind, the one terrible, heartbroken, angry, justified lament:

"Why don't you just tell me to *leave?*"

"I don't want...I don't know...I..." I try to speak, but there are only two words I can say that are both true and not so hurtful as to be lethal to both of us. So I sob out all my guilt and love and hurt and sorrow, shuddering. "I'm sorry, so sorry, I'm so sorry..."

And we cry ourselves back to sleep. Awaking at eight thirty, groggy and swollen-eyed, to the yowls of indignant cats—the whine of a Siamese mix with a thyroid problem is *not* to be denied—and to the more affable but increasingly sneezy beseeches of a dog in deep need of a morning constitutional, we gingerly approach discussion as we move through our morning routines achily, as if we've both spent the night being beaten with bags full of oranges.

As he stands naked in the bathroom, waiting for the water in the shower to heat up: "We've just been doing this for so *long.*"

As I pull open a tin of Wellness cat food: "You think I don't wish I could stop?"

As he pauses at the door with his satchel over his shoulder, his hand on the knob: "Will you be home tonight?" (Dreading that the answer will be "no," but also relishing, in some dark place, the sharp, clean stab that "no" would bring.)

"I have nowhere else to be."

"Me neither."

"Maybe couples therapy." I repress a cringe at the suggestion. I don't know why it is that the prospect of counseling feels like a life imprisonment sentence.

"I love you."

"I love you."

The day is filled with e-mails and text messages that are tender and long and, because they are not imbued with the horrors of face-to-face discussion, more direct. We have our most probing talks in cyberspace. And yet mostly they are talks about needing to talk, and then sometime at around four o'clock I tell him I can't handle talking, not tonight, and so I'm going to buy wine instead. And he is kind, he says, "Take care of yourself." The rug lifts easily up to accept the settled dust, and we are okay for a while.

Though Eric, the one of us who yells and accuses, is not the only one with suspicions. I suspect that Eric is not being entirely honest when he says he has nowhere to go. I know that there is the other woman out there, still thinking of him. She's written him passionate, longing e-mails (I snoop too, I am no innocent, just moderately less technologically adept is all); she not only let him into her bed, but continues to speak to him, even after all this time, perhaps with frustration but also with affection and patience and sweetness. I am not angry with him for having her; I am not angry at the woman either, who after all can be accused of nothing more than having better taste in men than I do. I'm not angry, though I'm sure Eric would rather I was. I am simply envious.

In many ways, I think bitterly, he is far less alone than I am. Occasionally at least he can still "accidentally" make out in a cab after a party. At least he is occasionally told he is wanted. I have no one to make out with in a cab. I long just to be kissed.

But it's also not true that I have no place to go. I may not have the solace of sex. But I have Fleisher's. And I try to escape there as often as I can. My bribe to justify the ever-increasing length of my stays is the meat. Eric has grown exceedingly fond of the meat. But the fact is that Eric and I both use my trips upstate as one more way, besides the rivers of wine we dose ourselves with, to hide from each other.

I go, I cut, I drink both together with my friends and, more often, alone. I read and watch movies on my laptop at night. I don't troll for sex, I don't try to get off, I hardly even cry, anymore, and when I do it's quiet and slow. I eat lots of meat. Every now and again, Josh even forces one of his aged steaks on me.

Incredible things, these steaks, once you've trimmed off the blackened detritus that is an inevitable result of dry aging—it is in fact the key to what dry aging is. It's also why dry-aged meat is expensive.

A dry-aged strip steak isn't cherished for the same reason that, say, tenderloin is cherished. A tenderloin is pricey right off the animal. Once you've learned the trick of taking it off, a tenderloin is just about the easiest money you can make as a butcher. Perhaps a minute to remove it, you don't even have to clean it up, trim the fat or silver skin. Just throw it in a Cryovac bag and send it off to some big-city restaurant where some chef will cook it up with a minimum of fuss and a sauce he could make in his sleep, and charge top dollar for this tender, insipid meat his customers so clamor for, a muscle that the animal literally never uses, so that it never sees the exertion and struggle that makes for both toughness and flavor.

But a dry-aged steak is expensive for what's done to it. And, more specifically, what's taken away from it. Between the moment a rib section comes into the shop and when, after three weeks of aging, it is cut on the band saw and trimmed into steaks, it loses fifty percent of its weight. Some of this goes to loss of moisture. The muscles have literally dried out. More is lost to plain old unglamorous rot. The outside edges of the rib section get dark, even black, and slimy. If conditions are right, and Josh is meticulous about the conditions in his cooler, the decay—and that is what it is—continues at an even, controlled pace. There is no mold, no creepy crawlies. But there is the slow breaking down of flesh, some of the inevitabilities of what happens to dead things in the very best of circumstances. While the flavor of the muscle's interior is intensifying into the quintessence of beef, and growing impossibly, meltingly tender, the protective outside edges are merely drying, aging, "going over." It's inedible, it's got to go.

The result is the best meat you can buy. But there's a lot less of it.

So one night I am cooking up one of the steaks Josh has given me over my strong objections. He very nearly had to use force, which I would not put past him at all.

Cooking these steaks is a somewhat nerve-wracking business because they are so expensive, and while they are still delectable if a little overdone, it seems a heartbreaking shame to miss out on the melting, chewy, meaty perfection of an ideally medium-rare aged strip steak. I follow Josh's directions to the letter.

JOSH'S PERFECT STEAK

> 1 100% grass-fed, 21-day-aged, 1½-inch-thick bone-in
> New York strip steak
> 1 tablespoon canola or safflower oil (optional) for sea-
> soning the pan
> Coarse sea salt or kosher salt to taste
> Coarsely ground pepper to taste
> 1 teaspoon softened butter (Josh insists on butter from
> grass-fed cows)
> 2 teaspoons extra-virgin olive oil

Preheat the oven to 350°F.

Remove the steak from the refrigerator and let it stand uncovered for 20 to 30 minutes before cooking. Pat the steak dry to remove any excess moisture.

Place a heavy, ovenproof sauté pan, preferably stainless steel or cast iron, over very high heat. If the pan is not well seasoned, put 1 tablespoon canola or safflower oil in the pan.

(Use ovenproof pans *only!!!* "No plastic-handled pans!" Jessica always warns her customers, yet always there is some moron, irate or contrite, with stories of ruined cookware, burning plastic drooping, that horrid toxic smell...)

Generously season the steak with salt and pepper right before you put it in the pan. Sear one side of the steak until a nice brown crust starts to form, about 2 minutes. Do not move the steak or press down on it in any way. Then flip the steak gently, using tongs (never pierce the steak with a fork!), and sear the other side.

Remove the pan from the stovetop, top the steak with the butter and olive oil, and place the pan in the oven. Check the temperature of the steak after five minutes with a meat thermometer. For a rare steak, remove it from the oven at 115 to 120°F. Grass-fed meat, because it is so lean, will cook much more quickly than conventionally raised beef. (Not to get your nerves any more wracked or anything.) Place the steak on a cutting board or platter and let it rest for five minutes. The internal temperature of the steak will continue to rise. After five minutes, slice the steak into strips and arrange on a warmed platter. A New York strip can actually serve two people, but I will often eat this all by myself.

I have not even bothered with a salad. This steak will be all I need.

So I've cooked the steak, and as I'm standing there waiting with my glass of wine, just sort of staring at the meat as it rests, crusted brown and aromatic on a plate beside the stove, I'm dreamily imagining how it will soon melt richly in my mouth, make my head fall back with pleasure, and as I'm imagining this, something pops into my mind. A thought I immediately recognize as tortured, yet it remains somehow irresistible, a scab to be picked.

What the hell else am I doing up here, idling, alone, if not dry-aging myself? And if that's the case, what's going to wind up rotting and being cut away? Is it our marriage that must succumb? Or maybe it's all the rest that is expendable, that is the peeled-off age. The affairs, the hurt, D, all thrown away to find the tenderness of a new, sweeter marriage.

Or maybe even I myself, my whole being, must be sloughed off something or someone else. I am the part that has to be discarded to make for something great, in which I'll have no role.

I'm leaking tears now as I stand, tongs in hand, watching a pool of pink juice that's formed under the meat on the plate. Maybe when I've sat in my juices long enough, everything will come clear, I won't want the rot, whatever it is, will see it as useless, no longer necessary. Is anything outside of butchery, outside of metaphor, ever that clean?

The steak is beautiful. I take two home to New York the next day, to share with Eric. I don't share my thoughts with him. He wouldn't understand, or rather he would understand far too well. And for now it's enough, just the pleasure of giving him that flavor, maybe explaining a bit about the aging process, about the sacrifice. Of moisture, that is, of flesh and fat.

Two days later I am walking up Union Square from my yoga class along the east side of the park. And I see D.

It's not a surprise, exactly. The only surprise is that it took so long. I'm at Union Square at least three or four times a week, it's the center of my life in the city. This happens to New Yorkers a lot, I think—periods of life defined by, mapped out on, some string of blocks, some neighborhood. Though Eric and I lived in Brooklyn when we were first married, much of our lives during those years played out on a few blocks of the East Village, between First and Avenue C, between 7th Street and 10th. An earlier period had me daily frequenting the West Village, Bleecker between Sixth Avenue and Seventh, Carmine and Bedford. For the last few years now, it's been Union Square. I explain, when Gwen or another friend asks why this is, that it's where my therapist is, my yoga studio, Whole Foods and the greenmarket and Republic, where the bartender knows me and pours my Riesling before I get up on my barstool. And all these things are true. But it all started with D. D works around here. Our affair began here, was carried out here—meetings at the Barnes & Noble, make-out sessions at the entrance to the subway or sitting on the grass of the square. Ended here. And the truth is I've been lingering here ever since, waiting to see him again. The only real point of interest—and if it's not just my superstitious mind, this may make a sort of cosmic sense—is that it happens now, when for once, exhausted and maybe a bit blissed out by an hour and a half of inexpertly rendered warrior poses, I'm not thinking of him at all.

I had wondered if I'd even recognize him if I saw him walking down the street, but I spot him in an instant, from a block away, with a throng of people between us, just the top of his head with that crimson hat and a brief glimpse of his gait. He's coming right toward me. I've not seen him in months, I suddenly can't breathe at all, my ears are full of droning.

I stare desperately at the screen of my BlackBerry until he passes. I don't try to catch his eye, and he either doesn't see me or has pretended not to.

He's living in the world, the same world I'm living in, only I'm in this endless eddy and he's floated on. He's free. I'm sloughed off. I want to throw up.

My brother wrote another refrigerator magnet poem, when he was probably nineteen or twenty:

> *When the flood comes*
> *I will swim to a symphony*
> *go by boat to some picture show*
> *and maybe I will forget about you*

Nineteen years old. How did he know, way back then? How is it I know only now?

11
Hanging Up the Knife

"As long as this candle burns, that's how long we'll be missing you here at Fleisher's.... So, approximately twenty-four to twenty-six hours."

"Ba-da-BUMP!"

We are standing in a circle in the middle of the shop half an hour past closing, drinking champagne out of chipped ceramic mugs. The table has been wiped and salted, our aprons are in the dirty laundry bin, my leather hat sits atop my packed bag. It's my last day at the shop; I'd agreed to apprentice for six months, and I've done it. The sublet is up on my apartment; my husband is expecting me home, for good.

The candle is one of Aaron's latest endeavors, a golden pillar about six inches high. It's made from beef tallow I helped him render. He hands it to me with a flourish. His mustache is by now a dark Snidely Whiplash thing that actually curls up at the ends. Colin now sports great long muttonchop sideburns. Josh of course still has his porntastic facial hair. (One of his favorite T-shirts reads: GUNS DON'T KILL PEOPLE. PEOPLE WITH MUSTACHES KILL PEOPLE.) The Great Facial Hair Face-off approaches. People are beginning to make bets, and Aaron is pondering prizes.

I've received other gifts today as well. From Jesse, who has decided not to participate in any mustache growing, I get a carved marble egg, veined pink and black, and a small stand to set it on. "Maybe it will help your writing, I thought. Like a sort of object for meditation or something."

Josh hands me a CD in a case labeled A GOODBYE MIX FOR JULIE—♥ JUAN. "He was in the store the other day. I told him you were following him, back out into the bad old world. He dropped this by."

"How is he? I miss him."

"You and me both, sister. But he's doing good. The new char-cuterie job pays more than I ever could. He'd have been crazy to pass it up. Onward and upward, y'know?"

"I suppose so." Last night I had a dream that I was about halfway up a sheer cliff, endlessly high. Up ahead of me was, it seemed, every-one I'd ever known—the guys at the shop, my family, Gwen, Eric, D—and they were pulling ahead, climbing fast, leaving me behind. I tried to call out but found I had no voice, that my words slurred and died in my mouth, that I could not be heard. I awoke with a terrified lurch, unable to scream. I have this dream all the time.

In addition to the candle, Aaron has also presented me with a small, ornate gilt frame in which he has placed a picture of a cow, and over it the same motto that he says hangs on the wall of the office at the slaugh-terhouse where he has been training for the last couple of months: "If we are not suppose to eat animals, why are they made of meat?"

"It took me forever to get that right, just like it is in John's office. Spell check kept switching 'suppose' to 'supposed.' But I had to have it exactly."

"How very you. Well, it's fantastic. Thank you. Will go right on my desk."

My desk at home, I mean, which has become a cluttered altar

to at least one of my obsessions. A vintage Spanish poster is pinned up over it—an advertisement with an image of Don Quixote riding a hog, a fat ham skewered on his lance. The surface is stacked with butchery manuals and cookbooks and stacks of papers held down by a black stone, carefully shaped, round, concave on both sides. It's called a "chunkee stone."

"*C'mon. There have got to be like a thousand of those in that cabinet.*"

Eric remained firm. "Nine hundred and seventy-seven, actually. You know how I know that?"

"*No one is going to miss one itty-bitty ancient artifact. It would be really romantic…*"

"*Julie. I can't.*"

"*You can't, or you won't?*"

"*I can't because I won't.*"

"*One early Native American field hockey puck. It doesn't seem so much to ask.*"

It was his first job in the city, at the Museum of Natural History; he catalogued their North American archaeology collection. Lots of beads, lots of chunkee stones, which are in fact exactly what I say—ancient field hockey pucks. I coveted them, loved the way they felt, heavy and cool in the hand.

Eric wound up hiring a stoneworker to make one for me. Which was a beautiful, touching gesture. Part of me still wishes he'd just stolen one.

I LOVE all the gifts I've been given today, but the best one came hours ago.

All morning I'd been "helping" Aaron make a *porchetta* he was giving some friends for their wedding reception. A whole pig, boned out, seasoned, and stuffed with an insane mélange of indulgence—garlic, onions, truffles, and several brined pork loins wrapped in bacon—then rolled up around a huge spit worked through the hog's open mouth and down the length of the creature.

I'd done nothing much more than help slice garlic and watch, agog, as he took all of the bones but for the skull out of the animal, keeping it all in one piece, until it was a gigantic, limp shawl of pork flesh. I did help roll the loins in bacon, and line them up end to end inside the carcass, and strew the entire thing with garlic and truffle slices; did help pull the pig around the spit and truss it tightly, a loop of heavy-duty wire in the place of the usual twine, every six inches, yanked until we had produced a long hog-cylinder, six feet of it, the head on one end the only variation to what was otherwise a completely uniform, skin-on, yellowish pink tube of meat. It looked so much like a penis that there was no joke to be made among even these embracers of the obvious. All you could really do was raise your eyebrows at it, and say, in high-pitched Josh style, "Oh-kaaaay..."

Aaron had headed back to try to clear out a space in the cooler for the giant thing, a neat trick given that the cooler was overflowing with meat as it was. It took him a while to reemerge, and when he did it was just to poke his head around the steel door and call to me, "Hey, Jules, come back here for a sec. Need some help."

So I headed back to the cooler, where I found Aaron, Josh, and Jessica all crowded in among the shelves of bagged subprimals, great heaps of bottom rounds and chuck eyes. They were all three atwinkle with anticipation. "Close your eyes." I did. Waited. "Okay, now you can open them."

When I did, Josh was holding out a black canvas cutlery case, with a shoulder strap, the kind every culinary student possesses, as ubiquitous as chef's checks and clogs.

"Ah, thanks, guys."

"Open it."

I tore open the Velcro fasteners and unfolded the thing, laying it out on the table. There were three knives inside. A five-inch boning knife, a foot-long scimitar, and a hugely heavy cleaver. "Oh!" I breathed. "These are great!"

Josh was practically bouncing up and down. "Read the inscription."

Each of the knives had words engraved on the blade, in delicate letters. *Julie Powell, Loufoque.*

"It's *louchébem.* You know, what Aaron was talking about, French-butcher pig latin? It means 'crazy lady.'"

I burst into tears.

"Oh no. You are *not* going to start bawling on me like a little bitch." Josh turned on his heel and marched out of the cooler.

Jessica hooted. "He is such a pussy."

"Jules!" Aaron pulled me in for a hug. "You're a butcher now! The apprenticeship is over."

"Thank you, guys, so, so much. Really."

"And look!" Aaron took out the cleaver and pointed at the brand name carved into the other side of the blade.

"Awesome. Just what I always wanted, my own big Dick."

"Ba-da-BUMP."

"I'm here all week."

"Yeah, I wish."

I teared up again, just a tad. "Yeah, me too."

"All right, all right," said Jessica. "Enough already. Back to work, guys. It's not even three o'clock yet."

NOW IT'S close to eight p.m., and we're well on our way to finishing off the champagne. I eye the rapidly emptying bottle, knowing I'll not be able to avoid the inevitable much longer, the good-bye speech, the drive home, the moment when I acknowledge that I don't have a place at this table anymore. I'm afraid I'm going to cry again. In fact I know I will; I'm just hoping I can wait until I'm alone in the car to do it.

"Julie, it's been really great having you here." It's getting to be toast time. Jessica holds up her mug. "Just having another woman around, for one thing. My *God,* the testosterone overload around here sometimes, *Jesus.*" She gives me a tight hug. "Seriously. We're going to miss you."

"Nah, she'll be back. She can't stay away." Josh pours me a

refill. The champagne is cheap and pink and I wish I could stay here all night drinking it. Wish I didn't have to go home.

"So, Jules, what did you learn today?"

"Um...that Josh is a big wimp who freaks out at a few tears?"

"That, and?"

"That, and...oh, well, there was the porchetta. But I didn't really learn how to do it. I just watched you."

"I promise, next time you need to bone out a whole pig and tie it to a spit, you'll be able to figure it out."

"I suppose so. Man, I've seen some *pretty* phallic things around here, but that took the cake, I have to say."

"Sometimes a six-foot-long tube of pig is just a six-foot-long tube of pig."

"Uh-huh. And then sometimes not."

Hailey, sweet little strawberry-blond Hailey, sips with responsible conservatism at the wine she is too young to drink legally. "So you're going to be coming back, right?"

"If you guys'll have me, yes. I don't have a place to stay anymore, but I'll come visit."

Josh flipped his hands at me dismissively. "There's always our couch to sleep on, until you buy your own place."

"Buy my own place?"

"Real estate shopping, you and me. Next time you're up. And you know what else, crazy butcher lady?" Josh points at the time sheets in their slots hung on the wall just behind the counter. "From now on, you're on the clock."

"Oh please."

"Fuck you, 'Oh please.' I'm not having any unpaid slackers on my table. I'm going to put you to serious work. None of this an-hour-to-break-down-a-shoulder crap."

"All right, all right..." Finally I raise my glass, reluctantly. "You guys, thank you so much for letting me stick around here. I've...this has been just the greatest...I..." I'm not going to start bawling, I'm not. "I don't want to leave."

Josh pulls his lips down and his eyebrows up into a sad clown face that he manages to make at once mocking and sincere, almost a little teary himself. "Awww...now if you cry again, I'm going to bitch-slap you with Aaron's *porchetta*."

It's completely dark outside now. I have my duffel bag and my big grocery sack of meat, my candle and my marble egg and my little picture frame and my inscribed knives. It's getting late. Eric is waiting. I've got to go home. My throat constricts.

I sit in the driver's seat with one hand on the wheel and the other fitting the key in the ignition, in the parking lot around the corner from Fleisher's. My eyes cloud with tears as I begin to turn the key, and then I just allow myself to sob, forehead on the wheel, shoulders hitching as I suck in air. I cry and cry.

There's a knock on the passenger seat window. I straighten up with a start; it's Jessica. Hurriedly wiping away tears, I reach over to open the door, and she climbs right in.

"Okay. Are you seriously crying in a parking lot because it's your last day?"

"Uh-huh. Or, no. I don't know. I just...I can't even...I just want to...to run away, I guess." I squirm in embarrassment at this childish, childishly cruel, admission.

"So run away."

"No, no, I can't. I don't want to, really. I just—" I sob again, twice, ashamed of it. "I feel like I'm boxing myself back up or something."

"Julie, I know we haven't really talked about this since, you know, dinner that time. But maybe you ought to, I don't know—"

I surprise myself with a vehement shake of the head, don't even let her get out the sentence I know she's forming, my words coming in a rush through harsh breathing. "No! I mean...yes, maybe...but...look. I don't want to...I don't know...lose...anyone. It's just...I don't want to lose myself either. That's just so horrifically cheesy, God." My forehead falls back onto the steering wheel. After a minute I feel Jessica's palm light on my back.

"Why don't you take a trip? Just by yourself, I mean. You

know I spent, like, six months in Japan? Best thing I ever did. Stay in a love hotel. I'm telling you, you haven't *lived*."

I sniffle. "A love hotel?"

"Oh, yeah. They're great. These hotels where you can go for just an hour or the whole night. You pick your room from a panel of buttons, like a vending machine or something. And the rooms are all decorated with, like, disco balls and anime and shit."

I start trying to steady my breathing. "Do you know I've never been to a foreign country by myself?"

"Well, there you go! That settles it. I know what you need to do. You need to go on a Grand Meat Tour. Go to Japan. Try horse sashimi or, like, feed some beer to a Kobe beef steer or some craziness. Go to Vancouver, Josh knows a guy who does great charcuterie there, or—wait! Argentina! One of the chefs we sell meat to, Ignacio, used to live in Argentina, I think. He could totally hook you up down there. Where have you always wanted to go?"

"I don't know. Eastern Europe maybe? Africa? Tons of places."

"Well, I think this is the time to do it. You're going to miss the butcher shop? So go find more!"

I shrug, wipe my face smearily. "I couldn't leave Eric like that."

"Julie? You're leaving him now. You think he can't feel that?"

Jessica climbs back out of the car once I've gotten myself cleaned up a little and we've hugged our good-byes. I finally start the car. The drive goes by quickly and uneventfully, the usual slide, down through the dark across the Tappan Zee, into the sodium orange haze of the Bronx, over the Triborough, where, instead of heading into Queens as I should, I take a right, making a detour into Manhattan. I trawl past D's building, peer through the windows into the foyer. I put the car into park for a moment or two but don't turn off the ignition. It's an old, torturing comfort of mine to idle there, half cringing in anticipation of actually catching sight of him, of him catching sight of me, imagining some world in which I take what I want, where I could do more than just pine, where I could walk through that door, ring up to his apartment, find him there for me with a ribbon around his neck like a puppy.

After a moment I put the car back in drive and pull away. Twenty minutes later I'm climbing the stairs to my apartment. My eyes are no longer puffy enough for Eric to notice; he just calls out his usual greeting: "Mommy's home!"

"At last."

Robert the Dog sniffs me perfunctorily and lies arthritically back down. Maxine the Cat reaches out a paw to beg affection from her perch on the kitchen island. Eric is drinking Charles de Fère, the same cheap pink champagne I'd brought upstate for our good-bye toasts. It's known at our local wine store as "Julie Juice," I drink it so often. He puts down his glass as I walk in the door, and he hugs me. Not a hard hug, just a long one, with his chin resting on the top of my head. "At last." He doesn't comment on my meat smell, and now, I suppose, he won't ever have to, not for a long while.

Aping the actions of contentment can, sometimes, get to feeling almost like contentment itself, something I've learned in the last two and a half years. So I get busy roasting a chicken while Eric pours me a glass. "I'm so glad you're home."

"I know. I'm glad too."

And it's not that I'm lying, not that the chicken roasting doesn't smell like home, that the cat purring on the kitchen counter doesn't sound like comfort, that my husband's embrace doesn't feel like love. It's not that at all. It's just that the world was feeling bigger to me, and here it begins to seem small, sometimes.

"HOME AT LAST" CHICKEN

    4 red potatoes, not peeled, coarsely chopped
    1 medium onion, coarsely chopped
    Extra-virgin olive oil
    Salt
    Pepper
    1 whole chicken, about 3 pounds, rinsed and patted dry
    Hot paprika
    1 half lemon

Preheat the oven to 400°F.

Place the chopped potatoes and onions in a bowl. Pour a healthy glug of olive oil over them, season with salt and pepper, and toss with your hands or a spoon to coat. Set a rack in a roasting pan and arrange the vegetables around and under the rack.

Smear the chicken skin with more olive oil and season it fairly aggressively, inside and out, with salt, pepper, and paprika. Tuck the lemon half up its bum and place it on the rack. If you want to ensure that the breast meat turns out moist, place it breast down. (Eric and I are dark meat people, so we don't care so much about the breast meat—crackly skin is more important. We roast it breast side up.)

Allow 15 minutes per pound of bird, plus 10 minutes or so to grow on. Open your first bottle of wine and watch something on the TV while you're waiting—nothing too fraught with difficult emotions or likely to bring up uncomfortable memories or situations. Nothing from the seventies, no *Dog Day Afternoon* or *Rosemary's Baby*. Something familiar, with the sort of sharp dialogue that you and your husband enjoy most particularly and particularly enjoy enjoying together. A little Joss Whedon something, perhaps, to soothe the soul. Press the Pause button a time or two to get up and stir the potatoes and onions around, so they don't stick.

The chicken is done when the legs wiggle easily in their sockets. Cut off the legs and thighs, all in one piece, the whole limb, and plate along with a scoop of the potatoes and onions, a handful of bagged salad. This can serve as many as six people, but a hungry husband and wife can make serious inroads themselves.

Eat in front of the TV, with more wine—something cheap and pink and reliable—until you fall asleep. Tomorrow, start trying to live in your life again.

PART II

Journeywoman

Our two souls therefore, which are one,
Though I must go, endure not yet
A breach, but an expansion,
Like gold to aery thinness beat.

—JOHN DONNE,
"A Valediction Forbidding Mourning"

This is the world we've made. Isn't it wonderful?
—ANYA THE VENGEANCE DEMON,
Buffy the Vampire Slayer

12

Carnicería

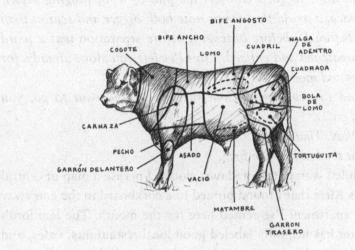

I'M STANDING ON an empty street corner in the Congreso district of Buenos Aires, well before dawn. It's very cold, my breath is showing. I hadn't counted on northern Argentina ever being cold, mostly because it almost never is. I've layered the heaviest clothes I brought with me here, a long-sleeved T-shirt under a sweater under my Brooklyn Industries sweatshirt, but it still isn't quite enough to keep out the chill. I'm waiting for a man. My heart is beating furiously.

"You should do it. You've never really traveled alone. One of those unexpected consequences of being with the same frakking person your entire adult life."

With the exception of D, he doesn't say, an exception like that of the one meteor that gets through and destroys 830 square miles of the Russian taiga.

"You've traveled." I am staring at the screen of my laptop, where a Mobissimo.com reservation for a flight to Buenos Aires

awaits a single click from my hesitant finger to be confirmed.
"You've been everywhere."

"Well, exactly. I've done my wandering. You should have your
chance. It's a big bad old world out there."

"So everyone keeps telling me."

*I do want to go. I can feel the pull of it, of flinging myself
into space, a world that seems now both bigger and scarier than
it did before D, before butchery, before separation was a word
that threatened and enticed.* "But I've left you alone already, for
months and months—"

"And I've survived. I will survive. If you want to go, you
should go."

"Okay. Thank you."

I hit the button. Confirm.

While I wait in the predawn gloom, I peruse a map of central
Buenos Aires that I found pinned to a corkboard in the entryway
of the apartment I've rented here for the month. The landlord's
daughter has helpfully labeled good local restaurants, cafés, and
tango bars, with neat dots. I knew that I would become instantly
disoriented once I stepped out onto the street, so I unpinned the
map, folded it up, and stuffed it in my pocket, along with the
apartment key, which is large and old-fashioned, like a key that
would open up a secret room in a Harry Potter book, before I left
this morning. The pointy end of the key I have tucked between
fore- and index fingers, much as I'd hold a meat hook. It's an old
self-defense trick I learned ages ago in some silly woman's mag,
and though I don't expect any sort of harassment, it's become a
habit of mine when I'm alone in unfamiliar surroundings, which
usually means the East Village after midnight or some gas station
parking lot that seems a little dark, but now means an entire new
city on an entire new continent, more alone than I've ever been.

I'm waiting at the edge of the Plaza del Congreso, a broad
expanse of grass and statues at the end of Avenida de Mayo, but-
tressed on one end by the Congress building. It clearly was aiming

for grandiosity when it was constructed but has instead wound up sort of wilted and sketchy. Under a tree near a statue of someone or other, there is gathered a group of guys bundled up in heavy coats, huddled around a fire in an oil can. They do not notice me or seem in any way threatening, but of course solo American women have it built into our DNA to avoid men gathered around oil can fires. The plaza is dotted with well-fed-looking, shiny-coated dogs, most of them colored like Rottweilers but small and basically terrier-shaped, who seem very much the home-is-where-I-lay-my-hat sort. They negotiate the broken sidewalks, the trash cans from which they glean scraps, the traffic, heavy even at this early hour, the blare of honking cabs, about ten times better than I think I ever could. They look both ways before crossing the street, they know when the walk sign turns green, they never stumble, and they always know where they're going.

Despite all this evidence of decrepitude, the buildings and avenues and people that move among them exude a slightly tired, European elegance. A few blocks to the south, if I'm reading the map correctly, if know where in the world I am, is Avenida Corrientes, a long strip of cafés and intellectual bookstores, where poets and students and political revolutionaries once drank and argued and wrote before dictators rounded them up, drugged them, and dumped them out of planes into the wide Río de la Plata. It is something nearly impossible to imagine, here in this city that today feels far more like Paris than anyplace else. I suppose visitors to Paris in, say, 1965 must have felt the same way, back before the Occupation was ancient history, was a more unbelievable, and appallingly recent, atrocity.

Santiago pulls up in the back of a taxi and I climb in beside him. He is a handsome man, perhaps even gorgeous, tall and lean with a shaved head (the stubble is dark), large brown eyes, and a ready yet slightly shy smile. I've met him once before, at his restaurant, Standard, a stylish bistro in the chichi neighborhood of Palermo, and I've already developed a bit of a crush. He speaks inexpert English, and my Spanish is nearly nonexistent. It doesn't matter. The cabbie pulls away from the curb. "Are you ready?" Santiago asks as he leans over to kiss my cheek in greeting.

I widen my eyes and shrug with a saucy smile. "Ready as I'll ever be."

I speak in the sparkling voice I've found myself employing since I arrived in Argentina, the flirtatious, humorous tone of an American Dame. Traveling by myself is so far proving to be rather like playing dress-up. No one here knows anything about me, so I can be anyone I want. Here I've decided to be all twinkle and sass and arched eyebrows, blithe drinking and sunny disregard. I wish I had a jaunty Katharine Hepburn–style pants suit with shoulder pads, a cigarette holder, a little dog to carry around in my purse. Maybe an eye patch.

When we first met, I told Santiago that I was a butcher, or wanted to be, and that I wanted to learn all about meat in Argentina. And with an inexplicable dedication to fulfilling the whim of the friend of a friend—he's a friend of Ignacio, the chef in New York who Jessica and Josh work with—he's arranged to show me all sorts of things. This morning we're headed to Mercado de Liniers, the largest cattle market in Argentina, a country of cattle markets. Mercado de Liniers is so famous that the whole neighborhood—a working-class place far from the classy neighborhoods of central Buenos Aires, chockablock with down-and-dirty *carnicerías* and *salumerías*—is named after it. The Mercado district. It's famous like Wall Street is famous; what happens in the early morning hours at Mercado de Liniers determines how much beef is going to cost in every restaurant and grocery store in the country, and in Europe as well, where Argentine beef is a coveted import. Santiago, a prominent chef, has agreed to take me on a tour.

It's still not yet dawn when the cab pulls onto the cobblestone drive around the market. I hop from one foot to another in the chill as Santiago talks to a guy in a down jacket at a guard post. He doesn't seem particularly happy to see me, though maybe I'm just paranoid and it's too damned early in the morning. I'm not sure where I get the feeling that I have no business being here, whether it's just a delusion of mine or if I'm picking up on some actual hesitancy, because I'm a girl or an American or a writer or just funny-looking.

But after a bit of back-and-forth, Santiago nodding deferentially and occasionally cutting his brown eyes briefly over to me, the guy shrugs, points past the fence to something or other, then thumbs us through the turnstile. Beyond, there is a wide boulevard of packed dirt, smelling pleasantly, pungently, of cow shit, lined on either side with metal railings punctuated by cattle gates that open onto warrens of corrals. Dogs loll about, not pets who have the slightest interest in getting a scratch behind the ears, but workers waiting for their job to begin. Honest-to-God cowboys on horseback are hanging around too—not called "cowboys," of course, but rather *gauchos*—wearing jeans and windbreakers and sneakers or rubber boots, and distinctive berets, red or black.

There are prefab buildings here and there alongside the gates, the offices of the various meat vendors, and stairways up to a winding network of catwalks, covered over with simple tin roofs. When we climb up to walk one, I realize just how vast this place really is, an immense maze of chutes and stock pens I can't see to the end of, illuminated at this hour when the sky is still a dark though lightening purple by massive sodium lamps, and every inch of the place is filled, it seems, with teeming cow flesh, pressed in close, lowing, flicking tails and shifting, shitting, drinking from great troughs of water.

Not every inch, though, really. Santiago explains, leaning against the railing beside me as we gaze out at the view. "The Mercado can hold thirty thousand head. Today? Maybe ten thousand today. Not too busy."

We are waiting for a call from Santiago's friend, one of the purveyors who works the market. Before too much time has passed, as the sun is finally just beginning to render the harsh lighting unnecessary, his cell goes off in his pocket, and he answers. "Okay, let's go." We head back down the stairs, and across the cobbled road that runs through the center of the market, to one of the prefab buildings where a barrel-chested guy in a parka and hefty boots stands waiting by the door. We all shake hands and do the cheek kiss thing, as if we were standing outside a restaurant instead of in the middle of a vast corral smelling of cow manure. Then he lets us into his office.

I get a quick lesson in beef selling, as done in the Mercado de Liniers. The sales forms to be filled out, which corral, number of animals, and type—*norcilla, vacilla, tornero*—all commanding different prices, depending on the quality, of course, the fat ratio, and conformation. He talks about the sometimes-checkered history of the market, a Wild West sort of past that involves cheating ranchers and unscrupulous middlemen. He himself is a middleman, though not unscrupulous. He is in fact proud of the good name he has maintained in the industry. Santiago claps him on the back with a wide smile. "I only buy beef from him. He is the *best*."

Outside, a bell is clanging. That's the signal for us to pull our coats back on and head out the door again. The sun has fully risen by now. It's a bright fall morning. We climb back up onto the catwalks that thread around every corral. There's now a small crowd of people—men, actually, all men, I seem to be the only woman around—trailing in a line behind a guy in a Mercado de Liniers fleece vest and a beret. He carries hooked under one arm a battery-powered bullhorn, with a CB-like attachment at the end of a spiraling cord, which he speaks into. In his other hand he holds a small metal hammer, like something the snooping detective might get hit over the head with in an old noir film. He's followed by a man with a legal pad.

Before each animal pen, crammed with a herd of cattle from a different seller, the man stops, beats the mallet twice against the railing, and begins rattling off numbers in Spanish: "*Ocho cinco, ocho cinco, nueve? Nueve, nueve cinco? Nueve cinco. Diez? Diez?*" Men are murmuring to him, raising their hands to catch his attention. Then the bidding fizzles out and the auctioneer hammers the mallet once more against the railing, calls, *"Diez."* The guy with the legal pad makes a note, and everyone moves on to the next corral. The whole process takes about thirty seconds, which is good because there are untold cattle to sell. Once the highest bid has been accepted, the successful buyer gestures to one of his *gauchos*, who dips what looks like a branding iron into one of the buckets of white paint that are strapped to the railings of the stock pens below and commences to mark every animal in the lot that's just been purchased. Then the cattle are herded out of the corral and off to some other part of the market to be put on trucks. There is a sudden racket of hooves on stone and shouts from the *gauchos,* which accentuates the relative quiet of the auction's proceedings. Everything moves with brisk efficiency and solemnity. There's no joking about, no extraneous conversation.

Most of the buyers are up on the catwalks, but a few prefer to move down among the cattle and *gauchos*. Santiago points out a handsome older man on a good-looking chestnut horse; he wears a beret and wool poncho and has glasses perched on his round nose and a cell phone hanging from his neck. "You see him?" he asks, speaking low so as not to interrupt the flow of bidding. "He is the buyer for Argentina's oldest and largest grocery chain. He is like the mayor here. He sees something he likes, he make a call? His guy up here"—he pats the railing of the catwalk—"buys it for him."

Because I don't understand much of what's being said in the course of the auction, my thoughts stray to the animals themselves. The cattle are…cute. Really cute. They look up at us with liquid eyes, blinking with lovable stupidity. For not the first time in my life, I vow that I'm going to one day buy myself a rescue cow and until the day it dies feed it carrots or whatever it is that cows like. But my sentimentality, here, makes me feel foolish.

The auction is over by ten a.m. "Now. The slaughterhouses close at four o'clock in the afternoon. There are maybe thirty? Maybe thirty slaughterhouses within fifty kilometers of here. All these animals here go there now, and by four thirty they are entirely all killed and cut."

"Damn." That's ten thousand animals, trucked off, slaughtered, and processed in six hours. I myself could break down maybe six chuck shoulders in that length of time, and I would need some serious Darvocet afterward.

We leave the market and walk around the Mercado neighborhood. Broad dusty streets, factories, train tracks. *Carnicerías* with grimy linoleum floors and sour smells, selling cheap meat to poor people. Dump trucks drive by, their beds piled high with cleaned and trimmed bones. The sun is finally warming up the air. Santiago takes me to a *salumería* where he's made an appointment for us.

The *salumería* is something else. Josh would lose it if he got to see this place, honestly. His twin loves of meat and of big, terrifying machinery would achieve a grand apotheosis, like looking into the face of God, that might actually drive him mad. Down long hallways, doors open onto room after room, dim and redolent of the tang of curing meat, ceilings twenty feet high, full of rows and rows of tall scaffolds from which hang thousands upon thousands of aging sausages. Prosciutto in another room, thousands of hog legs hanging. I watch men dressed in whites and hats like Oompa Loompas in Wonka's Television Room filling pig's bladders with finely ground pork for bologna, out of a stuffer ten feet high. Back in his cramped office overlooking the *salumería* floor, the owner feeds us eight varieties of sausage, taking slices off links with a pocketknife and laying them out on a crumpled paper bag.

By now it's lunchtime. Santiago takes me to Parrilla de los Corrales, his favorite spot in the neighborhood. It is bustling with people. With Santiago guiding, we order two plates of beef ribs, grilled sweetbreads, a white bean salad, a bottle of wine, and two coffees. It costs about twenty-seven dollars for the both of us and is wonderful. The wine is decent, the food simple and good, the conversation a bit stilted because of the language thing, but. I find myself bringing out my American Dame act, but Santiago doesn't seem to be as affected by it as I might like him to be. Oh, it's probably for the best. She's going to get me in trouble one day. I've only been in Argentina a week or so, and she already almost has. Thank God she's so good at getting herself out of scrapes.

"Oh darn." The American Dame does a mean Rosalind Russell.

The rotund, grizzled, and well-meaning Brazilian gentleman is drunker than she, by quite a lot. The American Dame can drink men twice her size under the table. He leans up against the doorframe to her charming Buenos Aires apartment, practically panting in his eagerness to get inside. He wants into her pants like a six-year-old wants the biggest teddy bear at the fairground.

The American Dame stops fiddling with her keys and turns on her most sparkling smile. "I just remembered. I was going to buy cigarettes. Do you know where to get them this time of night? Marlboro Lights?"

The American Dame flutters her eyelashes. The gentleman is too charmed to be put out by the implied request. "I will get you cigarettes. Marlboros." He smiles expansively.

"Oh, I couldn't possibly ask you...well, thank you." The American Dame rummages in her purse, pretending to look for pesos. "How much do I owe you?"

The gentleman holds up his hands. "Please, don't insult. I am bringing cigarettes for you."

"Thank you so much!" The American Dame twinkles, kissing a furry cheek. "I'll see you in a bit, then!"

As he stumbles down the stairs, the American Dame unlocks her door and walks inside her cozy studio, kicks off her teetering heels, collapses on her belly onto one of her two single beds, and, most conveniently, passes out. Convenient because, while she sometimes enjoys making a spectacle of herself, letting a man old enough to be her father buy her a drink or an elegant dinner, walk her home and maybe cop a feel on the street in front of her apartment, she doesn't always want to make good on rash promises.

The next morning there is a pack of Marlboro Lights and a matchbook resting on the windowsill outside her apartment door. The American Dame smiles a little sheepishly, opens the package, and lights up, blowing the smoke out her window as she listens to children screaming in Spanish, happily, endlessly, in the schoolyard below.

But the American Dame is clearly not going to get any action today, unless she literally pushes Santiago up against a wall and ravishes the poor man. Instead, he and I finish up our lunch with cups of coffee, and then head out to our last stop of the day, a processing center for a meat distributor called Fura. Here we stand against the wall of a tall, cold, white-tiled room where a dozen Argentine butchers break down an endless line of beef sides.

Butchers, it seems, are butchers everywhere. Everywhere the same smells, the same sights, the same logic, the same sorts of men. Of course these guys are part of a commercial operation, they move fast, they very rarely crack fart jokes—well, that I can understand, anyway. They're always in motion. But there's something about the way they smile at me—it's not exactly welcoming but more a cheerful acceptance of the inconvenience of having me around. And there's something about the way they look at me, or don't look at me, something about the way they move their shoulders as they slice these carcasses into bits. I'd recognize them anywhere.

I've never seen a side of beef broken down like this, right off the hook. All beef comes to Fleisher's already reduced to its eight primal parts. What these guys are doing, or some of them anyway, is work that would be done for Josh at the slaughterhouse. He would love to do it himself, both for the macho thrill factor and because it would save him money, but he just doesn't have the space. His ceiling isn't high enough and can't bear enough weight. Whole sides of hanging beef are about six feet long or more. They hang off hooks that slide on a rail bolted to the ceiling, high enough off the ground that the men can work with them, without screwing up their backs or letting the primal cuts fall to the floor when they come off the carcass.

And it's easy to forget this, since everyone is moving so quickly and casually, and there is just so very much of it, but these things are *heavy*. As in very. Each side is about four hundred pounds, and there are at least a dozen of them hanging at this moment. That is two and a half *tons* of beef. You could make my Subaru Outback out of meat and still have some considerable poundage left over. If the ceiling did cave in, there would be a deadly avalanche of flesh.

The butchers assigned to taking the major pieces off the hook are younger than the men at the table, in their early twenties perhaps, presumably both stronger and less experienced. But they do their jobs assuredly. I'm pleased to recognize much of what they're doing, or at least recognize the results of their speedy slicing. But there's one thing I don't get. "Santiago?" I lean in so he can hear me in the chilly room echoing with sounds of hooks rumbling down their tracks, meat slapping on tables. "What is that flap of meat he's cutting off there? From the outside, near the rear leg?"

"That's the *matambre*. Very popular in Argentina. Very, very good."

"Really?" The *matambre* is one fatty, ragged, rough-looking piece of meat. I can see where it comes from on the animal, basically the outside of the loin, maybe including the flank steak, but also a lot of fatty, chewy, well, junk, in American butchery terms. "We throw that into the grind for hamburgers."

"No! Really?"

"Yup."

"Oh, no, that's terrible. You must have *matambre*. La Brigada, it's the best *parrilla* in Buenos Aires. Have you been to San Telmo yet?"

"Not yet." San Telmo is reputed to be one of the most picturesque neighborhoods in the city, funkier and shabbier than Palermo—where the hip, young, and rich come to play—but with an arty, Left Bank feel to it, complete with antiques markets and tango bars and crooked little streets.

"I'll give you the address after we leave here." At his failure to suggest we go together, I feel a small pang of disappointment.

But now I am watching the older butchers at the table, like the old-world butcher of our imaginations, with massive biceps and hooks and knives that they wield like extensions of their fingers, which of course in a manner of speaking they are. These men can do something that takes me fifteen minutes at the table—peel the neck bone off the chuck eye, say—in fifteen *seconds*. No lie. It's unbelievable.

Every week I'm not cutting I'm losing more skills. The scrapes and scars on my hands and arms have almost entirely faded; I look at them in my mirror with just the same sadness that I did watching the last of D's bruises fading from my skin. I'd had this pipe dream, coming here, that I'd arrive at some *carnicería,* knives in hand, and join my brother craftsmen, united across divides of language and culture and gender by our common skill. But all I can do is stay out of the way.

Santiago and I stand around with our arms crossed, trying to make ourselves as small as possible, and watch until I get too cold, even in the windbreaker the plant's manager gave me, with the Fura logo printed on the back, a silk screen of a naked woman posing sultrily, apparently some actress, known as "the Brigitte Bardot of Argentina." We head back to the office and drink more Nescafé (Argentines love that crap) while Santiago talks shop in Spanish with the guy, a friendly blond man who tries to throw some English at me when he can. I in turn attempt to keep up with the flow of foreign language, but a few Michel Thomas audio lessons do not a competent Spanish speaker—or even listener—make. At least not if that listener is me. I am hopeless at languages, always have been. So I sit and sip and try to maintain a look of comprehension, and eventually the manager, whose name I never caught and am now too embarrassed to ask for, offers to drive us back to the city center, an offer we take him up on.

Santiago gets dropped off first. It's almost four by now, and he's got to get changed and head to the restaurant. We make the rest of the drive in near silence, simply because of the language barrier, though the guy does point out some sights along the way—a restaurant he supplies here, a particularly lovely park there, the racetrack, shops, and important buildings. He drops me off in front of my building with a cheerful *"Ciao!"* and cheek kiss, and once I've entered the vestibule, nodded, and murmured *"Buenos días"* to the doorman and climbed into the creaking elevator, I am, after a day of being with people, solitary again. I smell like meat for the first time in a while, the scent enhanced, as I consider it, by a faint green aroma of dust and cow shit.

Now it's the long slog toward Argentine dinnertime. Everyone here eats at ten or ten thirty. To go to a restaurant at nine, especially alone, especially as a woman, is to court undue, concerned attention from waiters and the one other person eating at that early hour.

Since arriving in Buenos Aires, moving into this small, comfortable apartment, I have developed a routine. I take my customary shower, in my customary but not much enjoyed lukewarm water, and then I take my customary nap. When I awake, I open my customary wine bottle, drink my two customary first glasses, and then, atop my single bed's comforter, attempt to distract myself from my thoughts in my customary fashion. Try to bring back the physical sensation of waking up with D's arms around me, his cheek resting on my shoulder, his reliable morning erection pressing against my thigh...

One character in *Buffy*, Willow, happens to be a witch, and when she is heartbroken over losing her girlfriend she can perform a spell to fill out some clothes left behind, as if they were being worn by an invisible, beloved body, and have them, simply, hold her. What I do is a bit like that, except I have no magical powers, and afterward there follows the inevitable result. A stupid bind, this general need tethered so closely to this particular desire, this one person. I wind up unable to get where I want to be at all, or if I do get there, it's only to find that no relief at all comes with the spasm and shudder—just tears and a bitter sense of senselessness.

I can't imagine D ever having such a problem, ever having any sort of problem with sex at all. Though maybe the way he paraglided right off my planet, as soundlessly and utterly as the ivory-billed woodpecker that birders will spend the rest of their

lonesome lives searching for, is a symptom of his own disease. I'd
like to believe that.

I splash water on my face and watch some TV, listlessly, down-
ing the rest of my bottle of wine with the steady efficiency of a
good butcher. At last it's nine thirty. I dress in something pretty,
go downstairs, catch a cab, manage to convey that I want to go to
the address Santiago has written out for me.

The restaurant is loud, bustling. Soccer pennants and pictures
and team shirts cover the walls. I am the only person eating alone,
and both the waiters and the other diners are very careful not to
stare at me, as if I'm an exotic, doomed creature, a dodo or some
such. I order the *matambre* as an appetizer, of course. It arrives at
my table prepared something like this. I have made up this recipe,
but I think it comes pretty close:

Matambre à la Pizza

 1 *matambre,* about 5 pounds (This is going to be nearly
  impossible for you to find. Call Josh, as I did, or use
  flank steak. Which won't really be the same thing,
  at all.)
 ½ gallon milk
 ½ gallon water
 Salt and pepper
 1½ cups tomato sauce
 2 cups mozzarella cheese
 Your choice of pizza toppings

Lay the *matambre* on a cutting board, fat side up. Trim off
some but not all of the extra fat.

On the stove, bring the milk and water to a boil in a pot
large enough to hold the meat. Once it's boiling, slip in the
meat and turn down the heat. Let it simmer for 30 minutes.

Meanwhile prepare a charcoal grill. You'll want it nice
and hot.

After 30 minutes, lift the *matambre* from the pot and pat it dry. Season with salt and pepper. Place it on the grill, fat side down, and cook it until the fat is golden brown, about 10 minutes. Turn the *matambre* and cook for about 10 minutes more.

While the second side is cooking, top the fat side with tomato sauce, mozzarella cheese, and any other pizza toppings you like—pepper, onions, hell, pepperoni if you want. If you do it right you'll wind up thinking there is a God, and he's an Italian stoner. It will feed the same number as a large pizza, whatever that means to you.

And there's more insane food to come. Specifically, steak. There are six or eight different cuts to choose from on the menu, as at most traditional *parrillas*. I've been reading up on this, so I know what to go for—*bife de chorizo*, the classic Argentine strip steak. Tourists, I've already figured out, generally go for the more expensive *lomo,* or tenderloin, but I still hold on to my high-handed butcher's contempt for such insipid flesh.

My waiter is a young man with a thin mustache who asks me in his broken English where I'm from and if I'm loving Buenos Aires as much as it deserves to be loved. He maintains the proprietary consideration that I have by now realized is an intrinsic part of the female solo-dining experience in this country. It's a strange reversal: the way he treats me reminds me of the way I used to watch D treat attractive waitresses in expensive restaurants, with a casual assured flirtatiousness that made me feel both a twinge of jealousy and a strange welling of pride. (It's one thing when I lie in bed, willing the memories—I deserve that anguish, bring it upon myself. But, dammit, why does my brain foist those remembrances on me when I'm in the middle of a perfectly pleasant meal, being talked up by a perfectly nice-looking waiter?) When I ask for my steak *jugosa,* he looks skeptical, or as if he hasn't understood me correctly, much as he looked when I ordered an entire bottle of wine for myself. I've gotten used to this. When I first got here, I would order my steaks *a punto* ("to the point," or medium rare). But for some reason, because I'm a tourist or a woman, waiters seem unwilling to believe I want a steak that hasn't been cooked halfway to oblivion. Odd, since they don't blink an eye when I order *criadillas*—that would be lamb testicles, to you and me.

I repeat my request. *"Sí, jugosa, por favor."* My waiter shrugs, smiles, writes something down on his pad, then refills my glass of Malbec and goes to put in my order.

The steak, when it comes, is divine—deeply flavorful, slightly chewy, with a crackling layer of golden brown fat along one edge, which, after I have devoured every last bit of meat, I suck at blissfully.

By the time I'm winding down with the last of the wine and a double espresso to see me home, the restaurant has gotten a little quieter. Finally I've successfully timed my meal to Argentine standards. The difference being of course that all these gorgeous Argentines, after stuffing themselves with extraordinary quantities of protein, will proceed to hit the dance clubs and tango bars and house parties that keep people on the streets of Buenos Aires until dawn, whereas I'm going home to my bed, a little drunk (though not so drunk as some might expect from two bottles of wine in the course of an evening—here's to Irish genes and alcoholism) and exhausted from my day of meat tourism. My waiter, whose name, I've learned, is Marco, lingers at my table.

He tells me he's from La Boca, a working-class neighborhood in the southern part of the city, the center of the rabid Argentine *futbol* culture. The stadium is there, and people have a tradition of painting their houses in the garish colors of their favorite teams. I've been told before this that I can't leave Argentina without taking in a football game, but due to my sports phobia I doubt that I will. Still, I nod enthusiastically at his semicoherent chatter about teams and players, assure him I will indeed catch a game when I can, don't demur too much when he tells me he will show me around "all the most good parts of my neighborhood." With my check he delivers a La Brigada business card with his name printed on it, and on the back, handwritten, "Tango." And a phone number.

"I teach also. You know tango?"

The American Dame gives a half smile. "I know *of* it. But I don't know how."

"I will teach you. Call me, okay, Julie?" I pocket the card with a smile and say yes. Though I know that I won't.

It's a long cab ride home, the cabbie a quiet, grandfatherly man in a *gaucho*-style beret. We don't talk. Staring out the window as we drive down the broad Avenida 9 de Julio, perhaps drifting on the rippling wake of my meal, I find myself falling into a reverie, a tender swell of self-pity and melancholy that isn't entirely unpleasant, a gentle, guilty feeling that I don't wish Eric were here, combined with a furtive enjoyment of being alone, and even lonely. It's not that I don't miss him; I do. But I realize I rather love the little tug of it. I feel like a witch who has sent her familiar away from her to do her bidding, but still knows exactly where in the world it is. Rather painful, and at the same time rather a relief.

Certainly, spending any time with another man, any other man—D usually, but not always, the exception—reminds me that I love my husband down to the guts and marrow. ("Eyeballs to entrails, my sweet" is what Spike would say, and Spike might have been a vampire on a cult TV show with a bad peroxide helmet of hair, but he knew a little something of love.) Rotund Brazilians and goofy tango-dancing waiters, even Santiago, I hold up, in retrospect or at the time, as further evidence that Eric is someone other and above, someone singular.

I use that word advisedly. I don't just mean "special," like you always think the person you love is special. I think Eric is special because he always has these insane ideas for projects he wants to embark upon, which sound totally bonkers until you think about them for ten minutes and suddenly realize they're fucking brilliant. I think he's special because he hates his eyebrows even though they're fantastic and he has no idea how beautiful he is and his obsessions range from the national treasure that is Fran

Drescher to conspiracy theories about museum fakes. And I think D is special too, because of how fiercely he fucks me, because he masturbates with his left hand and eats with his right, because I adore his nasty, sneaky sense of humor and sly smirk and the way he can make you laugh even while boring you to tears as he holds forth on some obscure filmmaker or TV show or eighties hair metal band, and because he always wears the same two sweaters and walks in this gliding, unhurried way, like he's on rails.

But this is not what I'm talking about. I'm talking about an objective recognition of a truly extraordinary person, the sort of person anyone with a brain and a heart understands is someone she is lucky to know. Not because he's smarter or purer or kinder or gentler than everyone else—though of course Eric is often all of these things—but because he...glows. I don't really like getting into talking about souls and crap like that, but *something* shines out of Eric. He lives his life so close to the surface of his skin somehow—not like a daredevil, more like the shoot of a plant, transparent and tender. That's not quite right either. He isn't fragile, not someone to be coddled, even though he elicits from me such a ferocious protectiveness that it's probably not good for either of us. God, what is it? He's *honest.* Not in the bullshit way that he always says what's true or doesn't cheat people or whatever. There's just no bullshit about him at all. He's got his hang-ups and self-delusions and esteem issues like everyone else, but he has also got this purity of self that I am so proud of. Proud as if it is my purity. As if he's my surrogate soul.

But something isn't right here. If I have a soul, it should be my own, I guess. My own to be proud of or ashamed of. It's just so much easier to take on his.

Maybe that's it. Why I don't want Eric here. Maybe I want to feel soulless for a while. Or not soulless, but with my soul at a distance, away from my errant body and mind. Maybe I just want to be unburdened.

It is nearly midnight, and the cabdriver has the radio turned to the football game. Just as the broadcast voice begins to grow more exercised, we pass a brightly lit café, which is suddenly exploding, as we drive by, with roaring male voices and leaping male bodies. "What on earth?"

The man smiles into the rearview mirror. "Goal."

ARMANDO COMES out of the gym the morning of our appointment talking into his cell phone, doesn't stop for any longer than it takes to give me a wave and air-kiss hello before gesturing to me to follow him to his car, which is valet-parked. He's a compact man, energetic, a stark contrast to Santiago's tall, thin frame and slightest hint of gentle melancholy. He has a broad, tanned face with a low forehead and a gap in his front teeth, close-cropped, Brillo-pad hair, and a scrub of beard kept at just the right degree of rakish unkemptness. Armando is Santiago's friend. He raises water buffalo, and today he's going to take me to see his herd.

As we drive south and west, he spends half his time on the phone and the other half explaining to me his operation, his plan to expand water buffalo sales into the domestic market, a tough sell because whereas Europeans are into healthful eating and whatnot, and find the lean, clean meat of buffalo desirable, Argentines just want their beef beefy and plentiful.

Once outside the city limits, the landscape quickly becomes empty and wide, fields of cattle separated by dirt roads lined with scrubby trees. The pampas, I suppose these are. It looks rather like south Texas, my parents' country, pale and dusty and flat. Cattle country.

Armando asks what I'm looking to see, to which I say, "Whatever you've got." He explains that right now we are going to a stockyard where one of his herds is being kept. It turns out it's been a very wet summer and fall. His land is marshier than most plots, which was the reason he decided to take a chance on water buffalo in the first place. He says he's the first in the country to try it. But this year has been too wet for even his muck-loving animals, so he's had to move them to a feedlot to keep them heavy and healthy. Problem is, according to import regulations in Europe, no animal that has spent even one day on a feedlot can be sold there. So now Armando is left with the dicey proposition of selling his meat domestically, which is neither as profitable nor as certain. Still, he maintains a positive, can-do attitude, is sure that he can make this go over big here, that Argentines are changing their lifestyle, becoming more concerned with their health and with the provenance of their food. He reminds me of Josh, always looking for the Big Idea, always full of plans that would seem grandiose if they did not so often come through in the end.

"Have you eaten at La Brigada?"

"I have. I love it!"

"La Brigada sells my *búfala* meat."

"Oh yeah? I should try it." (Not really believing I'll be able to resist ordering another big old strip steak the next time I go.)

"And Santiago's other restaurant, you have been there?"

Santiago also runs an Asian restaurant, a sort of noodle shop, catercorner to Standard. "No, haven't been yet."

"He serves my buffalo there as well. It's got a very good flavor."

After about an hour we arrive at the stockyard. Armando gets out of the car to unchain a gate and we turn onto a rutted road. On either side are churned-up muddy pastures. Chickens pick through the manure and smooshed hay. We pull up to a complex of barns and corrals and one low concrete building that I assume must be the office. We both climb out into the mud. While I greet the dogs that come trotting up, Armando shakes hands with a series of men in rubber mud boots and windbreakers. Some of these men work with the stockyard; others are buyers Armando is trying to tempt. There's much business he needs to do today, so after he introduces me to everyone, for the sake of politeness I recede into the background, following the group a few paces behind as we all move through a series of gates to a pen where Armando's water buffalo huddle together in a great glinting black mass of sleek hides and dark eyes and shiny, wide horns that curl down over their entire heads, giving the impression of brilliantined hair parted down the middle—a bunch of 1920s dandies.

A couple of guys start herding the buffalo into a chute at one end of the corral. The animals seem terribly nervous, but also terribly obedient. The biggest cause for panic for an individual buffalo appears to be being alone. Once the men have gotten the first few headed into the chute, the others seem content enough to simply follow, nose to tail, without protest, nothing but a few dumbly pleading glances over the wood-plank fence. Armando tells me to stand to one side, at a safe distance, and though I can't see that these guys are much of a danger to me, I do as he says.

In a neighboring pen, a cow has just given birth to a calf. As in *just* just. As in the calf, a lovely white creature with two parallel black marks across its cheek, like the healed scar of an encounter with a puma, is still wet and not yet on its feet, curled up napping, and the cow is still passing the placenta. As Aaron would say, you learn something new every day, because now I know what cows do with their afterbirth. Ew. She must be a Tom Cruise fan. A stockyard dog, a black mutt, manages to get some of the stuff, or at least lick up some of the blood. Which, again, ew. But she's a sweet dog, and when she comes up to me after gleaning what she can from the scene of the birth, I cannot deny her even though she still has thick crimson splashes across her muzzle.

Meanwhile Armando, with the help of his two assistants, is loading the buffalo one at a time into the scale at the end of the chute, just a cow-sized raised box with doors at each end that slide up and down, guillotine style. One by one they load the cows onto the scale. Often a second one will try to squeeze in with the first. I guess for cattle, claustrophobia doesn't trump the fear of being left behind. The stockyard workers force them back with quirts and shouts, then shut the door on the beast inside. The scale's needle swings back and forth until it settles on a weight. If the number is high enough, the buffalo heavy enough, Armando marks the animal with a swath of white paint by reaching through the narrow spaces between the planks with a brush lashed to a three-foot dowel. Then the door on the other side of the box is raised and the creature trots out hastily down the ramp, its hooves clopping loudly on concrete as it hurries to the farthest corner of the enclosure. One by one the *búfula* clomp into the chute and back out again in half panic, some of them slipping alarmingly, falling to their knees or even over onto their sides, then scrambling up again in terror and dashing to press close together. Once there, they stare at us humans as if they know we're apt to grab one of them and take them down like a lion taking a wildebeest. They, of course, have had millennia to develop the sense that this is the sort of death most likely for them, but it's terribly unhelpful now. I wonder what evolutionary leap would suffice to free the herds, to teach them to free themselves. They all look identical to my eyes but for their spangled white marks. In this particular case, it's the star-bellied, or star-flanked, Sneetches that are going to lose out sooner rather than later. But not just yet.

It takes about forty-five minutes for Armando to weigh out his herd, choose those ready for the abattoir. I stand with a foot on a rail of the fence, sometimes watching the calf, who is bright white and spindly legged and cow-licked in the senses of both its hair being whorled and its mother being attentive, as it slowly gains its feet. And sometimes I watch the watchful, shining black, nervously shifting mass of buffalo, their hooves clacking brightly on the asphalt, their breath steaming and tails whooshing testily. When the family's all together again, for now, the gates are opened and they all trudge on up the hill toward a barn twenty yards away up a muddy track. A guy in galoshes and a dog follow them, but the herd knows where it's going and needs no encouragement. And then we head back to the city, and I return to my apartment smelling like cattle, again.

That night, on TV, miraculously, my favorite episode ever of *Buffy* is on. "The Wish." It's dubbed into Spanish, but it doesn't matter; I've seen this episode so many times I know it nearly line for line. The story is this: Cordelia Chase, high school queen bee who gave her love to a geeky boy and then lost it, as well as all her friends, when he fell in love with another, decides that Buffy Summers, vampire slayer, is the source of all her problems. Everything was right in Cordy's world until Buffy came to town. Unfortunately, she makes the wish that Buffy had never come to Sunnydale in front of a vengeance demon, who immediately grants her request. At first it seems the wish is a great success. Her social standing is restored: boys ask her out on dates instead of treating her like sloppy seconds. But it turns out a world without Buffy is not a nice one to be in at all.

I wonder: is this new world a nice one to be in? It seems so, sometimes, when I'm petting a sweet dog flecked with afterbirth, in this beautiful foreign place surrounded by cattle. But then there are the other times, the after-nap times, the predinner times. What am I supposed to be doing now that I'm here?

The next morning, July 9, Día de la Independencia, it snows in Buenos Aires. For the first time in a hundred years.

It's not much of a snow. And it kind of edges on toward slush at the end of the day. But all morning it falls, snow-globe, fairy-tale flakes, and the effect of it on everyone is magical. I leave my apartment after staring out my window for a bit, and on the street everything has stopped. No one is shopping in the shops or eating in the cafés. The furiously whizzing black taxis have disappeared. Everyone stands on the sidewalk, staring up, incandescent smiles on their lips. Children and adults alike raise their faces and stick out their tongues. They laugh in disbelief, they kiss, they take pictures. There's no accumulation on the ground, nowhere near enough to make a snowball, but everyone's having an imaginary snowball fight. Everyone is behaving as if there's a six-foot blanket of sparkling snow on the ground and he has nothing waiting at home but a bottle of wine or a mug of hot chocolate, a roaring fireplace, and a lover or a mom, whichever is appropriate for the age and situation, ready to share it.

I've no one to share a fireplace with now. But I think I'm fine with that. Because how many girls can say they've seen it snow in Buenos Aires, and in a world they've managed to crack open for themselves, like a bone saw exposing the marrow?

13

Still Undercooked

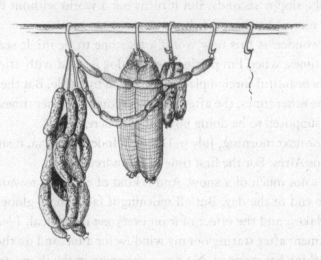

IT IS POSSIBLE that I haven't fully thought this through.

I mean, Argentina made sense. It's somewhat traditional, after all—at Fleisher's anyway—for butchers to travel after they've learned their trade, hit some of the world capitals of meat. Aaron went to Spain, Josh to Vancouver; Colin is planning a trip to Italy. But now here I am stretched out across the four seats of a middle aisle on Aerosvit Flight W132, direct to Kiev. I've got an enormous collection of Isaac Babel stories on my lap. I have just taken a sleeping pill, swallowed down with the worst wine I have ever tasted. The Cyrillic script on the bottle should have given me a clue; perhaps it actually would have, if only I could read one word of Cyrillic.

Scratch that. I have definitely not fully thought this through.

Seriously, why am I going to western Ukraine? If you asked me, I couldn't tell you. It's not as if it's some renowned mecca of cuisine, meaty or otherwise. I've always wanted to go to the Carpathians,

I suppose there's that. They're reputed to be beautiful, but that's not really the root of my fascination. Maybe it's a *Buffy* hangover. More likely it's an earlier, deeper yen, to see the place all the dark stories come from, Vlad the Impaler and holocausts and dictators people insultingly name "butchers" and dark Transylvanian castles on stormy nights. (Teri Garr in a dirndl tossing herself around in the back of a farm cart, trilling, "Roll, roll, roll in ze hay!" probably has a little something to do with it too.)

But that's not a good enough reason to go flying around the world again, not reason enough to buy another ticket almost as soon as I arrived back in New York. I think the reason is, really, that when I walked back into my apartment, I knew, knew, that I wasn't ready to be back. It wasn't Eric, it wasn't D or Robert the Dog, or New York itself. It was me. I felt undercooked, liquid in my center. I stayed a couple of months, veering between caged frustration at home and wild self-loathing. But I knew I had to get out again. The anguish in Eric's eyes when I tried to explain this almost made me quail, but there was a panic deeper, for once, than the panic at the thought of hurting him. To tell the truth, it didn't matter where I went, much. I excused my absence as a continuation of my butchery journeyman education. But in truth I might as well have thrown some darts at a map on the wall. I am going to the places I wanted to go at the moment when I bought the ticket—Ukraine, Tanzania, a brief stopover in Japan. Names on an itinerary, chosen very nearly at random.

A friend of my brother's has occasionally worked in Ukraine as a consultant for politicians who really almost definitely had nothing to do with the mysterious decapitation of their rivals. He's hooked me up with a young woman, Oksana, educated in the States, fluent in English, and by all accounts totally fantastic, who has agreed to do serve as my guide. The day after I fly into Kiev, she's going to meet me and we're going to take the train together to Kolimya, her hometown in the western part of the country. All I have to do by myself is get from the airport to the Tourist Hotel, near the Livoberezhna metro station on the left bank of the city, then manage to feed myself and get around for one day and night in Kiev without getting mugged or hit by a car, or falling down a manhole.

The pill doesn't seem to be working; you'd think the combination of it and a tower of Babel would do the trick, but I remain wakeful and restless. I fondle the phone in my pocket; a backlog of chatter is rising, and I have no prospect of soon easing the pressure. I wish my doctor had prescribed something stronger. Like, I don't know, OxyContin or something. Unfortunately, he knows just enough about my various addictions to know not to bring out the big guns, drugwise. I pull out one of the notebooks I've brought with me. I'm going low-tech for this trip. I haven't brought my laptop, and though I have my BlackBerry for emergencies, I'm going to endeavor not to use it—both because that phone has become so dangerous to me, a false lifeline that instead of keeping me from foundering threatens to pull me out to sea, and because I can't bear to even imagine the phone bill. So I'm taking up a little old-fashioned letter writing.

Dear Eric,

Well, I'm in the air, with my Babel and a bunch of sleeping pills that aren't working. Thinking about how sorry I am that getting to the airport was so hectic, that we didn't get to say a proper good-bye. I mean, misremembering the flight time by two hours? *This is how Julie self-destructs, not with a whimper but with a bang.*

After a while my hand cramps from all the unaccustomed writing, and I lie back. But I never do really get to sleep. Ten hours after frantically rushing down the gangway at JFK, I'm dully trudging up another one at Boryspil International Airport. It's a slightly shabby place, difficult to navigate, or that might just be exhaustion and Cyrillic. But I manage to find a cab, convey where I want to go, and get to the hotel room. After settling in I wander the streets, taking in the people and the feel of the place, but this not-knowing-the-alphabet thing has added a whole new layer of incomprehension. I can't even match up addresses from my guidebook to street signs. This profound, basic level of ignorance does funny things to my brain, makes me feel physically dizzy, like I'm a little drunk, and paranoid. I get on the metro, managing to buy tokens and negotiate the turnstile, but first I board a train going in the wrong direction, farther into the suburbs, before turning around and getting on another one across the river to the city center. Here, the buildings are old and the metro stations deep and magnificent, immaculately white and gently lit, with an escalator ride to the street that takes a full five minutes. People sit on the moving steps to wait out the ride. Teenage couples make out. I don't think I can bear that—flashes to Union Square, the backseats of cabs....I look away.

By evening I've at least managed to return to my shabby Soviet-era hotel, with a bottle of water (I'm not supposed to drink the stuff out of the tap, apparently), a link of cured sausage from a babushka selling them by the train station, and a hunk of bread. I hole up in my room for the night with my pen and notebook, continue working on my letter to Eric, reporting on the grayness of the city, the stiletto boots and extravagant fur coats of the unsmiling women, until I fall asleep.

Luckily, I find when I meet her the next day, that Oksana is not one of those women. Twenty-two years old, tiny and obviously rather brilliant, she has picked up an American way of dressing, jeans and sensible shoes. One of the first things she says to me that day is "I can't imagine ever dressing like a Ukrainian woman now. Those heels!" But she's a very Ukrainian twenty-two, which is to say that essentially she's more mature and pulled together than I am.

We see untold churches—St. Sophia's, St. Andrei's, St. Michael's. They are painted gold and white and sky blue, and the oldest of them dates from the eleventh century. In front of each of the churches there are a dozen or more wedding parties, billowing white dresses and multihued bridesmaid's gowns and tuxedos and flowers and limos and photographers. Apparently it is the last auspicious day of the season, Saint Somebody-or-Other's Day, so all the couples are squeezing in their weddings before the winter.

Behind St. Michael's there is a small fountain under a cupola where people are crowded about. There is a superstition about the fountain that, later that night on the train to Kolimya, will prove too great a temptation for my epistle-loving soul:

So this fountain, it has a sort of marble column coming up from the center of it, and the story goes, if you can get a coin to stick to the side of the column, your wish will come true. And I managed it, on the first try even. If I believed you would read this, I know you wouldn't need three guesses to think what I wished for...

We also passed this famous house, called "House of the Demons." This baroque gray fantasia of a building with no right angles, encrusted with stone frogs, stone rhinoceroses, stone fairies and sea monsters and elephants. Oksana said there's a sad love story attached to it, involving the architect who built it. I believe that. It looks like the work of someone who's lost someone.

I don't know if it's the movement and noise of the train—a movement comforting and sexual, like being rocked in a cradle or in a lover's arms, with the regular clacking of the tracks that both calms with its regularity and suggests other rhythms—or if it's just my growing conviction that D is out of my reach—that he's blocked me from his e-mail account, that he throws away my texts—but in the letter I begin writing to him I allow myself these sentimental observations and heartbroken cries.

I've never traveled in an overnight train. We are in what's called a "coupe"—a sleeper car for four—and now I'm the only one still awake. I can't sleep, but I'm not unhappy about it. I like this train. It makes me want to fuck. You.

My reporting to Eric is cozier, more about the telling detail. To D, I write persuasive essays; to Eric I write like I would write in my journal, like I would write to myself:

Oksana has the top bunk, I have the bottom, a middle-aged blond woman has the other bottom, and a dark man the opposite top. We have not spoken at all to these people—Ukrainians are rather a grim-faced lot....The aisles of the cars are carpeted, the windows have old-fashioned, dusty curtains. Walking through them, from one car to the other, past one open compartment door after another, is a curious experience, like peeking into a series of dioramas—old men playing cards, a compartment overflowing with loud adolescent boys in blue-and-white soccer uniforms, one silent older couple staring at a young woman, who sips tea. Passing between the cars is a bit of an ordeal—one door opening into a small, deafening, pitch-black space about three feet square, nothing to hold on to, floor unsteady, cold air whooshing in and the speeding tracks below...all for a warm beer from the dining car, and the small pleasure of getting a smile from the woman behind the counter when I mangle my "dyakooya." (Ukrainian for "thank you"—Oksana told me to use that instead of "spasibo." Apparently Russians aren't looked on too fondly in western Ukraine.) She smiled at me like I was a basset puppy stepping on its own ears.

The train left Kiev at seven p.m.; we will arrive in Kolimya at seven a.m. I spend much of the night writing my letters under the solitary light over my bunk, until my hand is stained blue with ink and aching.

...one guy with too-white teeth, seventy years old if he was a day, blatantly grabbed my ass on the way back from the dining car. Seriously, Eric, it was weird.

...but I think that my longing for you is beginning, at last, to take on a different cast. It's gotten more bearable, sweeter, nearly pleasant. A sort of peace in hopelessness, maybe.

We get off the train in the dusky dawn in a bit of a daze, make our way by bus and then train to the House on the Corner, a pleasant bed-and-breakfast run by Vitaly, a brash blond man with excellent English, Western sensibilities, and great ambition, and his mother, Ira, a small woman with short hair, crinkly smiling eyes, and not a word of English, who foists upon me a deeply delicious omelet the moment I walk in the door.

This place is roomy and clean and modern. Vitaly's mother is an excellent *cook.* The bathroom, which I would share if there were other guests but for the time being have to myself, is a Westernized vision of white tile and modern fixtures and steaming hot water. Eric, who visited this part of the world ten years ago, warned me that I'd be beset by Turkish toilets and a grim standard of personal hygiene, but so far I've encountered nothing of the sort. I'm almost disappointed. Where's the challenge here?

Today I'll rest, and write, and maybe get hit upon by an older Ukrainian man when I walk into town for a coffee. No, that will definitely happen.

So, my silent darling, one thing I've noticed, here and in Argentina both, is that when you are a woman in early middle age, of no extraordinary good looks, traveling abroad alone, you will be hit on, repeatedly and exclusively, by fifty-five-year-old men. And their approach will always be the same:

1) *They will ask what religion I am. As if this is deeply vital to what it is they want from me. I have learned to say "I was raised Episcopalian, it's a little like being Catholic," so as not to risk conversion speeches or the offense that might be taken should I speak what I think, which is "I'm an atheist, which should make you happy, since I've heard Catholic girls can be a little hesitant to screw random old men they meet in coffee shops."*

2) *They will comment on how young I look. The median age quoted to me is twenty-five, which is just patently absurd.*

3) *Once they learn my true age, they will ask me how many children I have, and when I say "none, yet" (I've quickly learned that the "yet" is key), they will very seriously*

*inquire as to the reasons behind this strategy, insist that I
have several, immediately, and more often than not insin-
uate that my problem is that I need a real man, an Argen-
tine/Ukrainian/whatever man, to impregnate me.*

And I will laugh the laugh of a fish working her way politely off
a hook and say, "Thanks so much. But men in my life is one thing I
do have, more's the pity. I think I'll stick with what I've got."

And then tomorrow, I'll go see some sausage.

When I contacted Oksana about this trip, I told her I wanted
to see meat, if there was meat to be seen. She didn't blink—which
frankly I thought was odd—and immediately set about finding
some places, especially for me to see sausage making, western
Ukrainians taking great pride in their sausages. This morning we
are going to visit a plant some ways out of town, in a small village, down a crooked, potholed country road lined with cattle and
sheep farms. The owners, Katerina and Myroslav, meet us at the
modest front door. *"Vitayu, vitayu—budlaska!"* Welcome! They
are both middle-aged, perhaps in their fifties, attractive, and they
both have wide, hospitable smiles. They shake our hands and usher
us eagerly inside. Oksana and I don white paper hats and butcher
coats matching the ones Katerina and Myroslav are already wearing, and they give us the big tour. It's much smaller than the sausage factory I saw in Argentina—more on the scale of Fleisher's
operations. Questions of size aside, it is much the same as every
meat-processing facility I've ever visited—the same salted meat in
plastic bins, the same white tiled walls and spray-washed floors,
the same funky curing smell mixed with a faint hint of bleach. The
same cutting bowls and sausage stuffers and smokers. Around the
table, the cutters stand breaking down beef shoulders, trimming
the meat off into chunks the grinder can handle. There is, though,
one important difference—most of the butchers at the table are
young, blond women. This is very nearly the first time outside of
Fleisher's that I've actually seen a woman butchering. Even there,
a female at the table who was not me was a rare phenomenon. But

here, it seems, butchering is not a job for men only. The fruits of communism, I guess. They smile at Oksana and me when we come up to the table to watch, but do not for a moment stop working.

Back in the office after the tour, Myroslav opens up a bottle of cognac while Katerina lays out a mountain of food—rye bread, cheese, olives, and at least ten kinds of sausage, representing a quarter of the varieties they make at the factory. There's headcheese, which is very popular in Ukraine, in part because it's cheap. *Cervelat* is a lean sausage made primarily of high-quality beef with a bit of pork fat; it's Myroslav's favorite. *Tsyhanska,* or "gypsy sausage," is somewhat fattier, at seventy percent beef and thirty percent pork fat. (Katerina can rattle off proportions from memory; Oksana then translates for me.) *Drohobytska* is a sausage that was traditionally made entirely of pork, but now often has veal mixed in. Myroslav explains that their *drohobytska* is in fact mostly beef, because in Ukraine pork is the more expensive meat.

"There is a saying about Hutsuls," Oksana translates as Katerina chats. Katerina does actually speak a bit of English. She has a daughter and grandchildren in New Jersey and is trying to learn the language. But she still feels more comfortable with Oksana in between us.

"What's a Hutsul?"

"We're Hutsuls. People from the mountains here, in western Ukraine. Real Ukrainians. People from the east part of the country are Russians, not Ukrainian."

"Okay. What's the saying?"

Katerina is looking at my face with expectation. She has a ready grin and a nimbus of reddish blond hair, and I find myself wishing I could speak to her directly. As deft a translator as Oksana is, quick and nuanced, I find I want to talk to these people without filter. It's the international brethren of butchers, I suppose. We are of the same cloth, I can tell.

"Hutsuls would rather have good sausage and no bread. Eastern Ukrainians want bread; they don't care if the sausage is good."

"I come down on the Hutsul side of that one."

Myroslav and Katerina both laugh, nodding, before Oksana has the chance to translate. It's funny—whenever we're talking about food, we seem closer to speaking one another's language.

Domashnia is beef, pork, and veal. "Doctor's sausage," *likarska,* is pork with milk, eggs, and seasonings. "Children's sausage" is finely pureed for a soft consistency and is made without any preservatives. *Krovianka* is blood sausage, from beef blood, which is delivered to Myroslav and Katerina directly from the slaughterhouse, along with the meat. I am beginning to get dangerously full now, and the cognac bottle is almost emptied, mostly by Katerina, Myroslav, and me, Oksana being as nearly a teetotaler as is really possible in Ukraine. Toasts have been made to each of us in turn, to the international brotherhood of sausage makers, to our two countries. I'm pleasantly buzzed and getting sentimental in the Ukrainian fashion, or the Irish one, take your pick.

"You should come visit me in the States. I want to take you to my butcher shop. You'd love it. And they'd love you!"

"Next time I visit I will see you too!" Katerina's English seems to have gotten better with the cognac. She takes a picture cut from a magazine that she has tucked into the edge of a picture frame on her desk. "My granddaughter." The photo is of a stunning teen model with long blond hair and candy-colored lipstick. "*Seventeen* magazine!"

"She's beautiful!"

"Yes! Thank you!"

"Please call me when you come to visit. I'll take you to my butcher shop." I write down my name, phone number, and e-mail address. This is all very much like some ten-year college reunion, meeting someone you'd completely forgotten about and, under the influence of finger foods and copious liquor, deciding you were obviously meant to be soul mates, and the digits are exchanged and the faces are wide with wondrous mutual recognition and there are teary hugs and laughing fare-thee-wells. And more often than not, the digits are lost and the soul mating never occurs. But then again, sometimes it does.

At last it's time for us to leave. We all embrace and kiss cheeks in the parking lot in front of their office door.

"Thank you! Come again!"

"*Dyakuyu!* I will!" Katerina sends us off with a giant bag of sausages.

We drive slowly to avoid the truly epic holes in the road, which are filled with water that in the light of the first sunny afternoon sky I've seen in Ukraine vividly reflect the yellow leaves of the autumn trees lining the road. It's rather lovely, or that might again be the cognac and sentimentality.

When we get back to Vitaly's, he is in the kitchen visiting with a young American woman who introduces herself as Andrea. When we unload our great sack of gifted meat, she moans, and says, "That is so wrong." This of course doesn't get us off on the right foot, because I myself can think of nothing more wrong than a vegetarian in Ukraine. But she's a Peace Corps volunteer, so I guess a few misguided liberal lifestylings go with the territory. I hand the bag over to Ira, who's much more than appropriately grateful. She pulls out some of the *cervelat* and slices it thin, putting it on the small kitchen table with some bread. Oksana and I both sit, and though we've had far too much sausage already, we each take a little nibble more.

We chat back and forth for a couple of hours, Oksana, Vitaly, Andrea, and I, while Ira continuously putters about the kitchen. Last night she made, just for me, some beef-stuffed cabbage rolls, which should have been stodgy and Soviet-tasting, but instead were ineffably lovely, light and brightly flavored. They entirely made up for the way I began to feel like Miss Havisham in her rotting wedding dress, sitting there at the table by myself, being served by a woman I could not speak to, taking small bites to put off the moment when I'd finish my meal and there would be nothing left for me to do that evening. And this morning I got eight airy, crisp, tiny pancakes, with jam. Ira is cleaning up now, though the kitchen seems pretty much spotless to me; she's one of those women who cannot bring herself to sit until she's wiped every surface and offered every guest every possible pleasantry.

Andrea, it quickly becomes clear, spends *a lot* of time here. She's nearing the end of her two-year stint in Kolimya, working at the same school Oksana's boyfriend works at, and she could not be more ready to go. She doesn't like Ukraine. She doesn't like the people: "The women are all skanky and the men are all disgusting-looking misogynists—except for you guys, of course!" She doesn't like the food: "Everything is so heavy, and there's meat in *everything*. The only thing I like is Ira's potato *varenyky*. I *live* off them."

Oksana exchanges a glance with Ira over Andrea's head that only I catch, and Ira speaks a few words to her in Ukrainian. With a wry headshake, Oksana translates for me. "Later," she says, with a sort of cryptic smirk, "Ira will show you how to make the *varenyky*. They're very good."

The next day Oksana and I tool around Kolimya's museums and shops. For lunch, at a café and beer garden that is charming even in the dripping chill, and that Oksana assures me is "where everyone goes" in summer, I eat borscht while she has something called *banosh*, a traditional western Ukrainian dish that looks rather like garlic cheese grits, that comforting staple back in Texas which I've not tasted in probably a decade. When Oksana lets me have a bite, I swear I will not rest until I learn how to make it.

Which I finally have done. And here it is!

Ukrainian Banosh

2 cups or more sour cream
1 cup white or yellow cornmeal
2 tablespoons butter
Salt to taste
¼ cup crumbled goat's milk feta (optional)

Place the 2 cups of sour cream in a small pan over medium-low heat, stirring constantly, until hot but not yet boiling.

Gradually add the cornmeal, stirring often, not letting the mixture come to a boil. Cook for about 15 minutes. The consistency should remain somewhat liquid; if it begins to get too dense, stir in more sour cream, a couple of tablespoons at a time.

When you judge it to be about done, stir in the butter and salt to taste and take off heat. Let sit, covered, for 5 minutes.

Serve in four bowls with cheese crumbled on top, if desired. This dish is like a Ukrainian translation of your favorite childhood comfort food. It's a good way of remembering that, mostly, we're more alike than different.

As we linger over our meal, my tongue loosens in all the ways I always regret later. As I will write that night, in bed:

What is this thing I do, this popping myself inside out for random people all over the world? Wallowing in these filthy, heartbreaking memories of you and Eric both? Girths and proclivities, fights and tendernesses all microanalyzed over bad drinks with strangers. I don't think it's just the untapped oil fields of sympathy, no. It's not comfort I'm looking for. It's like pulling off a scab too early, or squeezing a cut to summon a few extra drops of blood. And maybe, too, it makes the enforced distance seem less pathetic than romantic. I like to think myself the subject of a tragic nineteenth-century novel rather than an Adrian Lyne potboiler about a man and his stalker.

"I think it's more of a problem in America," Oksana says decisively. She eats her *banosh* delicately, much more slowly than I have downed my spicy borscht.

"What is? Obsessive love affairs?"

"Infidelity. And confusion like this. In Ukraine, people get married, stay married. We don't expect so much, maybe. Or we're happier because we know what we want."

"Maybe." I take a slug off my second Czech beer. I wonder if this could really be true. Is Oksana just young, with the consequent confidence youth brings? Or could there actually be some particular circumstance of nationhood, of history and tradition and religion and persecution, that could result in a populace more inclined, as a whole, toward contentment? It seems doubtful, but who knows? It's as valid an explanation for the capricious bestowal of happiness as any other.

I wonder what's going on with you and Robert and the cats? "What news on the Rialto?" to quote Buffy quoting The Merchant of Venice. So, continuing this tome—God, this letter is becoming gargantuan—after lunch Oksana took me to the Easter Egg Museum, which is actually shaped like a giant Easter Egg. Inside, nothing but tens of thousands of intricately adorned eggshells— pysanka they're called; you know what they look like, right? All these crosshatched designs, stripes and swirls, in yellow and red and black? From all over the country, there are eggs, different traditional styles from different regions. There's an egg painted by Raisa Gorbachev; another one from Yulia Tymoshenko. We went to the Hutsul museum too, sort of a standard ethnographic museum that you'd have loved but that gave me museum fatigue. Then we went to Oksana's parents' house, as did her boyfriend, an American Peace Corps volunteer named Nathan.

Oksana has a dog that she keeps at her parents' apartment, a Japanese Chin named Onka, which means, apparently, "smartass." She is an adorable little thing that likes to fetch a stuffed animal that is nearly as big as she is. Oksana's mother is also an adorable thing, cheerful and dark-haired and small like Oksana. As soon as she gets home from work, she sets to more work making us dinner, leftovers and store-bought things, fried chicken cutlets, potatoes, tomato-pepper salad, mushroom spread, cheese, pickles—a seemingly endless array of nibblies, which we eat with the bottle of champagne Oksana and I picked out before coming over.

We play with Onka for twenty minutes or so, until the doorbell rings and Oksana rushes to greet Nathan. Nathan's Peace

Corps term is also nearly up. He and Oksana are sort of hilarious together, and sort of sad. She is endlessly teasing him, she is smiling but prickly, affectionate but just a bit standoffish. After a glass and a half of champagne, she is also a little flushed. "Tomorrow Nathan is getting a...what do you call the haircut?"

Nathan is grinning. He has his arm around her. "A mohawk."

"A mohawk." She turns to her mother and speaks in Ukrainian, running a hand over the center of her head in explanation. "I told him I'm glad he's leaving so I don't have to look at him with stupid hair."

He grins wider and tries to kiss her, but she pushes him off, laughing. Perhaps this is just how she is, but I've never, in the days I've gotten to know her, seen her so barbed, and I wonder if it's because Nathan's leaving soon. I feel sorry for him. I know that feeling of being peeled away, with however much good cheer, and, let me tell you, it is no fun.

The next day, Oksana takes me to Sheshory, a resort town up in the mountains. "It's one of my favorite places," she explains as we climb onto the bus that will take us there. "A real traditional Hutsul village. In the summer there's a giant musical festival, and everyone goes. Old people, kids, long-haired, you know, hippies. Everyone camps or rents a cottage, and we swim in the river, the Pistynka River, and stay up all night."

The bus is packed and slow as I guess public buses all over the world are. The drive takes more than an hour. From the valley where Kolimya lies, we move through fields and small villages, along winding roads into the Carpathians. It's lusher up here, and chillier. Not truly cold, but brisk and with that mountain air that's not really damp, just ever so slightly moist—somehow, green. We disembark at the side of a narrow road by a restaurant and the tiny clutch of shops that make up the town "center." Behind the restaurant, across a footbridge, one dirt road climbs a slope upon which are clustered small wood-paneled houses, painted white or bright summery pastels, their eaves adorned with elaborate punched tinwork. Another path follows the river.

We spend the afternoon wandering the bank, dipping our feet in the cold water, teetering across rocky rapids. I have to imagine what it must be like during the busy summer tourist season; for now the town seems almost entirely deserted. We eat at the one restaurant, a rich stew of grilled pork, and by the time we finish, the light is beginning to take on the cast of evening.

"We should head back, I think. I made an appointment tonight at my friend's sauna. We shouldn't be late."

We walk out to the road, which seems as abandoned as the rest of the town. "It might be a while before the bus comes. It doesn't come so often. Let's walk. Then we can wave it down when it comes. Or we'll find someone to drive us."

"Sounds good."

"You will love the sauna. It is very healthy. Keeps you from getting sick. We won't use the *veniki*, though."

"*Veniki?*"

"Uh-huh." She grins sideways at me and makes a vigorous whipping motion. "Tree branches. Birch? You're supposed to beat against your back."

"Huh. What's that supposed to do?"

"It's very healthy. Makes you strong. But don't worry, we won't do that."

"Probably for the best."

We walk for twenty-five minutes. The bus never catches up to us, and hardly any other cars drive by. Oksana tries to hail a few of the ones that do, but at first she isn't successful. At last, though, just as we're getting nervous that we're not going to be able to get back to Kolimya in time, a blue Mercedes pulls up beside us, its window rolling down to reveal an older man with a paunch, an expensive-looking leather jacket, and a helmet of gray hair. Oksana sticks her head in the window, smiling in a way that on a young American hitchhiker would seem riskily flirtatious, but here just looks like a woman getting something done. She chats with him for a bit, then looks over her shoulder at me. "Get in. He's going to take us."

The man leans forward, looking at me over Oksana's shoulder, gesturing with his hand. "Yes, yes. Come in!"

I open the rear door and slide in.

The man's name is Misha. He and Oksana chatter in Ukrainian for a few minutes. I idiotically paste a wide-eyed listening look on my face, as if I can understand a word that's being said. Then Oksana gives a gasp and laughs. She turns back to face me from the front seat. "Misha raises pigs! No…not pigs. Um…" She asks Misha something.

"Boar," he says to me in English. "Like in the woods?"

"Really? For food?"

"No, no, no…my pets."

"But—" Oksana is looking very excited. "He makes sausage. He has a sausage factory!"

"Really?!"

I've never hitchhiked in my life, unless you want to count the time when I was nine and my brother was six and I put him and our next-door neighbor, pretty little Misty McNair with the perfect bows in her long blond hair, out by the side of the road in the yard, taught them how to stick out their thumbs for a ride, then left them there while I went to the kitchen for a snack. And now, the first time I get picked up, on the outskirts of a tiny resort town in western Ukraine, a thousand miles from my life, from Fleisher's, and, by God, it's a sausage maker.

We make plans to tour his facilities first thing the next morning.

We arrive at the sauna, which is really just a small wooden outbuilding in Oksana's friend's backyard, just in time for our appointment. I'd been expecting some vast tiled public bath full of naked middle-aged women and bad Soviet lighting, but instead it's just a tiny suite of rooms that Oksana and I have to ourselves—a bathroom with cubbies for our clothes, a pile of towels, plastic clogs, a resting area with bottles of water, a small fridge, and a table with four chairs, and the sauna itself. It's about the size of a very good New York City walk-in closet, lined in wood, with two tiers of benches and an oven in one corner. It is hotter than anywhere I have ever been in my entire, entire life. Unbelievable, the heat, like a fist squeezing us. Wrapped in our towels, we sit on the benches, or lie on them, or lean against the wall, trying to talk but mostly not being able to manage it. There is a pail of water with a scoop in it so that we can pour some over the hot top of the oven, but we do it once and feel like we might actually die from the steam, so after that we just sit in our sweat.

The thermostat says 110 degrees...centigrade. Healthful? This? It can't be. But my one-upmanship gene kicks in, I guess, because as long as Oksana stays in there, I'm not budging either. We stay for maybe thirty-five minutes, our first round. When she says, "I'm going to take a break now," I nearly leap out of the sauna with her. Just standing up leaves me dizzy and feeling a little sick. We retire to the other room, where we drink water for five minutes, wipe off some of the thick sheen of perspiration. When words return, I ask what's next.

"We go back in. We're supposed to keep going back in until we stop sweating. That's when we'll know all the poison's been flushed out of our bodies."

"Ah, okay, well, we'll see. I'm warning you, though, if that's the goal we could be here all night. I don't really stop sweating, as a general rule. Too much to flush, maybe."

In and out we go, for slightly shorter periods each time, for nearly two hours. By the end, my legs are noodles and I think I could sleep for days. It's true, though—I'm sweating almost not at all. We rinse off in the shower, dress, and get into the cab that Oksana's friend has waiting for us outside.

Back at the bed and breakfast, Oksana and I wave our hellos and good-nights to whomever is in the kitchen. It's Ira and Vitaly. Ira lights up when we walk in.

"My mother is ready to explain how to make *varenyky*," Vitaly says. "They are like, you know?" He holds up his thumb and forefinger to make a pinching gesture. "Little potato dumplings."

I literally think I could fall asleep standing up. My skin feels strange, buzzy, under my clothes. But I'm leaving Kolimya soon.

Leavin' on a jet plane, don't know when I'll be back again. "Oh! Great, thanks!"

Oksana, who must be exhausted herself, stays to translate as Ira, with an efficiency and delicacy and utter sense of comfort that I've never seen the like of among home cooks, shows me, step by step, how to make:

POTATO VARENYKY

    2 medium russet potatoes
    ⅛ cup finely chopped salt pork, rinsed
    ½ cup finely chopped onion
    1¾ cups flour (or more if necessary)
    2 large eggs
    Pinch of salt

Peel the potatoes, quarter them, and boil them in salted water until soft, maybe half an hour. Meanwhile heat the salt pork in a skillet, and when the fat is rendered out, lift the golden brown cracklings with a slotted spoon and set aside in a bowl. Sauté the onion in the rendered fat until golden brown. Set aside.

Drain the potatoes and mash them thoroughly, stirring in the onion mixture.

(Here Oksana raises her thin, arched eyebrows at me, and says something to Ira in Ukrainian that makes her laugh. "I told Ira she's been tricking Andrea for two years." "Love it. 'Honey? You know why Ira's varenyky are so good? One hint—it ain't the potatoes.'")

Set aside until ready to fill the dumplings.

Using your hands, mix together the flour, eggs, and pinch of salt with about a cup of water, adding more flour if it's too sticky to handle. Turn the mixture out onto a floured board and, adding flour as necessary, knead until you have a stretchy dough. Divide the dough into two balls.

Roll out half the dough on the board until it's pretty thin—

an eighth of an inch or less—but not so thin that it's in danger of tearing. Cut into rounds about two inches in diameter. If you don't have a cookie cutter handy, you can also just cut them into squares.

To fill the dumplings, put two to three teaspoons of the potato mixture on top of each round and squoosh it flat with the back of a spoon until it covers most of the piece of dough, leaving a clean edge all around. Form the round into a half-moon and pinch the edges closed. Repeat this process with the second half of the dough.

Then just drop the dumplings into a big pot of salted, boiling water. They will sink to the bottom at first, then float to the top after about three to five minutes. Once most or all of the dumplings have risen to the surface of the water, that means they're done. Drain them and rinse them with hot water from the tap.

Toss dumplings gently in a bowl with the cracklings and any further fat that has rendered off them. Makes enough dumplings for four. Serve with a scoop of sour cream or crème fraîche on top.

It takes me a long time to make these *varenyky*, but then, I am not Ira. Her nimble fingers stuff and fold and pinch the dough at a flying pace. Oksana translates quickly, but as Ira demonstrates she and I begin to outpace the words, Ira answering my questions directly. Of course we don't exchange actual words, but with a single gesture, a mimed pinching motion or a finger point and questioning eyebrows, she can see what I'm after, can nod her head yes or shake it no. I'm not the cook Ira is, but I'm a cook just the same. It's like with the butchers I've met; though I can't understand the words she's saying, we share a language. By ten o'clock we are all sitting together at the dinner table eating potato dumplings with pork cracklings and sour cream. They are divine.

Upstairs I get ready for bed. Pen and notebook are on the nightstand, and though my eyelids are drooping aggressively, I take a moment to write Eric a good-night.

So after the sauna, I have this disturbing rash I see spreading across my arms and shoulders, a sort of latticework of red lines, like perhaps my blood has been boiled to the surface. Oksana says that the sauna's "flushing out the poisons," but this can't be good, right? Maybe the poisons are better off unflushed. Well, if I die in my sleep, I guess we'll know why.

"COME IN, come in!" Misha motions to us as we ascend the concrete steps through early morning light into a stairwell that smells ripely of apples. He kisses us both on each cheek and ushers us up the stairs. "You'll have breakfast now?"

"Oh, I already...no, I mean, yes, please. Thanks." Ira has fed me breakfast this morning, an omelet with sausages, but there is no denying a Ukrainian who wants to feed you.

While Misha putters about in his small kitchen, we examine the other main room of the house. It is packed full of all manner of stuff, the most prominent categories being taxidermy animals and Yulia Tymoshenko paraphernalia. There's a stuffed wildcat stalking on a shelf up high near the ceiling. Tucked into a knickknack case is a Tymoshenko poster, showing the Ukrainian politician with her familiar blond braids. "So what's with the hairdo, anyway?"

"She didn't always wear her hair like that. It's a traditional Ukrainian style, to prove she's very Ukrainian."

"And what's with the white robes, and the two guys with the swords?"

"You know...for young men, I guess." Oksana shrugs, rolls her eyes. "Politics."

"Huh." I suppose if I were a gorgeous blonde running for prime minister of an Eastern bloc country, I'd be gunning for the D&D crowd too, but it's still a bit laughable, and creepy.

There are stuffed birds of all persuasions, stuffed rodents and snakes. A stuffed rabbit holds a snapshot of Yulia between its paws.

Breakfast is—well, Jesus. First Misha serves us each six potato

pancakes with his homemade jarred mushrooms, gathered from
his land. We each get a teacup full of kefir, and he urges upon us
a "liver salad"—basically a great mound of chopped liver layered
with peppers, onions, mushrooms, other unidentifiable strata.
Delicious—and, again, homemade—but like plutonium in the
stomach. Then he finishes us off with some apple cake and tea. Is
this really how Ukrainians eat every day?

Next he takes us downstairs again, where we all stomp back
into the shoes we'd removed at the door and head across the little
rutted road to his plant.

It's a Soviet construction, which he's bought to renovate. It's
dilapidated now, with old black smokers and ice crusting over the
walls of the walk-in freezer. Misha's got big plans, though—he's
putting in a new cooler and is purchasing all sorts of other new
equipment, grinders and stuffers and band saws. But the meat is
just one part of his ambition. Misha also is planning to build a big
public sauna and, rising above it, a graded ski slope. He thinks he
can start raking in the Sheshory tourist dollars, maybe build a hotel.
Oksana and I nod as he explains to us where everything will go, and
how this will become the greatest new complex in the whole town.

The first thing we hear when we step into the muddy courtyard
in the center of the plant is a raucous chorus of howls and barks
from a kennel in one corner. "My guard dogs. Hunting dogs,
too." He's got a Saint Bernard in one pen, a German shepherd
in another, and two leaping and yipping fox terriers. He speaks
to each of them briefly, but doesn't encourage me to say hello.
"They're trained not to like strangers. With me, they are angels."

In another large pen is a chaotic roil of mud and roots, and two
wild boars, who snuffle up to the fence as we approach, nudging
their snouts against the chain-link. "I found them in the mountains here, as babies," Misha says, as he presses a palm to the fence
for them to nuzzle at. "Their mother was dead." One of Misha's
employees gingerly edges into the pen to dump a big bucket of
meat trim, apples, and vegetable cuttings into their trough. They
busily attack—the meal, I mean, not the employee.

In yet another pen, built up off the ground like a rabbit hutch, are two foxes. "These also I rescued as babies. I used to keep them in the house, but they shit all over everything." The pen smells wincingly noxious. "I tried to let go, but they keep coming back. So now they live here."

The pair of foxes dash in endless, frantic circles around their cage, their eyes wide and their heads darting back and forth, trying to see everything at once. They've clearly been driven insane. I feel sorry for them.

At the end of the tour, which probably took most of an hour, we head back to his house again, this time to eat some of his "meat bread"—a dense meat loaf that edges into pâté territory— and drink some of his cognac. (Oksana takes only one sip out of politeness. Misha and I have several small glasses each.) He goes through his photo collection, which highlights vacation snapshots by lakes and a complete history of the dogs he's owned through the years. Then he takes us back to town.

"Oh, and on the way, I have something to show you that you will like very much!"

So on the way back, we pull into a complex of buildings that looks rather like an old fairground. He talks to a man through his window at a security point, who then unlocks a gate for us and swings it open so we can pull into a wide courtyard with booths all around the perimeter. All are empty now; there's no one around, but there is a cage about the size of a horse trailer in the center of the lawn of tamped-down dried grass. Inside, we can see as we step closer, are two enormous brown bears. They too pace, and snuffle the air through shiny black noses. Their coats are bedraggled with mangy balls of fur hanging off. Their eyes are sad, and insane too.

"These were rescued, as babies. Their mother was killed." Misha makes a mournful face that I believe, but there's the glow of fascination there as well as he watches the mad bears pace, murmuring to them under his breath. I'm beginning to get wise to this whole rescued-orphan routine. But nonetheless, I feel a little

sorry for Misha. I know what killing with kindness feels like—
like there's no good option. You have to save what you've made
bereft. You have to look after them. Even if it drives them bat-shit
crazy. I too have felt the irrational urge, the one that leads people
to climb into gorilla pits or to commune with large animals in
remote Alaskan meadows, to comfort and befriend creatures that
can and often will rip them to shreds. I want to dig my hands deep
into the bears' fur and figure out how to make them okay. The
gratifications of cutting down a side of pork are not so different,
really—it's a facing up to your crimes, an attempt to make things
right. And with the added benefit of some nice plump pork chops
to show for your work when you're done.

Enough sad-sack mammals for the day. We head back to
Vitaly's. Misha comes in with us and is surprised to see Ira, a
childhood friend. We all crowd into the kitchen and drink tea,
and I zone out a little in a digestive fugue while Misha and Ira
chatter away. After a while, Oksana and I go to the post office and
do a bit of souvenir shopping. I buy a few wooden eggs, painted
pysanka style; the real eggs are more expensive and, more important, would inevitably shatter someplace between Kolimya, Kiev,
Tanzania, Sapporo, and home. I also buy a sheer black peasant
blouse with gold and silver embroidery that I will either keep or
give to my mother. Then we go in search of *sala*.

When Eric visited Ukraine just a year or so out of college, he
came back raving about *sala,* which is some sort of seasoned salt
pork, eaten with bread. "It's everywhere," he tells me. "It's like
the Ukrainian national food!" I've gotten several e-mails from
him since I've been here, whenever I've been able to get to a cyber-
café to check, asking if I've yet sampled it.

The problem is, there's no *sala* to be found for love or money.
I've been keeping my eye out, I really have. I've looked in grocery
store deli counters, on restaurant menus. I've asked Oksana about
it and she's assured me we will find it at some point, somewhere in
Kolimya. But so far, bubkes. We make a concerted attempt today,
our last in western Ukraine. We visit groceries and markets and

one semi-enclosed butcher shop, just a large room with double doors open onto the street, with men and women in aprons standing behind a series of wooden tables piled high with meat. A yellow dog wanders, mostly unmolested, under the tables, feasting on whatever scraps fall. Oksana explains to one of the women what we are looking for.

"*Sala?*" The woman looks just the slightest bit flummoxed, but she slices a wedge of a snowy white hunk of pork belly with her enormous knife. It doesn't look salted, but I pop it into my mouth anyway.

So it turns out *sala* doesn't just mean a seasoned Ukrainian delicacy. It also means, well, pig fat.

"I think that now, people don't want to serve visitors such things, peasant food, unsophisticated," explains Oksana as I smack the sheen off my lips and tongue.

I couldn't do it, sweetie. I tried. But there's no sala to be had. The country has changed since your time, I guess. I feel like I let you down. But if it makes you feel better, your wife ingested raw pig fat in front of an incredulous Ukrainian butcher-woman. So there's that.

I'm on the train back to Kiev. Next, Tanzania. I miss you.

I SPEND a day with Oksana in Kiev, mostly shopping. Ukrainians love to shop, and there's much of it to do. The clothes are trendy, often not particularly well made—one cute dress I buy loses two buttons before I've worn it once—and not as cheap as you'd expect. But, at Oksana's urging, I do make one purchase I'm entirely pleased with. A black pleated skirt, in a very fine-wale corduroy, much shorter than any skirt I've worn in a decade or more. A sexy schoolgirl look. When I put it on, my legs suddenly look a mile long, and I don't think it's just the shop's mirrors. That night I pack it up, visions of saucy heels and kneesocks and pigtails dancing in my head.

The next day, I'm on a plane from Kiev to Dubai. We're flying over the Persian Gulf, and it's pitch-black but for the dim glint of a narrow moon off the waves and an occasional greenish blink of light, a beacon. Two sheaves of papers sit on my lap.

Well, Ukraine was fascinating, as you said. I think very different from when you were here, though. I'd love to bring you back sometime, would love for you to meet Ira and Katerina and Myroslav and Misha and, most especially, Oksana. And you should see the skirt I bought for twenty bucks!

What I don't write about to Eric is the vague sense of anxiety that's settled over me since I boarded the plane. It's not just nervousness about visiting Africa for the first time, and all alone, and it's not just my fear of flying. It's another sort of dread I can't quite work out. I don't want to burden Eric with such things. With D, I have no compunction, since writing a letter to him is like writing down a prayer and then lighting it on fire.

As the plane rose, I gripped my armrests and begged to live. Me, praying—so hypocritical. I'm so much more afraid of flying than I used to be, I wonder why? Last night, the night before leaving Kiev, I dreamed that Eric and I were on a plane that was going down. Just as it was about to crash nose-first into a swamp, time was frozen, and we were told by some omniscient voice projected from the future that we had precisely nineteen minutes to resolve all of our affairs. For a sickening moment I was alone in the plane's bathroom, naked and shivering, stabbing your number into my phone, too terrified to punch the Call button. But you came anyway. The bathroom was gone, my clothes were back on, and we stood on the bank of a creek. We both took off our shoes, dug our feet into the sand.

The dream was vivid, both the terror of the crash and D's eventual presence shocked through with the smack of reality, not a

D-shaped presence but D himself. A visitation. Every vocal nuance and glitter of the eye, his posture and smirk and the scattering of moles on his skin. I awoke in happiness that melted quickly into a backsliding resurgence of pain, and with a memory I'd forgotten. I think of it again now, my forehead pressed against the plastic of the plane window, staring into the liquid darkness. It happened toward the end, after a fight we'd had over what I can't now recall, some angry ultimatum or demand from me, no doubt. We parted with recriminations, and some hours later I got a text from him. He wrote, "I love you and I don't know what to do about that." I treasured those words at the time, found in them reassurance and a trail of bread crumbs to some future certainty.

But does anyone, ever, know? Does Eric, I wonder? Oksana or Gwen? For so many years, I thought it was so simple. I lived in a pop-up book, an Advent calendar, a place of doors and treats and clarity. Now I seem to live in another world entirely, fathomless and strange. I thought exploring it would help. But so far, so far from home, I still don't know what to do about that.

Passing over the Persian Gulf, moon glinting off the water, the only sight to see but for the light of an occasional boat, and then all of a sudden, bam! Bright necklaces of light, outlandish buildings and strange compounds and theme parks, and it's all out of nothing. And then I'm there. On the fucking Arabian Peninsula, man.

I pin my hopes on Africa.

14
When in Tanzania

IT IS FIVE thirty in the afternoon and I am resting in a pup tent that's been thrown up for me beside the cracked mud wall of one of the houses of Kesuma's father's sister's *boma.* Two girls, perhaps ten years old, elegant, thin, and small-boned, in red and purple robes, their necks and arms heavily draped with white beaded jewelry, are peering around the corner of the wall at me. They have their hands clasped up high near their faces to cover the brilliant grins and storms of giggles they break into every time I glance up from my letters to smile at them. Sometimes they wave, and when I wave back they are amazingly amused, as if they've just trained a dog to do a particularly smart trick.

It's been a long and wondrous day, and it's far from done. We left Kesuma's house in Arusha, Tanzania, at eight in the morning—me and Kesuma, Leyan, Elly, and Obed. Kesuma is a handsome, small man with a quick smile who wears his Maasai dress—red plaid robes, shoes made of motorcycle tires, an array of white

beaded necklaces and bracelets and anklets, a large knife in a red
leather scabbard around his waist and his beaded "Chief stick" in
his hand—whether he's in town riding his motor scooter, herding
goats in one of his family's villages, or speaking before hundreds of
people at Berkeley about his nonprofit organization, Kitumusote.
The mission of Kitumusote is to build educational and environ-
mental programs for the Maasai, a people fiercely dedicated to a
traditional lifestyle of cattle herding, which is increasingly difficult
to maintain in contemporary Africa. To raise money, Kesuma orga-
nizes "cultural safaris" like these. It's an uncomfortable phrase,
suggesting that I'm heading out in a Land Rover with my pith helmet and a thermos full of G&Ts, hoping for some human version
of the Battle at Kruger. But in fact what we're doing is something
far quieter and more personal—we are visiting with Kesuma's family. When we arrived at the village, the women were gathered under
the single large shade tree where they meet to take classes in Swahili
and basic mathematics. But they weren't studying at that moment;
they were singing. Kesuma's aunt, a handsome older woman, urged
me to join in the dancing, with a generous gesture of her arm and a
kind laugh that she sustained, even once it became clear that I was
quite a horrible dancer, spastic and awkward.

Now, after my afternoon rest, we seem to have come to the
question-and-answer period.

"Was your marriage arranged, or did your husband choose
you?"

"Um. I chose him." It seems a queer way of putting it, the concept of "choice" somehow just off correct, at once too trivial and
too indicative of will, but close enough, I suppose.

Kesuma translates, and the women erupt into scandalized
giggles and awestruck expressions, whispering among themselves.
God, if they only knew the half of it.

"Do you have children?"

"Not yet." They nod solemnly, with sympathetic, somewhat stricken looks on their faces, feeling the tragedy of my
childlessness.

"The center of our life is our herd, and our family, our children. What is the center of your life?"

Gosh. What on earth can I say to that? My husband? My lover? Sex? Money? My dog? Oy. I can't really explain that that's sort of exactly why I'm here with them in this remote village on an arid Tanzanian hillside. Essentially, *I was kind of hoping you would tell me.*

"What is your job in the home?"

"Well, in theory, the husband and the wife are meant to do equal parts of the work, cleaning, cooking. But actually I usually do more." When I'm not running off to some foreign country alone for months on end, of course.

The women giggle again at this notion, then grow serious. One of the older women, who looks tired, less vital and happy than Kesuma's aunt, begins to speak, and the others nod while Kesuma translates:

"You have so much freedom."

It's a startling statement. I'd just been thinking how I envied these women, their beauty and singing and bare feet in the dry red soil. Their romantically simple lives. I've been stupid.

"We have to do all the work. The men do nothing but go out with the cattle. And if we don't do something right, our husbands sometimes beat us."

It occurs to me that I have very little notion of how old any of these women are. A few of them seem to be children, perhaps sixteen years old. Others seem ancient. But most occupy an indeterminate middle ground. Kesuma's aunt could be forty or seventy. I ask Kesuma about this.

"I don't know. She doesn't even really know."

"She doesn't know?"

"We Maasai generally don't have birth certificates. It was a problem for me when I first tried to fly to the U.S.!" He laughs, as his head falls back and his shoulders duck forward in a gesture I've already recognized as characteristic of him. "I told the woman at the office I was twenty-seven, but I don't know. Do I look twenty-seven to you?"

"That seems about right." In honesty, Kesuma's age could be anywhere between twenty-one and thirty-five, his apparent physical youth tempered by a sense of gravity, not to mention his list of impressive accomplishments. Born in a remote village on the Tanzania-Kenya border, he has gone to school, become fluent in both English and Swahili, and saved the money to take college-level courses in filmmaking, computer literacy, and the effects of globalization. He's founded an international nonprofit organization, traveled to the United States to raise money and give talks, and made the kinds of friends, all over the world, who are happy to have him stay with them in their homes at short notice or no notice at all.

"We don't have birthdays like you. I'm the same age as everyone in my group of warriors. We were...I know the word...not *cut,* but...*circumcised!* All at the same time, and then we were all warriors. And we'll be warriors until the king of the Maasai decides that it is time for us to be elders. Then I can drink beer!" He laughs again. The women are all smiling at him in anticipation. They giggle when he translates, are fascinated that I could be confused by such a basic tenet of life as the marking of time and age. One of the younger women pipes up. "You don't have age groups? Warriors, elders?"

"No, not in the same way. We have something we call 'generations,' but that's more, I don't know, general. It's just everyone, man or woman, born within a certain period, about thirty years or so."

Kesuma translates, the women ponder my answer. Another woman asks, "But if you don't have age groups, how do you know how to show and receive proper respect?"

"Um...respect? I don't know. I guess maybe respect doesn't mean as much to us. Or it isn't the same somehow. I respect someone for what he's accomplished or who he is as a person, not because of how old he is."

The women look horrified. "But respect...respect is what makes us people. It's what holds together families. Respect is the most important thing!"

"For me, respect is nice, but I'd rather have, well—love, I guess."

For some minutes we try to bridge this terrible gulf between us; they are too polite to confess they think me a dangerously insolent heathen, and I am too polite to say I think they're trapped in some benighted patriarchy. But then I have a sort of revelation—more of an instinct than a reasoned explanation. "You say respect holds people together. I say love. I think—I don't know how to explain this. I think when I love someone, *really* love someone...not, um..." I turn to Kesuma. "Not, you know, sexual love, or a crush or something?" He translates, and the women giggle again. "But when I really love someone it's *because* I respect him. Or, my respect for him comes out of my love. I think maybe they're the same, really."

I don't know if this actually means something or not. But it seems to satisfy the women. There are smiling nods all around.

After our conversation, I decide to take a little walk around the *boma* and maybe find a quiet spot to take a piss. Kesuma has explained to me that each *boma*—a collection of several thatched mud huts, with a corral for cattle and another one for goats, the entire cluster surrounded by a fence that is really just a jumble of thorny branches—represents one family group, an elder and his wives and unmarried children, and the wives of his sons. Many *bomas* make up the village. They are spread out from one another, by quite a distance. As I walk around the *boma* I'll be staying the night at, there are a couple of others within sight, but only just. So actually the "village" is a sprawling thing with no real center, a vast scattering of homes up and down the mountainside. It seems a strange way to live, somehow at once lonesome and rather too rife with mothers-in-law.

It also proves a rather tricky place to pee. I get used to the notion of my ablutions being witnessed by a few incurious baby goats, but I'd rather not be witnessed by anyone at any of the *bomas* or by one of the children wandering about as I drop trow, revealing what to Maasai eyes must seem my hideously wide and pale ass. The trees and bushes dotting the landscape are both treacherously spiky and rather sparse, so it takes a bit of doing to find a good spot. But eventually I manage.

As I continue my walk back in the direction of the *boma,* I'm suddenly met by a small swarm of kids, waving and giggling and not attempting to exchange a word. They don't even call me *mzungu*—Swahili for "gringo," basically—the way the kids in Arusha do when I walk down the road, because they don't speak Swahili. Still, these guys—three girls between the ages of nine and twelve, I'd say, and a couple of small boys—know the drill. While one girl closely admires the beaded necklace and earrings Kesuma's aunt and the other women gave me when I arrived, the others rummage through my pockets for my camera and BlackBerry to play with. The Amy Winehouse ringtone on my phone—"You Know That I'm No Good"—is cause for many toothy grins and small spontaneous dances, and the camera of course has to be passed around. Everyone in the growing group needs to take a picture and then have everyone else gather around to see the result, the subject of the picture always receiving some congratulation or ridicule.

Then suddenly Kesuma's aunt is striding up to our group, linking her arm forcefully with mine, shooing the kids angrily away, showing special vehemence for a very small boy in a windbreaker that hangs down to his ankles, who runs off toward another *boma* some distance away, moaning. She pulls me back inside the *boma* walls to the pup tent that Obed and Leyan have erected for me to sleep in. (Kesuma has adamantly recommended that I stick to the tent, rather than brave a night in one of the huts. "Very, very dark and smoky. It's difficult, at first, for *mzungu* to get used to." Which makes me feel sheepish and wimpy, but I have acquiesced.)

"*Lala, lala…,*" Kesuma's aunt insists, making a universal gesture, palms pressed together under one tilted cheek. She wants me to have a little lie-down. The afternoon has grown hot, and either I'm looking a little wilted or the Maasai just assume all white folks are delicate flowers. I nod, smiling, and crawl into my tent. Kicking off my shoes, I lie down on my side, then have to roll over to take my BlackBerry out of my pocket. I glance down at its face as I do, and am appalled to see I have four bars of phone service. Even more astonishing, I can get online. Within moments I have logged onto Facebook, where I cannot resist updating my status to "Coming at you LIVE from a freakin' Maasai village." I also can't resist scrolling over to D's page, where I can see the only photo that exists of him in un-password-protected cyberspace. (Believe me, I've Google-stalked him enough to know for sure.) In it he's smiling in a very D-like way while wearing a Ben Sherman shirt I gave him. Just looking at it, here, makes me feel a little disgusted with myself. I turn off my phone and tuck it into my backpack. As I do, I come upon the chunkee stone, the one Eric had custom-carved for me. It is heavy and dark, with perfectly smooth concave faces like the inside of a cup-and-ball joint. I'm not certain why I brought it with me on this trip, risking losing it, but I enjoy holding it, running my fingers around its circumference or placing my forehead, briefly, to the cool stone. Beneath the chunkee are two bundles of pages, my two now-epic letters. I pull them out.

But I wind up not even writing in them. I just stare up at the fluttering sun-spackled walls of my tent. Outside, the light is gold on the hills past my netted window. Two girls continually creep up to the unzipped door of my tent, smiling and grabbing at the camera to see the pictures over and over again, then running off, either out of shyness or, more likely, fear of reprimand from Kesuma's daunting aunt.

And then all of a sudden, as if I was not sufficiently aware of how bizarre this whole situation is, there is a great explosion of bleating; the adult goats are returning from their day of grazing, and as the mothers enter their nighttime enclosure they call out to the kids, who were left behind near the village. A mournful, almost desperate call and response, which doesn't end until every mother and child is reunited. It's an oddly comforting sound, that blaring panic settling gradually into contented, suckling quiet. The sound of having everyone come home.

That night shortly after the sun finishes setting, I eat a dinner of goat ribs and potatoes that Obed and Elly make for me, banking their cooking fire immediately after. I'd imagined an African village lit by torches or campfires or gas lamps, but there is nothing. When the dark sets in, it sets in entirely. The only man-made light in evidence in the *boma*, or anywhere outside it, is my flashlight and a distant blinking red light atop a power line on another hillside that Kesuma tells me is across the border in Kenya. By my flashlight, I watch as the men show me their dances. Obed and Elly, the only other people here besides me in Western dress, watch too as Kesuma joins in. One of the songs and dances is like a competitive game; the story line is about skilled warriors who can leap straight up into trees to escape a charging lion, and that's what they do, one after the other, to the music. They jump straight into the air, pulling their knees up sharply, trying to get more height than the preceding man. The elders participate, as well as the warriors and the small boys. (I feel strange using those words, *warrior* and *elder,* but these are the words they use for themselves so I suppose I must follow suit.) The mood gets more and more exuberant, almost out of hand. The universal symptoms of testosterone poisoning. Elly, a beautiful young man who's prob-ably all of nineteen, shakes his head, laughing, and leans over to whisper in my ear, "These Maasai, they're *crazy.*"

Eventually I say my good-nights and return to my tent. I should stay up, it's not late and I'm not even terribly tired. I just suddenly want to be alone. So I lie down in my tent, staring up through the near pitch-black at the vague dim rippling of the nylon. The women have begun to sing, separately—I can hear that they are farther away, perhaps as far as the school tree. They are overlap-ping with the men, perhaps competing with them, or just comple-menting them. It is ravishingly beautiful, fiercely joyful and yet somehow evocative of yearning, and it goes on and on for hours into the night. I think of my phone, put away, its silence almost a part of the music. Lying there, sleepless, listening, I feel maybe the most peaceful I've felt in years, in forever.

Unlike Eric and I, who share almost the exact same taste in music and often wake up with the same song in our two heads, who can recognize instantly what the other is thinking from a bit of badly hummed tune or a couple of stray words from a single lyric, D and I did not often sing together. He'd have liked for us to, but I was shy about my voice, as D's was assured and pitch-perfect. Besides, none of the songs we knew the words to were the same. I remember one haunting melody he sang to me once in a parking lot in Florida. I had to go look up the lyrics later. It turned out to be a Beck song. I still don't know the words, though the tune sticks in my head and weaves in with all the other music inside and out. Something about *a strange invitation*...

I'm considering leaving the *boma* to go to the bathroom, which I have to do rather urgently. But then, rising over the sounds of the singers, comes a strange yelping cry, close by, like a woman calling out. I am damned near sure it's an actual hyena.

I think I'll wait until morning.

IT TURNS out that Elly used to work as a guide taking tourists up Kilimanjaro. I learn this the next day as he is driving us to our next destination—another village, another *boma,* this one belonging to Kesuma's father. Elly keeps the conversation lively on the long drive, informative and, just possibly, flirtatious. He alerts me to points of interest along the way: baobab trees; the tiny ante-lopes, no more than a foot high, called dik-diks; birds. There are these birds here, very common, just starlings, but their feathers are brilliant, sapphire blue, with bright orange breasts. An apparently suicidal eland races across the road just in front of us, avoiding by milliseconds a bus coming in the opposite direction. We ponder aloud about what could have gotten it so spooked, and I half expect to see a lioness or a cheetah racing behind it. Or perhaps that's just what elands do for fun.

We arrive at the *boma* over a treacherous track that almost isn't a track at all, up over the crest of a hill. I'd thought the village yesterday was lovely, but this is breathtaking. A long view out over a valley to another chain of mountains across the border in Kenya. One of the mountains is a volcano; it's smoking gently. The light is pink and gold; it is nearly sunset by the time we arrive, and we're greeted by small boys waving and the bleating of goats calling out to their mothers to nurse.

A sometimes violent act, this, the kids kneeling on their forelegs and then ramming their heads hard up against their mothers' underbellies. It looks like it hurts. One of the mothers, in fact, has decided she's had just about enough. She tries to run away from her hungry child. Kesuma enlists my help, getting me to hold her still by her horns while the kid kneels to feed.

Another goat acts rather like a naughty dog. He'll come try to eat out of your cup. I'm drinking a tea that Kesuma's wife has made me, Kesuma tells me, from the bark of a tree that grows nearby. It's a light, muddy color, but tastes like chocolate and cinnamon. The goat will try to get into the houses and is constantly being shooed away. There's also an actual dog, a friendly thing who Kesuma says is his. The Maasai in general don't seem much enamored of dogs. Kesuma and I are the only people who pet this one, and everyone looks at us like we're slightly loony.

Kesuma wears his traditional garb and motorcycle-tire Maasai shoes everywhere, but he's also got a degree in filmmaking and a keen interest in women's rights. He has visited San Francisco, New York, Europe. But he seems equally at home among the goats and *bomas* of his father's village, squatting on the ground with a cup of tea that his young wife brings to him before going back to her chores with the other women. And he keeps dogs as pets, a habit he says he picked up while visiting American friends in the States. Life must be strange and wonderful and big and treacherous for Kesuma, I think. But I suppose it is for us all, if we allow ourselves to pay attention.

Then it's time for the cows to come home. Maasai cattle are nothing like the prosaic Herefords back home. These are magnificent animals, enormous red and black and gray beasts with spreading horns and gleaming hides and great dewlaps. They have dignity; they even have grace. They come up the hill quietly, with very little lowing, the occasional clang of a bell.

Tonight, after I've eaten my dinner (a sort of spaghetti-

and-meatballs dish that Obed throws together) and the sun has gone down, we gather around a fire. It's cold up on this mountainside, and windy. I give Kesuma's father two beers I brought up from a town at the base of the mountain. Now that he's an elder, rather than a warrior, he enjoys a beer now and then, Kesuma has told me. Everyone else gets Cokes. We sit, and some of the men tell stories, which Kesuma translates. The stories are long and meander, and I don't follow them very well. They involve demons and evil spells, wives who try to save their children from fathers who want to kill them—standard mythical fare. I guess we are all of us worried about fathers eating us. Then they ask me to tell a story from America, and I'm flummoxed of course, but then I come upon the perfect solution:

"Into each generation a slayer is born, one girl in all the world with the strength and skill to fight the demons..."

So I tell them the story of Buffy, of vampires and fighting and heartbreak and wishes gone terribly awry. And I am pleased, no, amazed, that as we sit around the fire, as I speak and Kesuma translates, women and boys and girls and men lean forward to listen. Their faces light up. They gasp and laugh and shake their heads. My story too meanders a bit toward the end, and must be confusing—*Buffy*, as I've pointed out, can be a bitch of a thing to recap—but it's clear that the tale makes sense to them. And I end it as the Maasai ended their stories, with a moral.

"Be careful what you wish for. We all have to live in the worlds we make for ourselves."

I do not sleep well that night, not because I'm not tired, or because I'm moping or worrying or obsessing—surprisingly, I'm not doing any of these things. I do spend some time fantasizing about bringing Eric here, but it's a contented thought. And I'm pleased that I don't even want to entertain the notion of showing all of this to D; nothing could interest him less. No, the reason I'm not sleeping is that hurricane-force winds are buffeting my little tent. The noise of flapping nylon is unceasing, like sails in a gale. I fear the thing is going to come apart. For hours and hours this goes on, until finally Elly and Obed emerge from their own tent and come to tend to mine.

I see their flashlights coming toward me, and then they're shouting at me to stay inside, as the edges of the tent have come loose. They manage to tamp everything back down, ensuring that I'm not going to blow over the side of the mountain. At last, at around dawn, the wind abates and I'm able to sleep for an hour or two.

Kesuma greets me at the door of my tent as I stumble out. "We have a big, big day. Obed has your breakfast."

After I ingest a prepackaged cake and peanut butter on bread, pineapple juice, and a slice of mango, Kesuma takes me into the cattle pen so I can watch the men bleed a cow.

This is, at last, exactly the reason I've come to Tanzania in the first place. "I want to go to a Maasai village and drink cow blood!" I told Eric when I was trying to explain to him why I had to rip myself away from him again, and so soon. It wasn't about my unhappiness or his lack; it was experience I sought, exoticism. Just a touch of the utterly foreign, that's all. He wasn't convinced, but it made a good sound bite.

And I must say that as an experience to go halfway around the world for, cow bleeding doesn't disappoint. We crowd into the pen, the animals jostling to one side of the enclosure to get some distance between us and them. The men discuss which steer to choose; they want a male (for some reason they always bleed males) who is young and healthy enough to withstand the procedure and heal quickly. Once they decide on one, a midsized red creature, two of the men get a rope around its neck and drag it forward. They hold its head steady, and someone hooks an arm over its neck, around its horns, in a sort of headlock, pulling the rope tight so that the jugular vein swells. More warriors lean up hard against the steer's sides to keep it from dancing away. Kesuma has with him a bow-and-arrow set; the bow is only about two feet long, with a crude stick for an arrow, tied to the wood of the bow by a short length of twine. He leans down to get a good angle and then, at very close range, shoots the popping vein, pricking it. The steer jerks a bit, of course—there is now a gout of blood pouring out of its neck, after all—but mostly seems fairly resigned, like this is a bad trip to the dentist. The blood collects in a tall gourd, which holds, I'd imagine, a liter or more. The men fill it all the way to the top, and then Kesuma reaches down and grabs a big gob of mud and dung from the ground and pats it on the wound. They let the steer go and it trots off back into the herd, a little pissy perhaps but, apparently, not much the worse for wear.

One of the men picks up a longish stick, which has been shoved into the pen's thorny fence for safekeeping, and uses it to vigorously stir the blood in the gourd, for several minutes. When he lifts the stick back out again, it's covered in thready red goop, like meaty cotton candy, I suppose whatever solids there are in the blood. He hands it to a small boy, who begins eating the stuff off the stick with relish.

"Sometimes kids don't like the blood, so we give them this to get them used to it. It's more like meat."

"Uh. Okay." Well, so much for universality and *Buffy*. I guess this right here is what you call an unbridgeable cultural gap. Because that is just irretrievably nasty.

Kesuma's wife brings tin cups out for all of us adults, and each is filled about halfway. We drink. It's blood, all right. Salty and oddly familiar, like biting the inside of your cheek or having a tooth pulled.

Afterward Kesuma's wife brings us more of the cinnamony tea in a pot. I watch a tiny boy, perhaps four or five, take one of the cups we've just been drinking blood out of and studiously clean it out by squatting in the middle of the corral, scooping in dirt and dung, and tossing it around in the cup before emptying it out and getting some tea. Ah well. I guess this is the sort of thing you have to get used to. I drink my tea.

Then we pack up some stuff and start down the mountain, me and Kesuma, Elly and Obed, Leyan and a couple more young men from the *boma*. We're going to what Kesuma is calling the *orpul*, but I have no very clear understanding of what that is. I know only that they're going to kill me a goat once we get there. The day is already hot, and the climb down into the valley is rocky and steep. I keep slipping and nearly falling, while Kesuma and the other Maasai go tripping down the mountainside ahead of me like a bunch of brightly robed mountain goats. I grab onto spiky trees, try to keep from breathing too hard, and just manage to keep up, sort of. The hike down takes maybe half an hour, and winds up in a shaded ravine—a creek bed, actually, though only a trickle of water runs through now, at the end of the dry season. Another young guy from the village arrived a little before us, and with him the goat we'll be eating for dinner. It's a white goat, serene, seemingly not at all discomfited to be here in this rocky, narrow place, surrounded by men with very large knives strapped to their waists.

For a while the goat just munches contentedly on a stunted tree growing out of a crevice in the rock as some of the young men build a fire and Obed and Elly unpack the considerable supplies they've toted down the mountain to make the *mzungu* woman reasonably comfortable—Western-style food in Tupperware containers, a sleeping bag, cooking utensils, and bottles upon bottles of water, one of which Obed forces on me now. I've yet to see an African drink anything at all other than soda or beer. The sun is strong, even though broken into shafts by the spindly trees and sifted through by the breeze blowing down through the ravine; it's been a long walk down the mountain. I lap up the water greedily.

By the time the fire is built, on a little ledge above and across the tiny riverbed from the flattened-out spot, surrounded by thorny branches that evidently will serve as our sleeping area, one of the boys has gathered a large bunch of leafy twigs from downstream. They lay them out near the goat, who immediately turns to chew some of these fresher leaves. So it's not pondering death, at least it would not seem so to human eyes, when two of the Maasai grab it, one man taking the two forelegs in one hand, the other the two back, and toss it to the ground. It immediately begins to squeal, of course, being thrown about like that, but the men have it firmly in their grasp and hold it down without too much trouble, their scarlet and purple robes flung over their shoulders, out of their way, revealing lanky muscles. Kesuma squats and grabs the goat's head, holding its mouth closed and its nostrils shut.

The goat doesn't stop thrashing, not for several minutes. Neither does it quit vocally protesting, attempting to scream and grunt through Kesuma's muffling hand. The three Maasai chat among themselves, laughing, as the animal struggles.

The goats here are happy, I have to believe, fat and shiny-coated with the run of the countryside and no fear of their human keepers. But that doesn't mean that death is not painful and ugly. The creature wants life, desperately, won't let go of it for a long time. I wonder why the men laugh. I think it's because no matter how often you go through this ritual, how inured you become to killing animals with your own hands, if you are a decent human being you still hang on to that slight discomfort, that bit of shame over causing such distress. I had not thought I'd be so affected.

"Why can't you, you know, hit it over the head with a rock or something? Slit its throat?"

"The heart must stop beating before we open it up, so that we can collect the blood. The blood's the most important part."

Gradually, the animal ceases to grunt or jerk its head; as it does, the giggling stops, and the men grow watchful and considering. They squat over the animal, occasionally putting a hand out to touch the hide, softly, even tenderly, shaking the goat's shoulder gently as if trying to wake it from sleep. They are trying to feel something in the way the flesh moves under their hands, I guess, some indication of total release. Finally, after some muttered exchanges, after a moment more of quiet, Kesuma releases the goat's head. Its body is now limp; its neck seems boneless. They lift it onto the bier of green branches, rest it on its back with its head folded, like a swan tucking its head under its wing, and take their long knives from the scabbards at their waists.

One of the young men punches the dead goat hard in the stomach several times, ending each blow with a sort of brief massage with his knuckles. Kesuma looks up to explain, perhaps realizing that to my eyes, this pummeling looks a little harsh. "We want all the blood to be in the stomach." Punching a dead goat to make all its blood go into its stomach doesn't seem like a particularly scientifically sound process, but what the hell, these guys have slaughtered a lot more goats than I have. Then the three men, taking turns, begin to skin the animal.

I've never skinned a whole mammal. But I've boned out ducks and turkeys, and this begins to look a little like that. Kesuma makes a slit from the point just above the breastbone to the genitals—boy's parts, it was a he—which he cuts off. Then on either side of the slit, using their knives and their hands, the men start working the skin away from the fat and muscle. There is very little blood; a trickle or two from a nicked vein. From neck to tail, the skin comes away, down and down toward the joints of the legs. They cut a line through the hide on the inside of each leg, right to the hooves. These hooves they cut off, like Josh would work off the hooves of pigs. Kesuma hands them to one of the other boys, who takes them up to the fire to roast. The rest of the men continue to work the skin off the four haunches, until the hide is connected to the animal's body only along its backbone and at the nape of the neck. But the creature's head is still on and it still looks very much like a goat—and also a little like an illustration from a particularly gruesome Germanic retelling of "Little Red Riding Hood," with a small, mutilated body lying splayed on the tender pink cloak that was once its skin.

They take the leg joints off. Then one of the men breaks into the body cavity by pressing the tip of his long knife at the breastbone and banging down on the hilt with the palm of his hand until the bone cracks. They lift out the intestines, pale and still contained in their thin blue sac. They take out the liver, hand it around for each of them to take a bite of. Kesuma cuts off a piece for me to eat, which I do. It tastes much as I would expect, still warm, with a meltingly tender texture, like bloody cheesecake. There's something about the taste that is a little different from liver I've had in the past, but I can't quite put my finger on it. The rest of the liver he hands up to the guy by the fire.

Next he hands me a piece of kidney, which is...fine. Slightly urinous, but fine. Then some sort of greenish grayish glandular something; I'll just go out on a limb and say maybe pancreas? Also raw. And rubbery. But I swallow all bits offered without comment. Now they have a tin cup and are using it to scoop up cupfuls of the blood that has pooled in the body's cavity. We all wash down our bites of organ with it. I realize what I'd tasted about the liver that was different. Goat blood tastes different from beef blood, or my own. It's almost... well, it's...

"It's sweet!"

Kesuma nods as I return the cup. He takes a big swig and passes it on. "That's right. Sweet! Now, show me your hand." The other young men are continuing to break down the goat into parts, haunches and racks of ribs to be roasted or stored to take up the mountain to their families the next day. But Kesuma takes a break to do a little something for me. First he cuts a strip of hide from the edge of the flayed-open belly of the goat, perhaps five inches long and half an inch wide. He holds it up against the back of my hand, the slimy interior side against my skin, snowy white hair on the top side. He seems to make a measurement with his fingers, then takes the strip away and, working on a flat rock, makes two vertical slits in it; at one end, less than an inch long, and at the other, a bit longer. He beckons me to give him my left hand again, and when I do he slips the larger hole around it, works the hide down to the wrist, and slips my middle finger through the small slit.

"This is a tradition at the *orpul*. The young warriors come here once they are circumcised, to learn about herbs and barks to use for medicine, and to kill a cow. Sick men will come other times when they need to get well. And this"—he pats my hand, which now has a band of goatskin around it, stretching up in a sort of upside-down Y shape around my middle finger—"this is like...like a good-luck bracelet. If you get one of these when you're at the *orpul* and then you don't take it off until you come back, or until it falls off, you'll have good luck."

I pet the soft hair on the strip that runs from my wrist to middle finger. The skin is still wet on the underside.

We spend the heat of the day doing nothing much at all. Kesuma and the others make new goatskin bracelets for themselves, sharpen their knives idly on river stones, watch over the meat they are cooking for our dinner tonight (I'm fed some more liver, cooked this time). What they are not going to cook tonight, they wrap in leaves and tuck on top of more leaves, within a covered hutch of brambles which sits in the middle of our sleeping corral or whatever you'd call it. Within the hide are several round, fatty masses, about the size of golf balls. "Tonight," Kesuma explains, "we'll stay up to protect the meat in case any lions come looking for it." I'm ninety percent sure he's kidding, or at least exaggerating, but I think I'll take my potty break before the sun goes down.

In the afternoon Kesuma, Leyan, and I head up to the lip of the ravine to look for various roots and leaves and bark that Kesuma wants to show me. He is a strict teacher; he moves fast, expects me to keep up, as well as keep notes in the blue exercise notebook he gave me when I arrived in Tanzania. *Lokunonoi* is a bark used to treat stomach pain. The roots of the *orukiloriti* tree are boiled by warriors for a tea that makes them "bloodthirsty"; its thorny branches are used to build pens for the cattle and the protective fences around *bomas*. *Ogaki* is the "forgiveness tree"; you bring a branch of it to a neighbor when you want to ask forgiveness for some offense. You can chew on a branch of the *orkinyeye* tree to clean your teeth; it tastes fresh, almost minty. Most of these plants look to me very much alike. Most of them are thorny.

We ramble up and down the rocks of the ravine. I take notes, per Kesuma's command, as he explains things to me and as Leyan collects various roots and barks and branches. It is hot and dry work. By the time we arrive back at the *orpul,* Leyan is loaded down, but I'm the one dripping with sweat.

The sun goes down quickly. I eat a meal of grilled goat ribs and drink the crazy-making tea, which, because I'm not Maasai or because I'm crazy already, doesn't seem to change anything. A couple of Kesuma's friends gather some more of the green branches on which they'd killed the goat—now parceled away inside its little meat hut, the hide and the cooked meat and the raw meat that's been sitting out in the heat all day and the fat all bundled together, which seems to bother no one but me—and make a sort of bower for me to sleep on. We all lie down in the dark, I in my sleeping bag, everyone else just flat out on their backs. For a while they exchange stories and riddles, some of which Kesuma translates for me:

You are alone and slaughter a goat by yourself. Who is the first to taste the meat?

Your knife.

Perhaps the crazy-making tea did do a little something for me because the moment I drift off on the none-too-comfy leaves, I'm transported to some European city I've never seen before but that feels instantly like home, where Eric and I wander the tree-lined streets discussing whether to take in an art exhibit or lunch—and then I'm awake again, it must be three or four in the morning, and the men are all laughing and carrying on about something. I shut my eyes again and I'm in a bookstore, reading the blurb on the back of a book about D's and my lost love, and D is there too, and he asks me how I could have not known? And it's five thirty a.m., dawn, and I'm up for good, ready to climb that damned mountain and, if that doesn't kill me, get back to Arusha and Kesuma's house and a deeply necessary shower.

The hike back up the mountain is just as onerous as I thought it would be; within five minutes after starting up the wending, rocky path, I'm breathless and perspiring, and Kesuma has to fetch me a walking stick and get Elly to carry my backpack, in addition to his own. I'm humiliated, but Elly is kind enough to chat and flirt with me—he's definitely flirting with me—and keep up the conversation when I'm too winded to hold up my end. He talks about his jobs as a guide and a safari driver. In a few days he's going to be driving Kesuma and me on an overnight safari to Ngorongoro Crater. He's also worked as a mechanic.

Which, as it turns out, is going to come in handy. Since about an hour into our drive home, past Monduli, we run out of gas.

The truck comes to a rattling halt on a dusty road lined with acacia trees. A ridge rises above us to the north. There seems to be nothing in the vicinity resembling human civilization, but cars do occasionally pass. While Kesuma hitches a ride to the next gas station, Elly endeavors to get the car running again, which involves, first off, siphoning a liter of gasoline from the tank *with his mouth.* (Turns out the tank isn't empty, but the line inside doesn't go all the way to the bottom.) He puts this gasoline in an oilcan that he straps to the hood of the car, running a line from it straight to the engine. If he's trying to impress me with his derring-do, he's done it. If he's trying to make me very afraid of the perils of driving in Africa, well, he's done that too. I give him my last bottle of water and promise to buy him a beer once we get back to Arusha.

"Least I can do," I say as he spits mouthfuls of water out onto the pavement.

"Sounds good to me." He quits retching long enough to give me a smile and a wink.

That night, we do get that beer. Kesuma insists on coming with us, to a pool hall down the main road between his house and the Arusha town center, probably to protect me from any improper advances. He wears Western clothes, the only time I will ever see him in such during my entire trip—a white button-down shirt and black jeans, which combined with his white beaded jewelry and dark skin make him look awfully hip. A perfectly innocent time is had by all, but I feel Elly looking at me. I don't mind a bit.

I'M THE hippest white woman on the rim of Ngorongoro Crater tonight. I'd be hipper still if I wasn't so delightfully aware of my hipness, but we'll let that pass.

It's nearing sunset by the time we get to the campground where Kesuma, Elly, Leyan, and I will be setting up our tents, and the place is fairly crowded, with touring Westerners, their Tanzanian cooks and guides, and the occasional zebra. We've had a full day, having left Kesuma's house in Arusha some time after eight a.m. and driving first to Lake Manyara, a small park in a rift valley, about an hour from town. It was my first safari, and while I didn't see any brilliant Battle at Kruger–style kill scenarios—which is for the best, as I probably would have broken down like a little girl—I did thrill to the sights of elephants knocking down trees, families of rooting warthogs, wallowing hippos, and fighting giraffes. This last spectacle is a sight that, to quote yet another *Buffy* character, "puts fear in no one's hearts." Elly drove the Land Rover he'd rented for the trip, while Leyan and Kesuma and I stood up on the back seats to look out the pop-up roof.

I'd expected the sort of safari you think about when you read travel magazines and watch the Discovery Channel, led by an African guide in a pith helmet speaking into a microphone at a carload of tourists. "This is the African forest elephant. The tusks are longer than those of the bush elephant, and point downward..." But this wasn't like that at all. This was like a trip to the most amazing zoo in the world with a few friends. We pointed and whispered excitedly at elephants lumbering through the forest, stared, amazed, at the enormous snake—eight feet long if it was an inch—that we caught sight of near the picnic tables where we stopped for lunch, laughed and cooed over the tiny infant baboons in their mothers' arms. Afterward, on to Ngorongoro. On the way, we stopped for beers for Elly and me, Cokes for Kesuma and Leyan, at an outdoor bar next to a tiny open-air butcher shop, where halved and skinned goat carcasses were hung up against the wall like coats on hooks. Though Kesuma can't drink, I took a picture of him holding my beer bottle, to much hilarity. We talked, I remember particularly, about blue whales.

"Did you get good pictures of the elephants?" Kesuma took the Coke bottle metal cap between his teeth and cracked it off. I squeaked in indignation.

"Oh *God,* I wish you wouldn't do that. It makes my flesh crawl." I pulled out my cheap little digital camera and flipped through some of my shots, handed it over for Kesuma to see.

"They're beautiful, aren't they?"

"They really, really are."

"They're the biggest animals in the world, right?"

Elly took a swig off his second beer before jumping in. "No, they're not. Whales are bigger. Blue whales." I nodded my agreement.

"Whales?"

"Yeah. In the ocean. Like gigantic fish, but they're not fish, they're mammals."

"Bigger than *elephants*? No!" Kesuma made an exaggerated expression of amazement. He is so articulate and intelligent and well educated that it's startling when, as now and then happens, I discover some small gap in his knowledge. I tend to feel like he's having me on.

"When you come to visit New York, I'll take you to the Museum of Natural History. They have a life-sized model of one. It's *enormous*. Like a hundred feet long or something."

"No! Really?"

We loaded up onto the truck after Elly and I had finished our two beers, and I dozed for the final forty minutes or so of the drive to the campsite at the crater rim. Now we've arrived. Elly and Leyan put up my tent, simple, but an enormous thing for one woman. Their own, for three men, is half the size. I ask them to switch, but Kesuma won't hear of it. Then Elly goes off to cook our dinner—a fish for him and me, chicken and rice for Leyan and Kesuma. (Maasai, they tell me, don't eat fish.) While we wait for dinner to be ready, we sit at long concrete tables at the dining enclosure, a sort of shed with a roof but no walls. There are probably six or eight groups here at the campground with us. Kesuma and Leyan are the only Maasai. The other tables are set with fine china, tablecloths. I wouldn't be surprised to see candles. The other tourists are served by teams of cooks who set the plates down, then disappear into the cooking enclosure next door. Pasta, steak, sautéed chicken breasts.

Elly, Leyan, Kesuma, and I gather around a plastic plate and some Tupperware. We eat with our fingers, pulling bits of flesh from the fish's carcass, picking tiny bones out of our teeth, wiping our greasy hands on our pants legs. Elly and I drink the two beers we brought with us from the bar. Afterward we carry our dishes back to the kitchen area, which Elly washes while, as everyone else begins trickling out to tents and beds, Kesuma, Leyan, and I gather at our concrete table and play cards with the I ♥ NY deck I brought from home.

First Kesuma and Leyan teach me—well, try to teach me—a game called "lasty card." (For some reason people here have a tendency to add *y* to the end of all kinds of English words. "Lasty" for last, "chesty" for chest, "lefty" for leftovers. I find it odd and slightly grating.) I never really get my mind around lasty card. But I do impress them with my tremendous shuffling skills. This is something Eric has told me to expect. Apparently no one else in the world can do the arching style of shuffling that Americans do. I'm no good at it at all, though I learned at my grandmother's knee. (No matter how arthritic her hands got, Granny could always shuffle a mean deck of cards, and she was, to my ten-year-old eyes anyway, a regular sharp when it came to solitaire.) But though I'm no good, everyone grins in disbelief when I do it.

Then I try to teach poker, but I'm no better an instructor than I am a shuffler; Elly, who's by now joined us, is the only one who can really master it.

We're the last folks in the dining area. We play probably three or four hands before Kesuma and Leyan decide to head to their tent.

"You want to play a little more?" Elly asks. I'm pretty sure I know what's on his mind, but I pretend I don't.

"Sure. You think you could rustle us up another beer? Just one to share, maybe. And maybe a cigarette?" This is Julie tempering recklessness with caution. One beer. One cigarette. A few friendly hands of five-card draw. Perhaps I'll venture into the realm of stud poker, if I'm feeling crazy.

Elly does manage a beer. A heavy guy comes over, middle-aged and with a slightly leering look that would make me the tiniest bit uncomfortable if I were to think much about it, which I don't. He asks me the usual questions—my name, where I'm from, how old I am—then chats with Elly in Swahili before handing us the beer bottle, a cigarette from his crumpled pack, and a lighter for us to borrow. Then he leaves, off to bed as well, one presumes. The flicker of flashlights illuminates only one or two tents now; the only electric light on is here in the dining enclosure, with the exception of a couple of bare bulbs over the doors of the bathrooms a few steps away. We crack open the beer and, passing it back and forth between us, along with the cigarette, continue to play betless poker, mostly in silence, except when I occasionally explain at the end of each hand who has won. It's possible that our knees touch from time to time. We play until eleven, when the generator goes out, plunging us unexpectedly into darkness. I realize that the moon is strong, the stars unbelievable.

"Well, I guess that's our cue." I start to gather the cards into their plastic case. But Elly just sits there, straddling the bench, his elbows on his knees and his hands loosely clasped, looking up at me with a smilingly uncomfortable stare I try for a moment, unsuccessfully, to ignore. Maybe I don't really want to ignore it.

"What?"

Elly laughs a little, shakes his head. "I'm thinking about asking if I can kiss you."

I find myself thinking back, trying to remember if anyone has ever asked to kiss me. It seems like something that happens only in the movies. In real life, kisses always come after I've said something like "So, yeah, I gotta go home now," or "I've got a dentist appointment tomorrow," or "I think I'm drunk." Some sloppy air of inevitability is always there, mesmerizing but uncontrollable. I think maybe I like it this way, for a change.

"I've never kissed a *mzungu* before." He matches my wry grin with his own, and says, "May I?"

I pause a moment, pretend to consider, though of course I've already decided. "Sure."

And so he does. He kisses me, and his lips are soft and he tastes good. Since we both drank the same beer and smoked the same cigarette, I detect neither of these things, only a clean smoothness and perhaps the slight sweetness of a mint. It has been so long since I've kissed—or made out, actually, for that's rapidly what this is becoming, my knees between his, my hands running along the outsides of his thighs, our tongues tangling, his fingers in my dirty, dusty hair. I'd forgotten how fun it is.

After a while we stop. I'm not sure who stops first; I was just thinking about breaking off, but it seems that Elly pulls away just slightly ahead of me. "Whew," I say.

"That was nice. Thank you."

"No, thank you!"

"I have to finish packing up for tomorrow's lunch now. I'll walk you to your tent."

"Okay." We stand up and start off into the moonlight.

Elly takes his voice down several notches. "And you won't tell Kesuma? He wouldn't like it."

"I was just thinking the same thing."

"Good." By now we've reached my tent, which I unzip as Elly gives me a little wave and steps away. "Good night. See you tomorrow morning."

"Okay. Good night."

I'll admit that I'm feeling pretty proud of myself as I get ready for bed, changing out of my khakis, bra, and grimy long-sleeved T-shirt, into soft cotton pajama pants and another clean shirt. I'm proud that I was kissed, and by a gorgeous young man who must be ten years younger than I. I'm proud that I was brave enough to say yes, and then strong enough to bring things to a stop, or help them to a stop, anyway. I'm proud that I'm alone in a tent on the Ngorongoro Crater, far from everything I know, and that I like it. I could just about whistle a jaunty tune.

I've just finished taking out my contacts and running a toothbrush across my teeth a couple of times and am setting the alarm on my phone—I get no service here, but I still use it as my clock—when I hear a whisper at the door of my tent. "It's me."

Elly, back to say good night again or tell me something about tomorrow or, most likely, ask for another kiss or something more.

I'm nervous, amused, and irritated in equal measure when I scoot over to unzip the door.

But it isn't Elly. The moment the zipper comes down, a large man pushes his way into the tent, blocking the exit. It's nearly pitch-black inside the tent, but I know instantly, and with a violent lurch of the stomach, who it is. I have no flashlight. I scramble for my phone as the man who'd sold us the beer and cigarette grabs me by the arms, running his hands up and down them roughly in some absurd childish mimicry of passion. He's speaking to me, pleading rather:

"You are so beautiful. I have big dick for you, I have what you need, I'll be so good for you, yes, let me have the sex with you—"

I push a button on my BlackBerry to light up the screen and get a look at his face. He's pulling me to him, his tongue probing for my mouth, one of his hands abandoning my arm to grab at my breast. I wrap my arms tightly against my chest while still trying to let the little glow from my phone illuminate the room, and push him gently—*why gently?*—away.

"Why do you have that on? Turn off the light. It's okay. Relax." I've backed into the corner of the tent, but he's getting his hands everywhere he can manage.

"Hey, look. Look. I'm sorry if I"—if I *what?*—"gave you the wrong impression." *By being a white woman and staying up eating and playing cards with some black men.* "I'm sorry if you thought—" *I'm a slut because you saw me making out with Elly.* "Look. Thanks." *Thanks??!!* "I appreciate...um...well. I think you need to leave now."

"No. I'll stay. We'll have sex. It will be very good, I promise. I am good man, big dick—"

"No." Still shielding myself from his hands by clapping my arm across my bosom, with my other hand I push, a bit more firmly, against his biceps. My phone, still lit, clutched in that hand, illuminates the sleeve of his shirt as it presses against him. It is red. "You need to go. Please."

"But—"

"No. Really. Please go."

"Okay." His hands cease to grab at me. He's already backing up through the unzipped door of the tent.

I'm shining the light of my BlackBerry on his face like I'm interrogating him.

"It's okay. Calm down."

"I'm calm. Really. Just...thanks, but go now, please. Really." And he does.

I zip up the tent, and all the windows, which I'd had open to let in some air. Curl into my sleeping bag and zip it all the way too, though it is not at all cold. All the noises outside seem magnified. At one point I can hear something—one of the zebras, I presume—tearing up blades of grass with its teeth, seemingly right on the other side of the quivering tent wall near my face. I clutch my BlackBerry in my hand like it's a weapon.

It never once occurs to me to cry out.

Somehow, at last, I fall asleep. When I awake, it's still pitch-dark, with none of the morning sounds of coming dawn. But that's not what I take in. All I'm aware of, instantly, horrifyingly, is the smell, and the hot body pressing up against my back.

For an amazingly long time—seconds upon seconds—I feign sleep, curled up on myself like a possum, my breathing deliberately slow and deep and even, trying not to reveal myself to the man who has crept back into my tent while I slept and is now leaning over me like a lover. As if I could make him go away by just pretending he isn't there. I flash suddenly on those horrible nights, the worst nights, when Eric's rage boiled silently between us and I squeezed my eyes shut tight; I think about the dreams of not being able to scream.

But he's slipping his hands into my sleeping bag, he's panting loudly into my ear, he's muttering under his breath, and then, my God, he's clambering atop me, trying to work the sleeping bag down. I can feel his hard-on through the layers of polyester and fleece and denim. And at last, at last I fight.

At first it's just a few girlish pushes against his shoulders, a few mewling whispered protests and wriggling, which doubtless have the exact opposite effect I desire. But gradually I get more violent and, finally, angry. I end by slapping the top of his bald head repeatedly, while hissing, "What the *hell* are you doing?! *Get off!*"

He cowers when I hit him and sits up, holding his arms up over his head to evade my blows, but I'm too busy pawing around the floor of the tent for my phone to get in any more.

"What are you doing? What are you looking for?"

"I'm looking for my damned phone so I can see your face when I'm telling you to get *out of my tent.*"

"Stop looking. You'll find it in the morning."

It's nowhere to be found. I'm patting around inside my sleeping bag and under it, in the far corners of the tent where my clothes and backpack and shoes are bundled.

"I'll stay."

"No. You really, really won't." I've given up on the BlackBerry and am applying fairly heavy-duty pressure to his arms, forcing him slowly back toward the tent door.

"I won't do anything. We'll just lie down together."

"What the *fuck?* Get *out!*"

He gets truculent, which seems a dangerous sign, but I'm now too angry to care. He says, "You don't want me to stay?"

I bug my eyes out at him, actually laugh. "Are you kidding me? Not sure how I can be much more clear on this."

"But I'd be—"

"Look. Do you want me to call out to my guide? He's right in the next tent. He'll get you in trouble." As if I'm going to tell the teacher he pushed me down on the playground.

But that at last seems to do it. Finally he's scooting out butt-first, pouting as if I'd been the one to mortally offend him. "Fine. If you want me to, I'll go."

"Thank you. *Jesus.*" I zip up the tent door in a rage, pat around a bit more for my phone. It isn't here. I know the man took it. I have to piss, but I'm scared to venture out into the darkness.

I manage somehow to fitfully doze until dawn, having dug out my chunkee stone and clutched it to my chest. I figure if he comes back, this is my best choice of weapon. But he doesn't come, and soon enough I can hear people making reassuring noises, not the tiny creeping sounds that might be either zebras cropping grass or furtive footsteps, but creaking truck doors opening and slamming shut, the unzipping of tent doors, low conversations as the cooks from the various guide groups begin breaking out the breakfast supplies. Still, I'm afraid to leave my tent—or maybe *afraid* is the wrong word now. I get dressed, then huddle by the window that faces the cooking area, knowing Elly will be heading in that direction. I want to tell him first. I don't want to be the one who has to tell Kesuma.

It seems like hours—especially because my bladder is by now about to *burst*—but I probably spend less than ten minutes peering out the window before I spot him heading over from the tent to our truck. "Elly. Elly!" I call in a hoarse stage whisper. He looks up, glances around, finds the source of the call. I wave him over to the tent window with a sort of embarrassed grimace. "I've got a bit of a problem."

I tell him the short version first, just, you know, "That guy we bought the beer from last night got into my tent. He…" I'm having a tough time coming up with the word. Elly's eyes are already wide in alarm, and I don't want to make a big thing out of this. "He…well, he wanted to sleep with me, I guess."

"He came *into your tent?* Are you okay?"

"Yeah, yeah, it's fine. But the thing is, he took my phone. I don't want to make a big deal, I just—"

"Wait here."

Within minutes Kesuma, Leyan, and Elly are all gathered with me outside my tent, their faces taut with concern, as I go over the story again. Kesuma bites his thumbnail as he always does when deep in thought or concerned. "So you bought a beer from him."

"Yeah. Well, Elly did, really."

"And then he came into the tent after?"

"Right. Twice."

"Did you say anything to him to give him the idea you were—"

"I barely said anything at all."

"It's true, he was only there for a moment," Elly confirms. He's standing with his head bent, to hear everything I'm saying, but also, I know, I feel it coming off him, because he feels ashamed and responsible.

"Elly, would you be able to find this man?"

"Yes, he works with one of the other tour groups. He's a cook. I'll find him." And off he strides toward the cooking area.

Kesuma crosses his arms and looks this way and that, taking in the breadth of the campsite. Dawn has fully arrived now, and a steady trickle of tourists move back and forth from the dining area to the bathroom to the trucks. The tents are beginning to come down. Everyone wants to be at the park entrance the moment it opens. Obscurely, this delay makes me feel guilty, like I'm creating a mountain out of a molehill, making a scene.

"Look, he didn't hurt me, it's not a big deal, I just...I'd like to get my phone back."

Elly quickly finds the guy; a big man who looks sheepish and wide-eyed at once. As they walk toward us, Elly is talking to him intently, and the man is shaking his head in exaggerated innocence. I'm angry all over again at the sight of him. Kesuma straightens up as the two approach.

"Julie says you came into her tent twice last night. That you tried to take advantage of her."

"No, no, I swear—" His head is bobbing as if he's not sure if he wants to shake it or nod. "Okay, yes. I came to her tent. I wanted to be with her, and she is very beautiful—" Kesuma interrupts in rapid-fire Swahili, and the man answers back, and though of course I don't understand the words, it's clear that Kesuma is lambasting him. People are beginning to stare. The man switches back to English, turns to me. "I am very, very sorry. It was very wrong of me to come to your tent. But I went away, when you asked me to, yes?"

"Well, yes, but—"

"I one-hundred-percent swear, I didn't come a second time. Maybe it was another man, a bad man, it wasn't—"

"Look. I don't want to get you in trouble. I just want my phone back."

"I didn't . . . I don't have your—"

I'm being a castrating bitch, I think. *I'm ruining this guy's life.* Look how terrified he is. I feel like walking away, letting it go. But now Kesuma and Elly have surrounded him and are taking turns at him in rapid Swahili, maintaining a sort of good cop–bad cop routine, Elly clearly trying to persuade him to be reasonable, Kesuma barely refraining from shouting. At one point he directs an order in Maa to Leyan, who throws a threatening glance at the man before setting off for the park ranger's hut at the edge of the campground.

The man walks a few paces to sit heavily on a box of camping supplies a couple of yards off. Kesuma shakes his head in exasperation. "He insists he doesn't have your phone. He thinks we're stupid because we're Maasai. He is the stupid one. Why didn't you shout out? Then we could have just taken care of it then."

"I'm sorry. I know. I thought I could handle it myself."

"That's why we're here, to make sure you're okay. Okay?"

"Yeah. Okay."

Leyan comes back with a man in a ranger uniform, enormously tall, cheeks dotted with ritual scars, cheekbones high and eyes hooded and inscrutable. An intimidating man at the best of times. The same conversation happens all over again, this time mostly in Maa, the ranger looking at the two primary actors in this absurd plot out of a soap opera with evidently increasing anger. Both the man who snuck into my tent twice in the night and I have increasingly miserable looks on our faces. Almost everyone else in the campground has packed up and left, as the sun is getting high in the sky.

A ranger vehicle pulls up, and with a few grunts the ranger orders the man into the backseat. His fellow ranger drives off, and then he, Elly, Kesuma, and I get into our own truck, while

Leyan stays behind to do all the packing we've been too busy with this nonsense to take care of. Elly drives while Kesuma keeps talking to the ranger, who, as we follow the other truck down the road to the police station, becomes increasingly incensed. Both men's voices are raised now. Sometimes Elly tries to get a word in edgewise. Occasionally, the ranger gestures angrily in my direction. I hear the word *mzungu* several times, a word I'd never minded but that now sounds vicious. Wait—is he angry with *me*? My face goes hot and I feel tears in my eyes. What are they saying about me? That I was causing trouble? Dammit, I'd wanted to drop the whole thing. I didn't do anything wrong! Or if I did, they didn't know that. Unless Elly has told them? The only thing that is keeping me from bursting into tears now is my anger at the unfairness of it all. I stare fixedly out the window until we pull up at a low concrete building with a tin roof and Elly parks. Inside the ranger's station, a small room, there are perhaps seven or eight men gathered, plus the guy from my tent. There is still more back-and-forth between all these men. Occasionally one of them will ask me a question or two in English.

"What did he say to you the second time, when you woke to find him inside your tent?"

I struggle to be forthright. *This is not 1953, moron. What on earth do you have to be ashamed of?* "He got on top of me. He said he wanted to have sex with me."

Elly prodded. "He tried to rape you?"

"I don't want to use that word."

More talk, round and round. The questioning of the man gets more intense. It's clearly a cross-examination, and he's sweating and uncertain and finally he says something, a sort of protest, and everyone in the room suddenly reacts violently, all of them the same, throwing up their hands or rolling their heads to the sides with groans. At first I'm terrified—*what has he said about me?*—but Elly's shake of the head is accompanied by a covert grin in my direction, and Kesuma turns to me. "We'll get your phone. He has it. He's still lying, but we know he has it."

"How? What did he say?"

"He got caught in a lie. Don't worry." He says a few more words to the frightening ranger, who waves us away. "We'll go down to the park now. When we're finished seeing the wildlife, they'll have the phone for us."

And so that's what we do. We head back to the campground, pick up Leyan and our gear, and head down the road that winds along the steep wall of the crater. It's by now probably ten thirty. I don't know for sure because my phone is gone.

I'm relieved to concentrate on something else after that fretful morning, and Ngorongoro is an extraordinary thing to concentrate on. An enormous caldera, the site of a cataclysmic ancient volcanic explosion, it looks like an enormous bowl sunk into the earth, lined in soft greens and yellows, cast with the shadows of the cottony clouds that get hung up on the high cliff walls surrounding it, then free themselves to skitter across. The far rim is halfway obscured in the hazy distance; in the crater's center an alkaline lake glints a pale blue. Even from the top of the rim, you can see that the place is fairly teeming with animals, mostly water buffalo and wildebeests, ungulates of all varieties, all of them walking in the same direction, toward the central lake, as though they're participating in some grand Disney musical extravaganza. We catch sight of families of warthogs, adult couples with a child or two in tow, ridiculous creatures that somehow manage, when they kneel on their forelegs to root in the grass, grace and even elegance. There are herds of zebras, gazelles, tall birds with gorgeous and strange orange poms on their heads, ostriches, pairs of hyenas. I sink into a sort of blissed-out daze.

But I guess not everyone is so consumed. "I can't understand why he thought it was okay to go into a woman's tent. You're sure you didn't say something to him?" Kesuma asks again.

I try to hide my irritation, and luckily Elly, who I'm beginning to think of as my advocate on this matter, intercedes. "They barely talked at all. He was a crazy man."

"It makes me so mad. He thinks because we're Maasai we're

uneducated and foolish. So that's why he chooses you to bother, maybe." He turns around from the front seat to look me in the eyes. "African men aren't like Americans. They have different ideas about women. You have to be careful you don't make them think things."

Elly glances back in the rearview mirror and gives me a quick small smile, half-amused and half-apologetic.

"It's terrible this had to happen to you." We're approaching a pond shared by a flock of flamingos and a clutch of dark, wallowing hippos. We slow beside it to watch.

"It's okay. I kind of just want to enjoy the animals, you know?"

So that's what we did. We weaved our way around the circumference of the caldera. The highlight of our sightseeing was a group of four young male lions, magnificent and indolent, walking in a tough-guy gang right up to our truck. As I stand with my head and shoulders out the sunroof, one of the wonderful creatures pauses perhaps two feet away from the rear wheel of the automobile as we sit idling, looking up with those great, golden eyes—looking at *me,* I can't help thinking—until I avert my gaze, more than a little afraid that he might just decide to climb up and take off my arm for the insult of returning his stare. After spending some time circling our truck, lying in its shade, licking their paws, just like house cats' only as big as pie plates, they turn their backs on us and all saunter off together. No wonder they call it a pride of lions. "An arrogance of lions" just doesn't have the same ring.

By noon we've worked our way to the far end of the crater, where several picnic tables and a building with restrooms are set along the banks of another large pond, another family of hippos snorting in the water, elephants moving through the glade on the other side. Elly starts unloading our lunches while I use the bathroom.

But when I come back out, wiping wet hands on dirty khakis for lack of paper towels, a cluster of men has gathered around our truck. I see that another truck has pulled up, this one shiny and new. There are Maasai in traditional dress, other men in ranger uniforms. They glance at me as I walk past them, to a flat rock near the pond's edge, which I make a beeline for rather than attempting to get in on the conversation. I don't want to know, I really don't. But as I pass, and as I sit on the rock waiting for it to be over, I can't help hearing the words *mzungu* and *BlackBerry* and, I think, something that sounds like *sexual*. My ears ring as I stare out over the water.

After a few moments Elly comes over to me with my boxed lunch. He's grinning from ear to ear. "They got your phone!"

"Really?" I'd sort of picked up on that part. "How?"

"He told them he had it. He'd hidden it in the bathroom."

"What made him change his mind and tell?"

Elly laughs. "You don't mess with Maasai, man. They're crazy."

"Wait, you mean—"

"Yeah. Hit him until he changed his mind about the phone. Led them right to it."

"Oh, man." I cringe. The twinge of guilt, I'd be lying if I didn't say, doesn't entirely overwhelm another warmer feeling. The smug little voice that whispers, *Good.*

"Hey, it's his fault. We tried to be nice."

"I bet he wishes he'd just given us the phone."

"His head wouldn't be hurting so much now. And he'd have a job. He'll never work for anybody here ever again."

The other men leave and, after a light lunch, so do we, continuing our circuit of the crater. We see yet more rooting warthogs and a small herd of graceful, dark elephants grazing among a stand of widely spaced trees too lovely and composed to be properly named a "forest." On our way out of the park, we return to the ranger station to retrieve my phone, unscratched and in perfect working order, which is delivered with eloquent and extensive apologies.

That evening, back in Arusha, after a direly needed hot shower, I lie on my bed as insects buzz outside my window and Leyan and some of the other young warriors who make money guarding Kesuma's front gate have wrestling matches on the red dirt drive. In the kitchen, Suzie, a sixteen-year-old schoolgirl who lives next door and does chores for Kesuma, is making us *ugali* for dinner. A dish of cornmeal and greens, it's ubiquitous in Tanzania, served in every restaurant. Suzie has the wide smile of a kid, but the direct confidence of a woman twice her age (quite a bit more than some I could name). Tonight after dinner I'm going to practice English with her.

Tomorrow I'm off to Japan, for a couple of days of relaxation in a hotel with excellent room service and technologically advanced toilets and rampant slippers and 600-thread-count sheets, before heading back to New York. I've pulled out the two great sheaves of papers I've been compiling, for Eric and D, my twin journals of this trip, am flipping through them before mailing them off tomorrow. The crabbed handwriting is erratic, stretching out and squeezing together, sometimes illegible with exhaustion or emotion. For some reason, the writing has slowed down a bit since I've been in Tanzania. I'm not sure why, but it feels like a good sign. There's something about this country so far away; I feel like a Thanksgiving parade float out in this dry, high air, bobbing, seeking always to tear a tether loose from some keeper's grip. Still, in the aftermath of last night's—what would you call it?— "incident," I find myself needing to talk, to work out what exactly happened, and to these neglected letters is where I go.

When the two started out, each of them had wildly different tones—one solicitous and goofily gabby, the other fervid and extravagant. I would write to the two men utterly divergent accounts of the same experience or place, versions designed to cater to their two sensibilities, and I highlighted whatever a particular story had to do with what I wanted or didn't want from them. But now the two versions seem to be coming together. Reading the two side by side is like shakily bringing a pair of binoculars into focus. In the end, I relate to each what happened to me on the rim of Ngorongoro in almost exactly the same words.

Then I woke up in a couple of hours to find the guy basically on top of me. And for the longest time I didn't do anything, didn't move a muscle. And you know why? I think I thought this was what I'd earned. For all that I've done or felt over the last few years. In my half-awake animal brain, I deserved this. Even when I finally, finally got up the gumption to hit him, I kept my voice to a whisper. Even when I made him leave, even when I told my story, even when I was in the ranger station and the guy was being questioned, some little-girl piece of me figured this was my fault.

But now I've turned around on that. I'm not proud to say that finding out that the man had been beaten to the ground for what he'd done helped. It was like someone else could see that he was the one who deserved punishment. Not me, for once.

Maasai warriors are some good friends to have.

I fold Eric's pages into thirds, with some amount of effort. I can barely wedge them into the airmail envelope I bought for the purpose from a shop in town. I write down our address on the front, seal it, and set it aside to be mailed tomorrow. I begin to do the same with D's. "Julie?" Suzie comes to the door of my room, gesturing for me to come. "The *ugali* is ready."

"Great. I'll be right there."

I scal up the letter to be mailed. It's time to go home.

SUZIE'S TANZANIAN UGALI

> 1 small bunch michicha (actually, I have no idea what
> michicha is; you can use chard)
> 1 small bunch saro (ditto on this; use arugula, or a green
> with some bitterness)
> 1 small red onion
> 2 Roma tomatoes
> About ¼ cup vegetable oil
> Salt to taste
> About 6 cups water
> 3 cups *ugali* maize flour (or white cornmeal)

Thinly slice the greens, then thoroughly rinse both bunches together in a sieve. Shake off excess water and set aside.

Slice the onion into thin rings. Chunk the tomatoes.

Light a single-burner kerosene stove, or alternatively, your stovetop, to high, and set a largish saucepan atop it. Throw in the onions and a healthy glug of vegetable oil. I said a quarter cup in the ingredient list, but it's really your call. Cook the onions over high heat, stirring often, until good and golden brown, almost heading into burned territory. Add the tomatoes and continue cooking on high heat until they melt into a sauce. Salt to taste.

Add the greens and cook, stirring, until soft, perhaps 10 minutes. Turn the mixture out into a bowl and set aside. Rinse the saucepan. Add 6 cups of water and return to the burner.

When the water is just at the boiling point, slowly stir in about a cup and a half of the maize flour. Let boil, stirring often to avoid sticking, until quite thick, about 7 minutes. Add the remaining flour and cook another 7 minutes. By this time, the *ugali* will be almost a dough, more solid than liquid. As you stir, it will begin to pull away from the sides of the pan and form a ball. Turn this out onto a plate. Toss it over lightly a couple of times with a sort of flipping motion of the plate, forming a loaf.

This will serve four people. Cut thick slices of *ugali* and place them on plates, and spoon some greens to one side. You and your guests can eat with your fingers, pinching off a gob of the *ugali,* rolling it into a ball, and pressing an indentation into one side. Pinch some of the greens up into the depression and eat. Feed yourselves like this, bite by bite.

PART III

Master?

*Driven every kind of rig that's ever been made,
driven the back roads so I wouldn't get weighed.
And if you give me weed, whites, and wine, and
you show me a sign, I'll be willin', to be movin'.*
—LITTLE FEAT, "Willin'"

*Change has a way of just walking up and punching
me in the face.*
—VERONICA MARS

15

A Butcher Returns

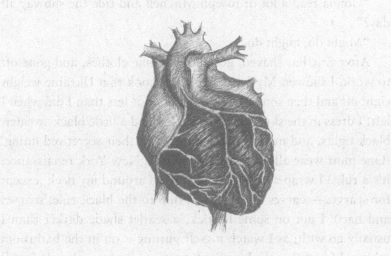

THE FIRST FULL day I'm back in New York is a crisp November one. I'd come back through rain clouds and met Eric with a long hug and short kiss in a gray drizzle in front of a JFK terminal while traffic cops dully shouted for us to pack up and move on. But in the night, all that blows away, and the sun the next morning makes the Chrysler Building across the river glitter like mica as I walk Robert for the first time in ages.

"How did it go?" Eric inquires when we get back to the apartment. He's using the excuse of my return to very much not get to work on time, mulling over the crossword and eating some eggs. I'd not known how things would be with us when I returned, and neither had he, I could tell the moment I first saw his face. But the next moment after that was easy, and we've slipped right back into life with astonishing, almost disturbing swiftness. There is something different going on under the surface, furniture moving around, air seeping in, perhaps. But we still fit together like puzzle pieces, with a snap.

"Rather marvelously, actually."

"Marvelous, eh?"

"Yes. I think I may be having a New York renaissance."

"Gonna read a lot of Joseph Mitchell and ride the subway all day?"

"Might do, might do."

After Eric has shaved, gotten into some clothes, and gone off to work, I shower. My Lord, Tanzania took that Ukraine weight right off and then some. I weigh ten pounds less than I did when I left! I dress in the skirt I got in Ukraine and a little black sweater, black tights, and my tall black boots with their secret red lining. (One must wear all black when having a New York renaissance; it's a rule.) I wrap a cunning green scarf around my neck (except for scarves—scarves are the exception to the black rule, scarves and hats). I put on some lipstick, a scarlet shade darker than I usually go with; as I watch myself putting it on in the bathroom mirror, I fancy that the bracelet Kesuma gave me—white hair still bright on the band, but beginning to wear off in places—looks rather mysterious and jaunty. I head out for the 7 train.

I don't get a block away from the apartment before the first man stops me.

"You are the most beautiful woman I have ever seen."

He is a bit older than I, well dressed, tweedy in that good, Giles-y sort of way. I find myself giving him a wide smile. "Thank you!" I walk on.

It keeps happening, all day. On the subway, in bookstores, in restaurants, on the street. I get whistles, open stares, extravagant compliments. From men young and old, wealthy and destitute, of every color. *Man, what a figure....You have a beautiful face....*I get hit on by a couple of guys at the bar at Republic, which I come by so I can say hello to Marcel, my favorite bartender. The guy collecting money for the homeless in a watercooler jug doesn't even give me the "*One* penny! *One* penny!" spiel. He just says, "You have amazing legs." A sultry dark-haired young man working at one of the greenmarket booths shoots me a bedroom smile from across a bin of apples. I've never gotten attention like this in my life. I could get used to it.

But the best part, the part that makes me feel like something strange is happening, is how I respond. I do not blush and sweat and turn away, and neither do I feel a pang of craving for more, more. To each man I nod with a small smile as I pass by without stopping, as if graciously receiving my due. *I am beautiful, yes, it's true, thank you for your kindness.* It feels utterly foreign, but as natural as sunshine.

That night, once I'm home and the spell has faded, I'm still all a-burble with the aftereffects, becoming giddy, as I'd not been when it was happening. "I swear to God, there was something otherworldly going on."

"Oh, come on. You're gorgeous."

"I'm really not. I'm telling you, it was weird. I wonder what it was?"

"Maybe that you're gorgeous?" Eric is making a stew, peering down into a big pot, at the bottom of which chunks of beef I bought at the greenmarket this afternoon sizzle merrily in bacon fat. It is a meal for a November night, a meal for home, and I'm ravenous.

"No, that's not it. I lost some weight, that could be part of it. But can't account for it all. The lipstick, maybe? No..."

"You're not listening to me....Ouch!" He jerks his hand back as fat splashes up. "You think these are brown enough?"

"Looks good." I'm sitting on a stool at the kitchen island, rather unable to let it all go. "Oh, well, duh! It's the skirt, of course."

Eric shrugs. He's fishing the stew meat out in batches as he sears them well on all sides. "It's a cute skirt."

"It's a magical skirt. My Ukrainian Magical Mystical Skirt, bestowing the power of instant irresistible sex appeal."

Now that all the beef is browned, Eric's scraping a hillock of chopped vegetables and herbs from a cutting board into the pot. There is a lively hiss as he begins to stir. "Great."

"I think so. That smells good."

"We may be eating just a wee bit late."

"Fine by me." My stomach is growling.

Once Eric has gotten his stew composed and in the oven, we retire to the couch with our bottle of wine (well, our second if you count what was left of the bottle he opened to add to the stew, which we've already finished off) to wait for it to come back out again.

I'd thought that after a month of relative teetotaling, and after coming home to find this new sense of comfort, this lack of dread, I'd not drink so much, and we have, after all, limited ourselves to one and a half bottles tonight, half our usual amount. But I've not counted on my reduced tolerance and the fact that I have had nothing but the two glasses of wine and the vegetable dumplings Marcel served me during my glamour spell at Republic. The next morning I'll not remember much of the DVDs we watched. As I recall, we started with an episode of Joss Whedon's sci-fi Western, but now *The Third Man* is in the machine—and I barely remember the stew, though at least we did manage to get it out of the oven without burning it to a crisp. It goes on to make a bizarre but delicious breakfast for us both. This is Eric's recipe:

ERIC'S BEEF STEW

> 3 pounds beef chuck stew meat, in 2-inch chunks
> ½ cup flour, in a shallow bowl or baking pan
> 3 tablespoons extra-virgin olive oil, plus some more
> 1 onion, sliced into thin half-moons
> 5 cloves garlic, minced
> 3 carrots, peeled and cut into ½-inch rounds
> 3 stalks celery, finely sliced
> 1½ tablespoons fresh thyme

2 cups red wine
1¼ cups beef stock
1 tablespoon tomato paste
Salt and pepper to taste

Preheat the oven to 300°F. Dry the stew meat with paper towels and toss them lightly with the flour until evenly dusted. On the stovetop, in a heavy soup pot, brown the meat in batches over high heat in the olive oil.

Once the meat has all been browned, remove it to a plate and set aside. Turn the heat down to medium, add another small glug of oil, and throw in the vegetables and thyme and cook, stirring often, until softened, about 10 minutes.

Return the beef to the pot, then add the wine, beef stock, and tomato paste. Stir in salt and pepper. Don't go light on either, but especially not the pepper, which ought to be freshly ground, really.

Cover the pot and slide it into the oven. Cook until the meat is meltingly tender, about 3 hours, or when you wake up on the couch, with the wife you still love like your own flesh snoring beside you, with her feet in your lap and a wineglass threatening to spill from her fingers. Rub her feet and remove the glass before rousing her enough to slip out from under her to fetch the stew. Two people can get three meals apiece out of this. Eat some, blearily, right away, then let cool thoroughly on the stovetop; all night long is fine. It will taste much better in the morning.

THANKSGIVING COMES EARLY this year, just three days after I arrive back home, so we decide on a quiet day, no family, just the two of us and Gwen at our apartment (her boyfriend is out of town), a turkey and dressing and a couple of vegetables. We've finally, finally seen about as much of *Buffy* as we can collectively stand. It's time to move on, so our postmeal TV watching consists of four or five episodes of our brand-new obsession, *Veronica*

Mars. We continue to drink and nibble and fall asleep on the couch, eventually. It's pleasant, easy, and just a tad morose.

How we approach Thanksgiving, it turns out, is how Eric and I seem to be approaching all aspects of fitting back into our life together. We don't have fights in the middle of the night anymore, I don't wake up in the morning to the heat of Eric's radiating anger. And neither do I feel that same trapped, claustrophobic feeling that used to overwhelm me in the evenings. This doesn't mean all is well, though. More like all is quiet and waiting to see.

"I think we should go to couples' therapy, Julie. Maybe start up after the holidays."

We've talked about this before, of course. For the first time the suggestion doesn't fill me with stark terror. But I'm still uncertain. "Okay. I don't know if that can fix things."

"You mean you don't know if you want to fix things."

"No! I love you, I want you in...I just don't know if I want to be—"

"Married."

I flinch a bit, pressing my lips into a thin pale line, and say nothing.

Since we didn't see family for Thanksgiving, we arrange a trip for Christmas with my folks, as last year, only this time we all come together in Santa Fe. There is, as usual, much eating and jig-saw puzzling. I buy Eric something carefully unromantic, a Bose dock for his iPod.

He gives me a knife.

Actually, it's a necklace, a delicate silver pendant on a chain, a charm of a knife, and the hilt is studded with tiny diamonds, the tip actually sharp enough to hurt just a bit when I press it into the flesh below my breastbone.

"Oh my God."

"I know it's not the right kind of knife. I wanted a cleaver or a—"

"It's perfect." I'm tearing up, and my parents and my brother think I'm being a little silly, sentimental over a thoughtful gift. But Eric and I know it's something else. I don't read aloud the small card he's tucked inside the box.

For my butcher wife. To do with as you will.

I AWAKE early on the morning of New Year's Eve, roused by a dream. I'm in a dark corner of a library or bookstore, and a man, someone faceless and irresistibly strong, is forcing himself upon me, holding me down, roughly fondling me. I try to scream out, there are people so close who could help, but my voice dies in my mouth. It is the most helpless feeling in the world, and familiar, and somehow my fault. But still I try to cry out, and try, and desperately try, and.... "Stop!!"

Eric jerks up in bed in terror. "What? What? Are you okay?"

I am, already, in the wake of the nightmare, smiling. "Yeah, actually. Sorry."

"You had a bad dream?"

"Yeah. But it's okay. I could scream."

"No shit."

I feel like I just woke from a dream of fine wine and warm summer evenings.

Eric tumbles back to his pillow. It's nearly dawn, the light outside our apartment window tender and growing. He and I are having a dinner party, eight people coming for our usual New Year's Cajun feast. There's cleaning and shopping and cooking to be done, and what with recovering from Christmas and traveling I've not gotten around to much of it.

Before getting out of bed I unplug my BlackBerry and scroll through e-mails, as is my habit, leaning up against Eric's bare back. In the past month or so, since returning from my trip, I've gotten used to the touch of Eric's skin again, am no longer afraid of him or his expectations. It helps that he has ceased to demand. Maybe he feels me slowly coming back to him, or pulling away, or whatever it is that's happening to me. Perhaps I seem to be doing both at once. But we are, for the first time in a long while, relatively content.

My in-box contains a message from iTunes. I think it's just a receipt for one of our latest purchases, a TV show or an album, but no. This is something else.

"You've received an iTunes gift."

I click to open. And have to will myself not to stiffen as I read what's inside.

> *Julie*
> *I shouldn't be writing you, but I've listened to this song*
> *230 times in the last week and it reminds me of you for*
> *some reason.*
> *Happy new year.*
> *Damian*

So, yes. This program has been brought to you by the letter D, but of course he has a name. It's a name that has often struck through me like lightning. But for the last year and more, in my phone, in my distraught e-mails, in my journals and letters, in my heart, he's been reduced to D. A reduction that has perversely seemed to make his power over me even more entire—symbolic, abstract. Godlike, in point of fact, the similarity underlined not least by his extreme absence, nor by the fact that the past few months have seen me beginning at last to add my ex-lover to the list of things I no longer believe in.

So to see his name there, unaccompanied but entire, at the bottom of an e-mail, is to be suddenly shocked into remembering: this is a man. Not some kind of sinister force, irresistible and fatal. I once looked up the meaning of his name. It is from the Greek, and it means "to tame." I took this much to heart. But this is just a guy. A guy who's weak too sometimes, a guy who's just said he shouldn't be doing something, but is going ahead and doing it anyway.

It's a little dizzying. I can't tell if I'm ecstatic or terrified or pissed to the eyeballs.

Yes, I can. I'm all those things.

The song is "Willin'" by Little Feat.

First of all: What the fuck?! Second: What. The. *Fuck?* *"Willin'"*? I know the song "Willin.'" It's a song about hopped-up truckers. What in the *hell* is that supposed to mean?

Also? *What the fuck?!!!!*

I get up and, while Eric is still in bed, download the song and listen to it several times with my earphones on, laughing sometimes, rolling my eyes, tearing up once or twice, letting my heartbeat slowly back off its hysterical beat.

It's a great song, one I know well. But it's a song about a fucking trucker. A trucker who sees his Alice in every headlight. A trucker who's been from Tucson to Tucumcari. A trucker who's willing. Willing to be moving. What does it *mean?*

So, yes, I microanalyze. The strange thing is, though, that by the time Eric arises and we begin discussing our plans for the day—a shopping trip for me, a bit of work and a run for him—I'm actually something close to calm. I wait several hours to respond to this strange missive. (That in itself a once unheard-of accomplishment.) Shortly before I leave to go into the city, I shoot out a quick e-mail:

> Damian
>   *I'm assuming that the song you've sent me was just a*
> *New Year's–related moment of weakness/douchebaggery.*
> *If not, though, and you want to talk, I will be at Union*
> *Square, at the greenmarket, at one o'clock.*
>   Julie

I don't expect him to show. I don't really dare to hope for it, am not even absolutely sure that I want it. I remember well the breakdown that seeing him once before inspired. And I have too much to do today for histrionics.

In summer, the greenmarket is an explosion of color and noise and crowds, a city of foodies descending like plagues upon bright piles of broad beans and bins of corn and glorious, knottily shaped tomatoes. In the winter, however, it's a tiny, quiet, gray affair. I don't have to wait in line at the bakery booth for a couple of baguettes, nor at the tent where a Korean woman I am on a smiling-basis with sells homemade kimchee and microgreens.

I spot him as I'm bagging up some salad. I've been trying not to look around for him, but when I glance up briefly from the Igloo cooler full of mesclun, he's right there, maybe twenty feet away, loitering at the corner of 17th and Union Square West. Standing there in his same old coat, same old hat, earbuds in his ears, head ducked in that same old way. I know he's determined that I see him before he sees me, that I be the one to approach.

My heart is pounding hard in my ears, I know I'm blushing, but I finish paying for my purchase, make myself go slowly, continue to breathe, count out exact change, and wish the woman behind the plastic folding table a happy new year. Make myself walk steadily, though I'm tempted to either rush at him or run in the other direction. I can feel the tiny smirk on my face, the smirk we both always used together. I come to a stop in front of him, perhaps a foot and a half away. He glances up at me, his head still tucked down. Those eyes.

You can say many things about what happened between Damian and me. But the look that passes between us now is a look full of history and ambivalence and knowingness and regret and, even, humor, even—could it be?—a muted sort of happiness. That exchange, whatever it all means, and it means too many things for me to immediately understand, is not to be faked. Why would we?

He slips his earbuds from his ears, slips his iPhone out of his coat pocket (of *course* he has an iPhone: if there is one thing I could bet my life on with confidence it would be that Damian would buy an iPhone *instantly*), wraps the white cord methodically around the shiny gadget, slides it back into his coat. With his head still bowed, he looks up at me again, that complicated look, somehow naked and questioning and sardonic and guarded all at once, and I know I look just the same. "Have you had lunch?"

"No."

"Good. Let's go."

I ARRIVE back at our apartment at around four thirty, hurried— late for starting dinner preparations—and loaded down, flushed. I greet Eric, who's sitting at his desk hunched over his laptop, with a kiss on the forehead before beginning to unload groceries. "If we're going to get this gumbo done before Paul and Amanda get here I'm going to have to get chopping."

"I'll help."

I pull out the celery, bell pepper, onion, my boning knife (I use it for everything, probably shouldn't but it fits so well in my hand, is a sort of comfort to me somehow), and I take a cutting board from behind the sink. I'm singing under my breath.

Driven every kind of rig that's ever been made,
driven the back roads so I wouldn't get weighed.

"I wish you wouldn't do that."

"Do what?"

Eric's come up to the kitchen sink to grab another board and a knife. As I roll the onion over to him, I look up and realize instantly that he knows—or thinks he does—just what has happened.

Well. Good.

"That song. I know he gave it to you. I didn't even have to go looking. It was right there in our iTunes file."

I set down my knife, rest my knuckles on the counter. Make myself look him in the eye. He's doing the same. For the second time in one day, one of those complex, gorgeous exchanges. "That's right."

I'm shocked to notice that I don't tear up, or cringe, though there's anger in my husband's look, and hurt. All I do is take a deep breath, blow it out through pursed lips.

"I had lunch with him today. Needed to."

It occurs to me that I am happy. That sounds horrible, but I am, about many things. I'm happy about the unexpected civility and calm of the lunch today, at the same Indian restaurant where Damian seduced me so long ago. It was not an easy conversation. He had quite a grocery list of my hurtful and unacceptable behaviors of the last year and more, of all the ways I had raged and pled and bargained and, frankly, lied, all those ways you speak to a God you don't really believe can hear you but still hope will surprise you. What I'd not realized, because I'd not credited him with the humanity to feel hurt or weakness or sympathy, was the toll these constant demands took on him, or how desperately he had to push against that suck of my need, how legitimately afraid he was, how legitimately angry that I kept trying to pull him to me. But even as I cringed as he pointed out each tyrannical, manipulative text and e-mail and late-night call, I also felt a strange equilibrium returning. I'd misused a power I didn't even know I had.

And with that realization, I find I'm also happy about both the still-present physical pull of him and my remarkable ability to resist it, about the hug and kiss on the cheek he gave me when we parted and the unbelievable truth that I didn't fall apart when he left.

I'm happy that I'm now about to open my mouth and speak with perfect honesty to my husband, from whom I've so often tried to hide.

But perhaps I'm most happy because I've suddenly realized just this. I can *see* these men, these dear, flawed men, my partners and lovers and friends. And they can see me. And none of us are going to die because of it.

I've steeled myself for Eric's response, for rage or guilt or tears. But he surprises me. He nods. "Okay." He doesn't look away, and he asks no probing questions. But I'm going to offer up something more. No gut-wrenching confessions of guilt. I don't feel any, for one thing—my God, I really don't. It's like getting a therapeutic massage for the first time and standing up afterward and realizing that I've spent my entire life with a knot in my back, or a tense neck. And now, just being human, just walking around the earth, feels entirely different. Except that analogy isn't quite right. Because let us be clear here. Damian is not the person who made me whole and well, just by swooping down from Jupiter and entering my life again like some glorious extraterrestrial masseur. No. All his return did was make me realize I'm somehow managing to heal myself. So, no guilt. Only what he, Eric, my husband, deserves.

"It was good to see him. We talked a lot. He's unhappy about how we left things, and obviously I have been too."

"I really don't need to know."

"Okay." I didn't say it was going to be easy. "I can't cut him out of me. Don't want to. I don't mean that he'll... or that I'll... I just need to accept it. He's in there. Buried in. Part of my... my experience, I guess. Like a tattoo. A scar."

Eric nods again. "I know."

"And you know you are too. Buried in, I mean."

"I know." His lower lip curls as it always has, for the sixteen years I have known him, when he is about to weep. His eyes are a sparkling blue when he cries. A hard thing to see, something I've always shied from seeing, but I don't look away now. "I love you, Julie. So, so much."

And I have tears in my eyes too. "I know." And I am happy. I am, in fact, overjoyed, filled with love—not love like a drug or a sickness or a hideous hidden thing or a painfully faraway one. Love like air. Like a dream of sand between my toes.

"I will probably see him again. I know I will. We have a lot to talk about. I won't be sleeping with him."

"You don't have to promise—"

"It's not for you. I'm not going to do it because I don't even know if he wants it, or if I do, and because it would be messy and—"

The embrace Eric encircles me in then is full and deep and both familiar and strange. I lean my head against his shoulder. I can feel his tears when they fall on my cheek, but he isn't racked with sobs, he isn't pulling me so tightly to him that it's like he wants me to slip back inside his skin. "You know what? I'm so fucking tired of being scared," he says.

"I don't want to scare you, I just need to—"

"That's not what I mean." He takes me lightly by the shoulders and pulls away to look at me. Our faces are wet, but we don't attempt to dry each other. "Life *is* messy. I'm tired of being scared of that. We'll deal with it. Things are going to happen, or not happen, and life is going to change, one way or the other, and I'm tired of being terrified, angry that I can't keep everything the same, the way it was. You know? I don't *want* everything to be the way it was. So this is what we're going to do. We're just going to *see*. It's uncertain, and it's probably going to hurt, and we just don't know, and you know what? I'm *fine* with that. I love you."

"I love you."

"And everything? It's going to be okay. It's going to be great. We're just going to see."

"Yes."

We kiss, for the first time in months really. And then we make gumbo. Eric chops, I devein shrimp, he looks over my shoulder with glee, as he always does, when I make the roux the Paul Prud-homme way, with fantastic heat and smoke and finesse. We know how to move around in the kitchen together. After all, we've been doing it our entire lives.

Epilogue

February 13, 2008

SO. MY JACK THE RIPPER theory. What I think is that when this poor, sick fucker looked at the frenzied destruction he'd wrought, when he saw what he'd done to these women, who he'd probably hated or feared simply because they possessed a uterus, maybe the tiny flicker of humanity remaining in him burned him. Maybe he opened them up, took out their insides, did his patient exploring, not as an extension of his savagery, but as a sort of ritual cleansing against it. Maybe he tried to soothe his horror of himself by bringing order to the chaos he'd created—cataloguing the parts, studying the way pieces came together. He could take the torn, bloody evidence of his sickness and worthlessness and transform her, transform *it,* into something recognizable, sane. Neat slices of meat ready for the butcher's window. Whoever this guy was, butcher by trade or not, he was too far gone to save himself. But what he did with his knife to these women's bodies was his attempt to anyway. His butchery was his last bid for salvation. I get that.

Then again, maybe I'm exactly wrong. Maybe he wasn't a butcher at all, and if he had been, women would have remained whole, he would have stayed in his shop contentedly feeding people, making something from something else, and his salvation would have been himself.

Once I've finished my coffee, I set the cup in the sink, wash my hands—thoroughly, up under my nails and under the leather of my Maasai bracelet. Then I slip a large translucent vacuum bag from a stack on a Metro shelf against the wall and return to the table.

A liver is unlike any other organ—not muscular and obvious like a heart, with its ventricles and aorta clues to its function; not like digestive organs, those tracts and sacs a passageway, concerned with the practicalities of nutrition and excretion. A liver is a mystery. It's a filter. The liver records experience, the indulgences and wrong turns; it contains within it a constantly updated state-of-the-union address. But it keeps what it knows a secret. Encoded. It cleans up after itself, too, will after a time purge files, dispensing with the unnecessary information, what's been relegated to the past, keeping what's needed. There are even some hopeful, possibly deluded souls who believe a cirrhotic liver can heal itself, with time, and with gentleness.

I shake the bag open with my right hand while lifting the liver into it with my left, my whole forearm supporting its sagging weight. As its surface sticks to the inside of the bag, I hoist it up in both hands, giving it a few jerks to weight it down to the bottom, well clear of the lip. Tote it over to the big Cryovac machine pushed up against the wall, lay it inside, line up the mouth of the bag flat against the raised metal sealing edge, and close the lid. Through the window at the top of the machine, I watch the bag swell slowly up, then shrink quickly, tightly, around the organ with a sound like the timbers of a ship in a heavy storm. The door of the machine hisses open, with horror-movie slowness. I take out the bagged liver, weigh it, slap the sticker that comes sliding out of the slot at the bottom of the scale, printed with the weight and today's date—"11.2 lbs, 2/13/08"—onto the cool surface of the bag, label it with the Sharpie stuck in my right rear pocket—"Beef Liver"—and haul it over to the walk-in freezer. Pulling up on the latch and edging the door open with my shoulder, I lean just far enough into the frigid darkness to place the package in a bin on the metal floor atop a pile of burgundy bags just like it, but frozen as hard as rock and rimed with frost.

I've just finished wiping down the table with a rag soaked in a bleach-water solution when Josh strides up and heaves a side of pork onto it. "Hey, your tattoo all healed?"

"Yeah. See?" I lift the hair off the back of my neck as Josh peers to see the small word inscribed there in black ink. *Loufoque.*

"Very nice!" He slaps the hog's haunch as I let my hair fall. "So, genius, you forget everything you ever knew about meat?"

"Oh, I imagine."

"Prove it."

I peer down at the pig for a moment, contemplating my first move. Today is only my second return to Fleisher's after a hiatus of many months. It's a Wednesday morning, the gentle midweek buzz of readying the shop to open instantly familiar when I walk in the door. Aaron is peeking down into a big pot of soup on the stove. Jessica and Hailey are talking over receipts near the cheese counter. Jessica has recently found out she's pregnant—which has been occasion for much amused contemplation of a toddler running around the shop with a cleaver dangling from his hand—and is grooming Hailey to handle things while she's out of the shop. Jesse is filling up the case.

The first time I returned was on a Saturday, and it was a bit of a disaster. Often, on the weekends, the shop is invaded by the Weekend Warriors, old friends or colleagues of Josh and Jessica, all of them guys, up from the city, who want to practice cutting meat because they think it's manly. On these days the wash of testosterone becomes a flood that threatens to float the table away. The conversation, which on an average Wednesday ebbs and flows, pours out in an unceasing torrent on these Saturdays. No talk of politics anymore, or movies. None of the usual self-aware riffs on the homoerotics of butchery and male competition. Now the chest-thumping becomes very nearly literal. Stories about guns and hunting begin to predominate, as cycling yarns fade into the background, unless they include viscera.

Aaron has one that does. He tells his tales with his whole body, standing in a biker's squat, holding imaginary handlebars, his eyes wide, then tightly shut, chin pulled back, as he reenacts the moment of stopping to see lovely deer crossing the road. One second later he witnesses their explosive death by high-speed collision, the grisly blowback dousing him from head to toe.

(Okay, I laughed.)

My femaleness becomes an issue on these days as it never has been during the week. It's not as if they're flirting with me, exactly. It's more like the mere presence of estrogen agitates them. In no way are any of these men interested in me sexually, but their animal brains take over, I guess, and somehow, quiet and small though I make myself, I become the axis of some strange male ritual, rams clashing horns, apes clapping their chests with their great leathery palms. People are suddenly calling me "sweetheart"—a familiarity an amateur butcher has not earned. Someone drops ice down my back. Thank God I have no pigtails and there are no inkpots around. Only Colin rises above their antics. He reminds me of Robert in a dog run with a bunch of little yappy dogs—Colin is a creature of a whole different magnitude, indifferent or amused. He and I exchange conspiratorially jaded glances.

It's an odd feeling. Of course I've witnessed this behavior before. So has any woman who's ever been a thirteen-year-old in a schoolyard at recess. And any woman can tell you it can be exhilarating. In the past few years, I've quite often loved being in the center of such a swarm, recognizing that I'm just a conduit through which macho, emphatically heterosexual men can goad one another, but wanting to be just that. It somehow made me feel worthwhile.

But not here. Fleisher's long ago became a haven for me from my womanliness, or at least from my frustrated need to feel womanly, seductive—and used. Used by men—by any man—to deliver whatever it is he really needs. I don't want that anymore. Here in the shop I want to be worth something because I know how to handle a knife and crack a dirty joke. Worth something because of who I am. So I like Wednesdays.

I flex my hands and eye the clock before I begin.

"Your hand bothering you?"

"Oh, not *so* so much. It aches a little. I'm getting back into the groove, you know."

"Momma, you're a butcher now. That ache is gonna be with you the rest of your life. What, by the way, is that fucking thing on your hand?"

"This? Oh. It's a Maasai bracelet. I ate the goat this skin came from. Look, you can still see a few hairs on it. If I wear it until it falls off, I get good luck."

Josh nods approvingly. "That's *disgusting*."

I snap off the kidney and its attendant fat, then attack the tenderloin, eyeing the clock. I'm not remotely ready, certainly not after the sabbatical I've been on, to challenge the Great Side-Breaking Record, currently held by Aaron at forty-four seconds. (A can of Colt 45 sitting on a high shelf, draped with a digital stopwatch, commemorates the great event. Aaron has taped over the "5." It now reads, "Colt 44," and a handmade label beneath it reads, "Refreshing piggy goodness brought to you by Aaron.") But I have aspirations. I pull out the tenderloin quickly, throw it to the table. Count down five ribs from the shoulder, wedge my knife tip between the tightly wound vertebrae, then, once through, pull my blade down to the table, as smoothly as I can, removing the shoulder.

"Oh, you still got it." Josh peers over my shoulder.

I shrug.

"So what's going on with that husband of yours?"

"You trying to distract me?" After raking my knife down the length of ribs, I set it into the scabbard strapped around my waist and pick up the butcher saw to break through the ribs and separate the belly from the loin.

"I just can't believe sweet Eric would do something like that."

After withholding all this drama for so long, in the last month or so I've told Josh quite a bit about what's going on. Not in that desperate, self-pitying barrage I used to be so good at, but just as one friend to another. Things are different now. There are no names I can't say without falling apart.

"What, you mean him seeing the girlfriend again? Oh, she's a nice girl. And she loves him. Gotta like that about her. They left things strange, I guess, trying to work stuff out."

"Good God, Momma. You need to take away his Wii until he snaps out of it."

"Heh." I'm through the ribs, and so I put down the saw and take up my knife again and finish the cut with it, curving up past the bottom of the rib cage and down to take off the belly. Throw that to the table.

"Meantime, if he's getting laid—"

"I don't know if he's getting laid."

"Well, you oughta be able to get some ass too. Stay with us for a few days. I'll hook you up. And we can do some house hunting."

"Thanks, but I'm okay for now. Though I will take you up on the real estate shopping." For the last month or so I've been having a look around up here. The idea of having a place in these curled mountains, a place of my own, makes any prospect of my future, paired or solitary, seem less frightening. I yank the remaining side around, leg hanging off the edge of the table.

"And what about this other asshole?"

I shake my head. "He's gone off again." After a month or so of conversations, conversations that seemed terribly healing and measured and Adult, D—Damian, I mean—has flown the coop, without explanation. "It's what he does. He's here and he's gone, he can't do anything else. And finally I've learned that, and I'm over it." I lean on the loin with one elbow and grab the animal's foot with the other, in readiness to break the joint.

"Bullshit."

I grunt as I push down hard on the leg. The joint wiggles and squeaks but doesn't break open. "Well, I'm not over *him*. Over *it*. He is who he is—"

"An asshole."

I shrug again, push down again, unsuccessfully, on the leg. "He's just the man he is, capable of just what he's capable of. And he's gonna do what he's gonna do. So am I, so is Eric. And we shall see."

"Fuck. You are like a Zen master."

On the third try, a decisive crack. With a single deep slice to wood, the leg is off the loin, in my strongly gripping hand. Sinovial fluid drips to the floor.

"Nah," I say with a grin. I slap the leg back onto the table.

Aaron calls from the kitchen. "What was the time on that, Jules?" Josh rolls his eyes.

"Oh, about a minute and a half." Actually, no. Actually, one minute, twenty-five seconds. Exactly.

"Halfway there. You're on your way, Jules."

I take a deep breath, smell the smells of meat as I run my fingers around that impossibly smooth white cup joint, that old, private pleasure of mine. "Yeah. Maybe so."

ACKNOWLEDGMENTS

There are so many people who've taught, supported, helped, and plain old put up with me during the writing of this book, I'm inevitably going to blank on some names here, so apologies in advance.

Thanks to the entire Fleisher's crew—Josh and Jessica Applestone, Aaron Lenz, Jesse, Colin, Hailey, Juan, and everybody else—who let me poke around the shop for six months, getting in the way, and gave me much undeserved free meat. Thanks to my guides and helpmeets on my travels—Santiago, Armando, Diego, Oksana, Kesuma, Leyan, Elly, and the park rangers of Ngorongoro Park in Tanzania, who managed to keep a clueless traveler alive and mostly well. Thanks to my family—Kay and John and Jordan Foster, Mary Jo and Jo Ann Powell, Carol Sander, Ethan and Elizabeth Powell—most of whom have declined to read this book, but in the most cheerful, loving way possible. Thanks to Emily Alexander-Wilmeth, Emily Farris, Eric Steel, and Amy Robinson, who plowed through drafts, gave great notes, and didn't hate me, as a general rule. Thanks to my "bleaders," you know who you are. Thanks to Robert, who's just the best dog in the world, and to Maxine, Lumi, and Cooper, who are the best cats, in no particular order. Thanks to my editor, Judy Clain, and her assistant, Nathan Rostron, who edit adroitly and remind me from time to time that there is such a thing as too much information. Thanks to Michelle Aielli, my "publicist" at Little, Brown; I use quotation marks not to denigrate her astounding PR powers, but rather to indicate my discomfort in attaching such an oft-mocked word to a friend who does such a remarkable job of keeping me sane. Thanks to therapist Anna and bartender Marcel, who also pull double shifts on sanity maintenance.

Most of all, I thank Eric and D. Writing your own story is easy enough; having your story written by another is hard. I am grateful down to my toes to you both, for your generosity and grace in handling a situation difficult and not of your choosing.

INDEX OF RECIPES

ABOUT THE AUTHOR

After a misspent youth involving loads of dead-end jobs and several questionable decisions, Julie Powell, the author of *Julie and Julia: My Year of Cooking Dangerously,* has found her calling as a writer-cum-butcher. She lives in Long Island City, Queens, when she isn't in Kingston, New York, cutting up animals.

READING GROUP GUIDE

CLEAVING

*A Story of
Marriage, Meat, and Obsession*

by

Julie Powell

A conversation with Julie Powell

How was the experience of writing Cleaving *different from that of writing your first memoir,* Julie and Julia? *When did you first decide to turn the experiences recounted in* Cleaving *into a book?*

Well, on a practical level, I came to *Julie and Julia* with a narrative in place, and a ton of background material, i.e., a year's worth of blogging. There was already a middle, a beginning, and an end. With *Cleaving,* I sort of started *in medias res.* I knew I wanted to learn to butcher and to write about it. At the same time, though, I was in the throes of this horrendous upheaval in my marriage, and the aftermath of this consuming affair, and it soon became clear that these circumstances were not only sneaking into the story, but were a huge part of what I needed to write about. When I began, I had no idea how it was all going to turn out. So that was a twist. I wasn't blogging the story, obviously, but in a way there was an immediacy to the writing, because I was working *as* I was figuring out what it all meant.

Julie and Julia *was made into a movie, released a few months before* Cleaving *hit the shelves. Do you think that the movie influenced readers of* Cleaving?

Oh, definitely, I think. For people whose first experience with my story was my first book or my blog, there's a certain thread that leads into *Cleaving,* even if the events depicted are upsetting. I mean, going back to my first book now, I see the seeds of a coming crisis in a way I was completely blind to at the time. But it's different for people who were first introduced to me through the movie. *Julie and Julia* is a wonderful film, but it is a considerably cleaned-up and simplified version of my story. It's also a touching if occasionally simplistic paean to two strong marriages. To watch that movie and then run out and pick up *Cleaving* is to risk some serious psychological whiplash. Visions of Amy Adams, 1) coated in meat schmutz and wielding a cleaver, and 2) being tied down and spanked by an adulterous lover? That could damage some folks.

What was the most significant life lesson you learned from working in a butcher shop? What was the most challenging aspect?

When I think about butchering, I think about seams. When butchers refer to seams, they're talking about the connective tissue that both connects and signals the separation between muscles. Seams are what make butchery an essentially gentle craft; they're what give it its poetry. Seventy-five percent of butchery can be done with the one-inch tip end of a boning knife, because most of the time, the seam will show you how the muscles are meant to peel apart from one another. As if they were meant to part in this way all along. For a girl who has trouble differentiating where she ends and those she loves begin, that's a pretty profound lesson.

As for most challenging? A beef chuck shoulder, no doubt, is the trickiest job for a butcher. One hundred fifty pounds, and a bear to take apart. I break into a sweat just thinking about it.

How did your ideas and feelings about your experiences change as you wrote Cleaving?

My working title for the book was *The Dying Art.* I was certain it was the perfect title, tying together marriage and the craft of butchery by what I saw at the time as their common threads: their inevitable extinction and their association with blood and misery. I was in a pretty dark place. But the publishers weren't happy with the title, and we wrangled for a long time over an alternative. Fortunately, by the time we settled upon *Cleaving,* I was feeling much more positive, about both butchery and marriage. Artisanal butchery is thriving again, thanks in no small part to Josh and Jessica Applestone, and I've learned that even a rocked and cracked marriage can not only be mended but also grow and change and thrive. "Cleave" is a wonderful word, meaning both to separate and to hold together. I found in the course of writing this book that sometimes you have to do the former to more successfully achieve the latter. Not to promote infidelity as a marital aid, but the crisis brought on by my relationship with "D" forced Eric and me to examine what wasn't working between us, and to ask ourselves tough questions about what we could do to change ourselves and our marriage.

Was there a surprising or instructive episode during your travels around the globe that didn't make it into the book?

Hmm! Well, most of the bits I've kept out of the book I've kept out for good reason, reason that holds for Q&As to be published in the back of the paperback. My travels to Argentina, Ukraine, and Tanzania constituted my first solo expeditions outside of the States, and the sheer wonder and trepidation of navigating the world on my own cannot be overstated. Oh, I didn't write about losing my camera, or about going to the bar in Arusha and getting gawked at on the dance floor for dancing maybe a bit too much like an

American sorority girl. (Ah, Kilimanjaro beer...) But other than that I tried to report my experience as faithfully as possible.

What will you write next? What will you cook next?

An excellent and frightening question. I'm working on a novel right now, which has me terrified out of my mind. As for cooking, I mean, who knows? I go where intuition leads me: I'm a leaf on the wind.

Questions and topics for discussion

1. Julie Powell takes us deep inside the intricacies of working in a butcher shop. What did you find particularly fascinating—or off-putting—about the details she relates?

2. Did reading *Cleaving* make you more inclined to visit a local butcher shop? Have you ever felt the same draw toward butchers that Julie feels?

3. Conscientious eating has been much in the news recently and is an increasingly prevalent part of our culture. How do the practices at Fleisher's measure up for you in this debate? What do you consider "eating well"?

4. Julie Powell witnesses a pig being slaughtered at a pig farm. What did you make of this scene in *Cleaving*? Would you be able to watch such a thing? Or partake?

5. In *Cleaving* we learn more about Julie's relationship with her husband, Eric, than was revealed in *Julie and Julia*. Why do you think Julie and Eric stay together, even after the trouble starts?

6. Imagine yourself in Julie's circumstances, faced with the return of a past lover. In what ways would you have reacted similarly—or differently—to the situation?

7. What do you make of Julie's decision to sequester herself in the Catskills and apprentice herself to a team of butchers? Have you ever plunged yourself into an obsessive project to make a change in your life? Did it work? Does it ever work?

8. What did you make of the crew at Fleisher's? Do you think it might be true that butchers are a different breed?

9. What was your response to Julie's affair with D? Was it understandable? Reprehensible? Were you sympathetic?

10. At a certain point Julie reveals that Eric is also seeing someone on the side. Did you consider this "only fair"? Did it cast Julie's own indiscretions in a different light?

11. What did you think about Julie's around-the-world journey to visit butchers? Where in the world would you want or be willing to go to experience food?

12. Do you think Julie Powell's travels abroad changed her? How?

13. What do you make of the memoir's title, *Cleaving*?

READING GROUP GUIDE

Julie Powell's
suggestions for further reading

The River Cottage Meat Book by Hugh Fearnley-Whittingstall
This gorgeous, exhaustive, and passionate tome on the importance of responsible husbandry and what to do with the meat that results from it is a must-read for all thoughtful meat eaters and courageous cooks.

The Whole Beast: Nose to Tail Eating by Fergus Henderson
UK chef Henderson is mad for offal, and determined to use every part of the animals he cooks, from lamb's brains to herring semen. Much of this book you'll read more to get the creative juices flowing than to glean for practical culinary information, but it will get you thinking about everything that every part of every animal has to offer. And there are some great and accessible recipes in there as well.

The Omnivore's Dilemma: A Natural History of Four Meals by Michael Pollan
Now a classic, this book really pushed the conversation about the transparency (or, mostly, the lack thereof) in the big business of American food production into the mainstream national

consciousness. Pollan continues to be a powerful advocate for making profound fundamental changes in the way Americans produce and consume food.

Eating Animals by Jonathan Safran Foer

I confess that I read this book with my eyes sort of permanently glued to the top of my head; there is something sanctimonious in the writings of many passionate vegetarians to which I am allergic. But Foer's rigorous pursuit of discovering just what he can face eating, ethically speaking, is engaging and authentic. Foer and I are not so different, as it turns out: we both have become extraordinarily concerned with the provenance of the food we feed ourselves and our families, and seek to address the moral questions that surround the eating of animals. It's just that I can live with eating the meat of a humanely slaughtered pig, and he can't.

What to Eat by Marion Nestle

A nutritionist and consumer advocate, Nestle in this book takes us on a disconcerting journey through our local supermarkets, pointing out all the ways that advertisers and corporations try to lure us away from wholesome foods to the processed, packaged, and empty. A disturbing read, it is also an empowering one; when grocery shopping, forewarned is forearmed.

Consider the Lobster by David Foster Wallace

I'm a huge DFW fan and think all his work is worth a careful read. He can be a daunting writer to tackle, and this collection of his essays seems an excellent way into his work. And the title essay, originally published in *Gourmet* magazine, is a conscientious examination of our relationships with iconic foods and the creatures sacrificed to create them.

The Nasty Bits by Anthony Bourdain

In his follow-up to *Kitchen Confidential,* Bourdain shows a (slightly) gentler side. But he's no softie, and he'll still crack on the head, metaphorically anyway, any culinary wusses who shy away from utter, wild ecstasy in the face of great, meaty, guts-and-all food.

Corked by Kathryn Borel

In this fantastic memoir with a bite, Borel, in the wake of a life-changing accident, tentatively explores and deepens her relationship with her difficult, fascinating father during a tipsy tour of the wine regions of France. This book is just what a food- (well, wine-) related memoir should be—honest and delicious.

Against Love: A Polemic by Laura Kipnis

Often thought-provoking, occasionally hilarious, and always firmly tongue-in-cheek, Kipnis's skewering of the institution we are all supposed to aspire to is ultimately less a disparagement of committed relationships than a criticism of our tendency to mindlessly swallow the Hallmark-ready conventions of contemporary marriage.